Freeman's
Home

D0527322

Previous Issues

Freeman's
Home

Est. 2015

Edited by

John Freeman

Grove Press UK

First published in the United States of America in 2017 by Grove/Atlantic Inc.

First published in Great Britain in 2017 by Grove Press UK, an imprint of Grove/
Atlantic Inc.

Copyright © John Freeman, 2017

Assistant Editor: Allison Malecha

"Alipašino" first appeared in Bosnian in Adisa Bašić's *Promotivni spot za moju
domovinu*. Sarajevo: Dobra knjiga, 2010; "Germany and Its Exiles" first appeared in
German in Herta Müller's *Der Spiegel* as "Herzwort und Kopfwort" in January 2013;
"The Committed" is excerpted from Viet Thanh Nguyen's forthcoming novel, which
will be published by Grove Atlantic; "A Land Without Borders" is excerpted from *A
Land Without Borders: My Journey Around East Jerusalem and the West Bank*, to
be published by Text Publishing in April 2017; "A Natural" copyright © 2017 by Ross
Raisin. Extracted from *A Natural* by Ross Raisin, published by Jonathan Cape; "Being
Here" is excerpted from Marie Darrieussecq's *Being Here*, to be published in English
by Text Publishing in 2017. Translation © 2017 Penny Hueston. Original French
publication: *Être ici est une splendeur* © P.O.L. Editeur, 2016; "E. A hymn bracing for
the end" is excerpted from *Concerto for Jerusalem* by Adonis, translated by Khaled
Mattawa, to be published by Yale University Press in the Margellos World Republic of
Letters series in fall 2017. Reproduced by permission.

The moral right of the authors contained herein to be identified as the authors of this
work has been asserted by them in accordance with the Copyright, Designs and Patents
Act of 1988.

All rights reserved. No part of this publication may be reproduced, stored in a
retrieval system, or transmitted in any form or by any means, electronic, mechanical,
photocopying, recording, or otherwise, without the prior permission of both the
copyright owner and the above publisher of the book.

Every effort has been made to trace or contact all copyright-holders. The publishers
will be pleased to make good any omissions or rectify any mistakes brought to their
attention at the earliest opportunity.

1 3 5 7 9 8 6 4 2

A CIP record for this book is available from the British Library.

Grove Press, UK
Ormond House
26–27 Boswell Street
London
WC1N 3JZ

www.groveatlantic.com

Trade paperback ISBN 978 1 61185 517 3
Ebook ISBN 978 1 61185 946 1

Printed and bound in Great Britain by Bell & Bain Ltd, Glasgow

Published in collaboration with the MFA in Creative Writing at The New School

THE NEW SCHOOL
CREATIVE WRITING

Cover and interior design by Michael Salu

Contents

Introduction

JOHN FREEMAN

For much of my life home has been elsewhere. Both of my parents grew up in cities they felt compelled to leave, so for a decade my family lived *elsewhere*: in Cleveland, where my parents met, then on Long Island, where my father found work, and later—for the longest stretch of time—in a small Pennsylvania town called Emmaus, where my mother and father made a home. There I walked to school on cracked sidewalks beneath maple trees so large my fearless brothers thought twice about climbing them. The Lehigh Valley rose above and around us like a smoke ring. Night felt like a well.

We lived in Emmaus for just six years but until recently it was the only home I'd known. It had the moody, memorable rhythms of a home. On clear afternoons our high school pep band marched the streets belting out songs, tossing batons. On snowy winter mornings my brothers and I curled around the radio, listening for school district closings. Upon hearing East Penn Schools, we bolted into the yard to build castles from chest-high drifts carved by snowplows. Summers, the soft June air would be pierced by the whine of far-off drag races.

I never knew there could be a difference between where you are from and what you call home until my family left Pennsylvania in 1984. My father had a new job in Sacramento. We were going home—to his home, and like almost every trip my family took, we drove. The United States unpeeled before our station wagon packed with coloring books and our springer spaniel Tracy, who curled up into a ball the size of a danish and slept most of the way. Everything else we owned was stuffed into a moving van driven ahead of us by a guy named Kool. As Ohio opened up into Iowa and then to the broad terrifying expanse of Kansas, I thought, this is where I'm from.

I didn't know it then but California would become where I was from. My family adapted to long, even seasons and shallow nights and hot lungfuls of valley air. It would be a decade before I felt again the lonesome hollow in my chest a fall day can give you. I lost my nickname and my brothers reinvented themselves too in minor ways. It wasn't odd to see palm trees or to think about everything east of us as "back there," to not even think about the past at all. To just get in a car and drive somewhere alone to see how fast the machine could go.

M ovement is a particularly American metaphor because agency is one of the nation's obsessions. It is part of America's mythology that you make your fate. You can decide, and then become, whatever or whoever it is you wish to be. In a country which takes such poor care of its weak—which has been and continues to be so hostile to visitors—it feels especially cruel to play this dream song. And yet everywhere the tune hums: in presidential speeches, advertisements, church services, in pop music and books and films. It is the melody of American life.

I have come to believe that home is the antidote to myths such as this one, myths that hover outside the reach of so much human life, creating a low pressure system of unhappiness in between the ground and sky. Perhaps we truly need to become in order to be, but however speedily or sluggishly that evolution proceeds, we need a narrative space in which we tell and live the story of our lives—and that space is called a home. In this sense, a home is not a fixed place, or even necessarily a stable one. The last decade of migration ought to tell us that. Rather, home is a space we have exerted ourselves against to make a corner of it ours. Home is a place we claim or allow ourselves to be claimed by.

Part of making and preserving this space is telling it. The writers collected in this issue of *Freeman's* are caught in the middle of that act. As readers, I invite you to eavesdrop on their narrative hammering, to watch them raise the roof beams. These are intimate, difficult, sometimes amusing, and beautifully textured stories—true and otherwise—poems, and photographs. For a child, a home is the original sensory map, and so several stories begin right there, with that first surveying of the territory.

Xiaolu Guo describes her childhood in a small fishing village in China, where she was raised by her frail grandmother and hard-drinking, cruel grandfather. For Thom Jones, home was the aisles of a general store which his grandmother ran during the Depression in Illinois. Passersby were so hungry she'd pack scoops of peanut butter to have at the ready for desperate visitors. Edwidge Danticat was born in Haiti and grew up in Brooklyn, and in her bittersweet essay she writes of something that happened in the interregnum between homes that instigated a crisis of faith in her life.

The building materials of home do not exist in a world of plain geometry; they are constantly changing shape and weight. Many stories here sketch out the quantum mechanics for living in a shifting field, when the need for safe space remains. Nowhere has this urge for safety and home been more powerfully under threat than in Syria and Libya. The novelist Rabih Alameddine travels in Lebanon and Greece where he witnesses the small and large ways Syrian refugees make a temporary space a home, and when conditions are too abject for this urge to take root.

A society is often defined by how it treats those seeking shelter, wanting to make a home. In her brilliant, furious essay, Herta Müller tells of her own migration into Germany in the worst days of Ceauşescu's regime in Romania and the awful ways she was treated upon arrival. She warns of the amendments made to Germany's sense of itself, of who counts as German after the war when exiles returned home. Then she compares this house of holes to the one Germany struggles with in the wake of mass migration into Europe from the Middle East.

Time and again the pieces here form a calculus of belonging, and wrestle with the ethics of addition. The poet Kay Ryan has a theory on home. It has to do with interior proximity, and a balance between our need for what is around us and for our ability to affect it. Emily Raboteau marries into a family and notes that when you become daughter-in-law to an immoveable object, such as a stubborn Ugandan mother, you take over the burden of channeling that tension into the creation of a new, larger home. In his elegiac short story, Barry Lopez writes of a lucky woman for whom the effort of maintaining a home has largely receded, and who funnels her remaining energy into preserving the health and vitality of a wider home, the natural world, which is home—she hopes—to all.

Would that there were more in the world who saw this way: sharing a home in many cases is a fractious, often dangerous matter. In his essay about life on the edge of Israel and Palestine, the novelist Nir Baram describes how a history joined by exclusionary definitions of home corrodes daily life along that border. In a chapter from his forthcoming novel, Viet Thanh Nguyen imagines the stories of people on boats coming from Vietnam to America in the 1970s, the terrifying Middle Passage of a huge wave of migration into the U.S.—and upon their arrival things will hardly get easier for them.

Whether it's war or pressures too great to bear, home is so often the place one needs to leave. In an excerpt of his upcoming novel, *A Natural*, Ross Raisin conjures a gay footballer traveling the low-level club circuits across England on his first trip away from home. Marie Darrieussecq writes of the painter Paula Modersohn-Becker, and how she had to leave her husband and children behind in Germany to get space to work in Paris. Juan Gabriel Vásquez made a similar trip to the city of light some eighty years later, following in the footsteps of Latin America's great novelists, only to discover home had followed him there. Gregory Pardlo signs up for the marines as a young man but spends most of his time not really wanting to leave where he is from.

Home can let you down more than any other place and still retain its hold over you. Kerri Arsenault comes from a paper mill town in Maine, a place created by its industry and then killed by the carcinogens that industry pumped into its air and water. Yet the town's residents remain loyal. In his poem, Danez Smith writes of the way new connective spaces between unlike people are created by the cruelly exclusionary logic of a home that won't let you in.

Since force is acting on it at all times, home must be claimed and arranged, catalogued and maintained. Adisa Bašić's poem speaks in the voice of a neighborhood which lures no tourists but means everything to those it raised. Amira Hass lives in the West Bank and notes how signs of what was once Palestine litter Jerusalem, most notably in the stone houses which were built before the creation of Israel. Lawrence Joseph has lived in lower Manhattan for several decades and his poem chronicles the turns of light like a painter who knows his palette. Writing of his childhood Austin, Benjamin Markovits recalls how if it was your home, you reserved the right to rename its streets, to mispronounce its landmarks, to make it yours.

There's a liturgy of home in these pages—a praise that goes beyond compliment and edges toward devotion. Aleksandar Hemon humorously describes the marathon singing sessions his family hosts at gatherings to keep their Ukrainian heritage alive. Rawi Hage describes how he began taking photographs during the civil war in Lebanon, hoping he might see a bomb dropping, an activity that may have preserved the trauma of that war for years to come. In a steamy prose poem, Stuart Dybek recalls driving home from a day at the beach, the tension of stopped traffic eclipsed by the erotic possibilities of a stopped car. In her exquisite, beautiful poem, Katie Ford shows how home is what you encode to a text: the poem becomes home itself.

To find a home sometimes we have to expand our notion of what that means. It can be one place, or it can be many, it can be one's own words, or it can be the words of another writer, as it is for the narrator of Leila Aboulela's story, who has lived the life of a conservative Muslim in Scotland but who finds air to breathe in the work of her favorite novelist, a woman who has lived a different life than hers. For the hero of Kjell Askildsen's brief story, a place becomes a home when he can finally add a person to it.

Ultimately, home is in the body and the voice for so many writers. In a stirring verse, the great poet Adonis sings the praises of the vessel which has carried him across nine decades, and the form which has made the world his home. And finally, in a speech accepting a prize that once came with a monetary award to be allocated for overseas travel, the Melbourne writer Gerald Murnane beats out a hymn to the places that have made and sustained him across six decades in the city he calls home.

Even though New York is now my home, these writers have convinced me home is ultimately not a singular place. That even if you make a new home, others can exist in minor keys. I have felt at home in London and in York, Maine for long stretches, and pretty much in every pool and on every cinder track I have stepped foot on, and strangely in the most remote parts of the American West which remind me of what was there before it was stolen.

I type this now from Chicago, not my city, but the home of Aleksandar Hemon and Teri Boyd, parents to my god-children, and therefore a home of sorts. It is probably my sixtieth visit to this strange, miraculous city of ziggurat skyscrapers and endless alleys, poetic talkers and well-curated mythologies. I last saw the Hemons in Sarajevo, their father's other home, and where four of the pieces in this issue were spoken aloud before the writers themselves knew they had a piece for this issue.

The kids are asleep upstairs now—ages four and nine—the exact ages I was when I lived in that small town in Pennsylvania thirty years ago. The ages at which you can watch children change before your very eyes, the thin membrane between now and then so slim it feels transparent. I wonder what they are thinking in their sleep, how large and permanent the city must feel crouched in the dark around them each night. Each day the world around them opens wider. Perhaps there will be a time when this city will become where they were from, but I hope they take a page from this book and realize they can call it home, too.

Six Shorts

She was scarcely five feet tall. Her hands and elbows were rough with callouses. Her hair was thin and gray and she always smelled vaguely of Bengay. She walked with a cane. They called her "Mag" and said that in her day she was a "looker" and that she loved to dance. She didn't seem the dancing type to me. To me she was "Gram." Every day she dragged herself from bed at dawn and set her aching body to work. The "Store" opened at six a.m.

The bread man came early with his redolent supplies. The milkman was next, followed by the meat man, and then customers began filing in, in a steady procession. I remember Stanley Kunchas, a cheerful Hungarian who came through the back door on his way to his shift at the Durabilt. He left his bulldog, Pete, on the back porch while he departed through the front door, strolling up Jericho Road, lunch pail in hand, in love with life and the whole world. Pete guarded Mag's back door for years.

The people came to buy and they came to visit. Mag was a skillful hostess/psychologist/entertainer—there was little TV in those days. There was no hurry. Still, the shelves got stocked, the stove got stoked with coal, laundry got done, meals were made, four daughters were raised, as were innumerable grandchildren.

Mag couldn't stand the sight of hunger or suffering. She saw the

Depression come and go and saw to it that her customers were fed. Located as the store was near the Burlington Railroad, hoboes were frequent visitors. They would do odd jobs for hot food and coffee and talk of their travels.

Mag started the store with fifty dollars she earned working in a glove factory. In my childlike way I helped in the store. I sacked red and white potatoes in ten-pound bags tied with cotton string. I blended yellow beads of dye in tubs of margarine. I would dab peanut butter from a tub onto a piece of wax paper. Mag gave it away as a kind of emergency food. I swept the floors. Hauled pop bottles down into the dark basement. There was a cistern down there. A cousin once told me that it was seven hundred feet deep with a powerful undercurrent.

There were other grocery store hazards. I killed the occasional jumping spider that arrived in the banana crates from Central America. The same cousin told me they could move at blinding speed. The excitement of such possibilities kept me on my toes. And then there were butcher knives. My grandmother taught me how to slice meat while keeping the knife blade moving away from my hands and body. It was my grandmother who taught me how to knot my shoes.

The years took their toll on Mag. Times changed. Customers moved and defected. The A&P was quicker and cheaper. There were two armed robberies and Mag's bladder ruptured from the stress of waiting for another. She had become an old woman, defenseless and alone. Her doctors told her she was too worn out to run a store and that she had to quit. The family agreed. "Enough," they said.

The store is torn down now. Mag is dead. Most of the people who traded with her are dead too. The store wasn't much to look at anyhow. There's a greenhouse on the property now. But the store lives on in my heart. It wasn't simply business. The store was about knowing and loving people. It was a time and era worth remembering.

—Thom Jones

Crispin was ticking like a little Geiger counter as she settled in on a pillow near my head this morning. I was her uranium. But of course with a real Geiger counter, the object isn't just to register the find; somebody has greedy designs on the uranium; somebody wants to get it and sell it. Somebody is getting excited, and the ticking is getting faster and faster.

The marvelous thing about Crispin is that she is not getting excited. She settles down, turns off the tick and shuts her eyes.

Not everything has to escalate.

I've tried to think about her purr. Why does it always happen at about the same nearness to my head? And why does she purr and then stop purring? What I think is that it's a perfect-proximity indicator; it turns on just as she crosses a certain border into perfect proximity, and its only function is to say, You're there. That's why it can quit.

What the cat wants isn't contact but something close to it. Or I could go a little further and blur the border between proximity and contact and say that being almost there (proximity) is the best sort of being there (contact).

Close but no cigar, people say, as though anybody wanted a cigar. Close is much better than a cigar, says Crispin.

This feeling about proximity is related to the exquisite force fields in a house. In the same way that the cat is made perfectly easy (perfectly easy!) by a certain magical relationship between herself and the head of her person, a person is made easy by the magical relationship of various intersecting vectors generated by her chair and table in concert with her lamp, say.

That's how we feel at home, ideally: we feel released to not pay any attention to where we are because we are suspended and weightless in a beautiful web made out of the sweet intersections of the familiar and thoroughly prevetted.

A house is a big skull, or at least mine is for me—the container of my brain. Really, I move around in my house disembodied, I'm sure.

Or I move around in parts of my house, that is. I wonder if other people are like this and only really use an embarrassingly small amount of their space? If there was an infrared tracker of my movements it would be so irradiated in my bed area that it would burn through the back of Fairfax. There would be serious hatchings in the kitchen and bathroom, lighter arcs out to the mailbox and the driveway for the papers, but the other rooms would be ghostly.

I could apparently sublet much of this lavish thousand-square-foot house.

No: that was a joke. I need all the space I'm not using, just as Crispin needs everything all the way out to the distant perimeter of the fence. She knows if some bad cat has snuck in, and it is very polluting to her rest. We need it empty.

I actually mean empty both physically and mentally.

I have always felt kind of embarrassed that I have to have so much brain I don't use, and even seem to have to aggressively defend the emptiness of. I've never quite come to terms with it because it's so un-American, so inattentive-to-my-bootstraps sounding. It sounds like a character flaw. Dare I say, I am in many, many ways *not* curious? That I do not care to add to my mental stores?

Or perhaps I could say, slightly less self-damningly, that though I *am* curious my curiosity is unserious, as if I am just pretending to be curious about, say, how tall hops plants can grow, because I know that hard little fact is going to drop through my mind just like pretty much everything else? In other words, it is a mind that cannot hold onto a lot but still it is a good mind in its way with long lines of sight unobscured by the heaps of stuff that build up in minds that can build them up.

What my kind of mind likes makes it tick like Crispin's perfect-proximity indicator.

My bedroom is full of books and as I pass my eye over them on a given morning, one or another of them is somehow just at the right distance from me, just perfect to open and allow that strange unmaking and remaking of the self, that weird interweaving of brains when things go permeable.

You have to have a lot of extra house around yourself to get this to happen and perhaps it is somehow happening in the extra-house part of the other mind that has become so attractive to me right then. Maybe we share some kind of room for entertaining.

—Kay Ryan

I have told this story many times since the events took place. As with many a trivial anecdote, I have come over the years to realize that this one is, in fact, not trivial at all; each new retelling brings me, I think, closer to its meaning. Perhaps one day I will understand it.

In 1999, after three years of trying to build a home in Paris, I decided to leave. The choice to settle in this city had been dictated by my vocation: In the sixties, Paris was the place where my literary forebears, particularly Mario Vargas Llosa, had written the masterpieces that informed my tradition, my language, and my tastes. But my Parisian experience was a discreet catastrophe. I spent the first months seriously ill and I failed at the basic task of writing books I could be proud of. After a few months of hiding away in someone else's home in the Belgian Ardennes, I arrived in Barcelona. There were material considerations behind this decision—here I could earn a living writing in my own language, or teaching literature, or translating it—but also a kind of unashamed superstition. The name of Vargas Llosa, perhaps my predominant influence at the time, was once again very much present in the mechanics of my decision. In the early seventies, he had written wonderful novels while living

5

here; his publisher was here, and so was his agent. He had built a home away from home, I thought, and I would try to do the same.

By the fall of 2000, I had joined a literary magazine, *Lateral,* as part of its editorial board. At the end of my second or third meeting, Juan Trejo, a fellow apprentice in the novelistic trade, approached me to tell me the following story: The day before, having left home to throw his garbage in the nearest trash bins, he spent some time going through the leftovers—the cast-off books, furniture, or appliances people leave by the containers for the benefit of others. Among the rejected stuff he found a VHS videocassette; on its label, typewritten, were the words *Interview with Mario Vargas Llosa.* He picked up the tape and the next day, gave it to me. It was, he said, a welcome present.

That evening, while I dined at home with my wife and my sister-in-law, I told them about the tape, and the three of us agreed that there was something unusual about Trejo's story. As he left home to throw out the garbage, he knew that the next day he would have a meeting with the rest of the editorial board; the new guy, a Colombian who also thought of himself as a writer, had expressed his admiration for Vargas Llosa; and the tape Trejo had found next to the garbage cans, among discarded things, was not merely about literature, which in itself would have been a major coincidence, but an interview with that same novelist who he knew was so important to the new guy. Trejo could have left the tape where he found it; or he could have picked it up but forgotten about his conversations with the Colombian newcomer; or he could have preferred, out of timidity or plain indifference, to keep it for himself. My wife and my sister-in-law marvelled at Trejo's thoughtfulness. I suggested we watch the interview, as a way of closing a nice evening, and they said it was a good idea.

Here the plot becomes intricate. Besides the name of the novelist, the label didn't reveal any particular information; it therefore felt like an eerie coincidence to realize, as we began the video, that the program in which Vargas Llosa would be interviewed was a well-known Colombian show called *Face to Face*. A lost tape found next to the garbage on a street in Barcelona contained a Colombian TV show about a Peruvian writer I happened to admire. What were the odds? In the interview, Vargas Llosa discussed his recent experience as a presidential candidate and his defeat by Alberto Fujimori. The interviewer announced he would also be discussing his most recent novel, *The Notebooks of Don Rigoberto*, which he was publicizing in Colombia at the time of the show. This is how I learned that the interview had taken place in 1998. Vargas Llosa had visited the Bogotá International Book Fair as part of his publicity tour that year; I was there, coincidentally, and had bought the book and thought of getting it autographed; but I'm not good at harassing the writers I like, and my copy of the book remained unsigned. My mother-in-law, more resourceful or less shy, had managed to get an autographed copy, and before I left for Belgium, where I was living in those days, offered to exchange it for my unsigned copy. It had taken me longer than usual to start reading the novel, and there it was at that very moment, on the floor next to my nightstand in Barcelona, along with the other five or six books that interested me. And so it came to pass that on my TV screen a writer was speaking, in 1998, about his book; in the year 2000, across the ocean from the continent where both of us were born, I was reading that book and had a signed copy within arms' reach. My wife, my sister-in-law, and I began speculating about the chain of events that would have made such a moment possible. But nothing could have prepared us for what happened next.

Vargas Llosa had started talking about *The Notebooks of Don Rigoberto;* the producers of the show, diligently, had found footage from the Bogotá Book Fair in which Vargas Llosa appears surrounded by multitudes of readers, or browsing books in neon-lighted stands, or walking along corridors, escorted by fellow writers such as R.H.

Moreno-Durán. After a close-up of the surrounding faces, the camera dived down to document their walking shoes. Suddenly, in the left part of the frame, a pair of new shoes arrived that didn't belong to the writers or to the accompanying journalists: they were ladies' shoes. The camera panned up again, perhaps out of sheer curiosity, and the frame was filled with the new actor, or rather actress: A woman approached Vargas Llosa with a copy of the new novel, smiling, and asked him for an autograph.

The woman was my mother-in-law.

And so it came to pass that the book Vargas Llosa was signing at that instant on my TV screen was the exact same book that my mother-in-law had given me. I had only to turn my head slightly to see it, but of course I did much more: I grabbed it, opened it, and read the inscription in Barcelona (in the year 2000) at the same time that Vargas Llosa (in the year 1998) wrote it out in Bogotá.

"Best wishes," it read. And then: "MVLL."

Every question became pertinent now. What circumstances had allowed that interview, recorded in my hometown of Bogotá while I was living in Belgium, to reach me at my new home in Barcelona? What made the editors of the show use the footage where my mother-in-law appeared suddenly to have her book signed, instead of another take of another moment? What chain of banal coincidences made me start reading the signed book two years after getting it and just a few days before Juan Trejo found the tape among the discarded objects of Barcelona life?

What happened that evening in my Barcelona apartment remains beyond my full grasp. I've told the story a thousand times, I've told it in writing and in interviews and to friends in casual conversations, and I'm fully aware that I still expect my listener or my reader to come up with a rational explanation. I know Juan Trejo gave me the tape as a welcoming present in the same way I know my mother-in-law gave me the book as a farewell gift: Both moments speak to the fact that I was living somewhere I wasn't intended to live. But maybe that's neither here nor there.

—Juan Gabriel Vásquez

At the age of sixteen, I convinced my cousin to chase the falling bombs in the streets of Beirut with me. The objective was to get a photograph of a bomb before it reached the ground or landed on a building, on a car, on a street, before it caused death and mayhem. The camera was his, but we shared it. The car that we drove in pursuit of the bombs was my father's. The images of falling bombs never revealed anything. After we sent them off to get developed, all we had were photographs of blue skies, a few clouds, roads, and the tops of buildings.

The "decisive moment," to use the French photographer Henri Cartier-Bresson's famous expression, was not determined by a visual anticipation of what would appear within the poised frame of the camera, but by the sound of the bomb's whistle. We stood on highways, in alleys between buildings, aiming our lens toward the trajectory of whistles.

I left Beirut, and twenty years later, upon my return to the Mediterranean city, I reminded my cousin of our madness and the time we rushed after the falling bombs. He nodded and said, It's a miracle that we are still alive. Miracles, I said, do not exist. They do, he said, the proof is that we are here and alive in spite of people's stupidity and the terror we endured. You believed in miracles back then, he reminded me.

In Montreal, I had no job to fall back on and had spent all my savings on that last trip to Lebanon. I stayed in bed for weeks not able to move and I began to contemplate suicide.

Then one day I decided to get up. I walked from my Côte-des-Neiges apartment to a government clinic. The social worker who interviewed me there happened to be an acquaintance from my university days. We both completed a degree in Fine Arts, and like the majority of people who studied liberal arts, discovered that it was hard to get a job in the field afterward. Marc, the social worker, went back to college and finished a degree in social work, and I drifted for a while, holding many small, inconsequential jobs. In class Marc had always seemed arrogant, with an air of superiority. He was well read, eloquent, but had no talent as an artist. He seduced men and women equally. His critiques of people's artwork were very perceptive and analytical, but he was always dismissive.

At the clinic, Marc asked me about the method of suicide that I was considering.

A bullet, I said.

You have a gun? he asked.

Yes, I replied.

You would be the person pulling the trigger.

Yes.

Can you imagine where you would be standing?

On the balcony.

And you would be looking in which direction? he asked.

The sky, I guess.

And what part of the body would you aim at?

His interrogation lasted for a while, and continued with the purpose of assessing the seriousness of my intention.

He asked me what I was doing before I had thought of ending my life.

I told him that I had just come back from Beirut.

It could well be post-traumatic stress, he said, but that has to be determined by a psychologist. I am here to gauge what channels and options are open to you, and what your obligations are. Is there anything in particular that happened in Beirut that you would like to discuss?

Nothing in particular, I said. I just met with family.

Anything in particular you remember? he said.

A few dinners with family members and old friends. I visited a cousin who was a childhood friend.

What did you talk about?

We were reminiscing about the time I carried a camera with the intention of capturing the image of a falling bomb.

And did you capture it? Marc asked.

No, we never did.

And why do you think you wanted to capture the image of a bomb in a photograph?

Death, I said, and laughed at the vagueness of my answer.

No laughing matter, he said. Photography is about death, he added.

Barthes, *Camera Lucida,* I said, and we both smiled, having read the same books in university.

You were not afraid? he asked me.

No, I said.

Did you think of it as a suicidal mission?

No, I said, I wouldn't have brought my cousin with me, I guess, if that was my intention.

So suicide is a private matter to you.

Yes, I said. It should be, or else it's murder or an intention to harm somebody.

And what would you have done with the photograph if you happened to have captured a bomb falling from the sky?

A trophy, I said. Undeniably a rare image.

Your interest in image-making seems to have started in your youth, he said.

Yes.

But the camera was your cousin's, you mentioned.

Yes, but we shared it. The car we drove on our mission was my father's.

Marc paused and said to me, Listen, these are the options: I have to assign you to a specialist to further assess your situation.

And then? I asked.

The psychologist will determine what to do next.

And what would that entail? I said.

Anything from medical treatment to hospitalization.

But I have never actually owned a gun, or a bullet for that matter. It's all hypothetical, I said.

It is out of our hands now, he said, and stretched back in his revolving chair. What did you expect from your visit here?

To talk it over, I said, not to be potentially incarcerated.

I am curious, he continued. What is your cousin's situation now?

He stayed, he never left home.

And what has he been doing for the rest of his life, since chasing the bombs with you?

Nothing. He continuously whistles, it's irritating, he has stayed home ever since then. Never got a job, borrowed money, and he lives at his parents' house with his sister who provides for him with her secretarial job.

Was he the one driving the car when you chased bombs?

No, I did the driving.

Was he the one who took the photographs?

No, I did.

There was a pause, and we both looked into each other's eyes.

He didn't come of his own free will, did he? Marc asked. You dragged him along, you forced him, and he must have been terrified, he didn't want to die. Did he come of his own volition? Marc repeated.

No, I said, defiant now.

What did you do to him?

I called him a coward, I said, and I stood up to walk to the door. What else did you tell him? I told him if he has faith nothing will ever happen to him. And nothing has happened to him ever since, Marc sneered. We'll be in touch, he said. Your file will be assessed soon.

—Rawi Hage

Where they should be wading, skeletal birds step, marionettes operated by an unseen hand. In the glare you can almost catch the glisten of their strings. Stooped as if shawled in blue-gray wings, herons cross a brackish marsh that once threw reflections of their grace, but now stares up blind, the cracked face of a mummy unwrapped, scarred by bleached fish bones.

We drink more beer, shower less, and save the dishwater to spill on flowers. Love, they still bloom only below the kitchen sill. Last night, thirsting bees chased us home, dive-bombing madly as we ran, flashlights bobbing in one hand, foaming sweaty bottles of Heineken in the other.

Traffic stops on Signal Hill for a tarantula to cross the road. One more mirage crawling across shimmered concrete. "Do you think a mirage is aware of what it is? If it ever wonders if we're real?" She's only asking to kill time. We're crawling in an overheated Dodge, backed up behind a bloated convoy of water trucks. Their hoses dangle like deflated trunks, a circus line of elephants sloshing as they rumba around scorched, suicidal curves. They drizzle as they grind through gears and trail a slick that hisses beneath our tires like a rainy night.

At twilight, the herons' folded wings make it appear as if they're outfitted like Fred Astaire, in tails. Their beaks look as if they've strapped on masks and are on their way to a Venetian masquerade. Or perhaps they're wearing nose flutes or some archaic instrument, about to sardonically toot a troubadour *canso* about the plague. Those once lethal, fish-spearing beaks droop as if they might be used to prod like canes. "What's a metaphor but a mirage?" she asks, although it's not a question.

In a dream we're crossing the Mackinac Bridge in a misty drizzle again, on our way to camp in the Porcupine Mountains, and stop as we once did at Crisp Point Lighthouse to fish the whitefish run. We saw old agate hunters in the fog, remember, retirees from shuttered Rust Belt auto plants, arriving in Winnebagos to prod with canes for gems and Petoskey stones along the pebbled beach where a branch of the rusty Two Hearted pours into Lake Superior. Is it merely another symptom of drought when even in dreams that stormy North Atlantic up in Michigan appears more real than this shimmering mangrove coast where waterbirds scavenge a cracked mudflat and a parching heat somehow ascends with enough vapor to warp the shapes of light?

Mount Sage, Tortola's highest hump, has trapped a cloud. It's green there the way mountains are capped with snow.

—Stuart Dybek

I still keep a pair of basketball shoes in the closet of the entrance hall in my parents' house in Austin, Texas. These are the only high-tops I still own. Most of the time I live in London and don't play, but whenever I go home, I dust off the shoes and head out to the half-court in the backyard that my father put in when I was a kid, and shoot around. Every day for pretty much every year of my childhood I spent a couple of hours there after school, sometimes hanging out with friends, but often just working on my jump shot. I guess I could add up the time. About a year of my life.

A sycamore spreads its leaves over the court, so even on hot afternoons you can play in the shade, but these days the branches hang heavy enough that there are only certain spots where you can shoot your shot without worrying about being blocked by nature. There's a telephone wire, too, which sags across at the level of the free-throw line. The concrete paint is peeling, leaf matter has collected in the cracks, twigs crackle underfoot. On warm days, which means most of the year, you get bitten by mosquitoes. A converted apartment looks over the court on one side, where the latest renter can sit out on the balcony drinking a beer in the evening and watch me play if he wants to. On the other side, the bamboo hedge has grown too tall to look over. Depending where the wind is blowing from, you can smell the smoker from Ruby's BBQ a couple of blocks away, which is where we got the chopped beef my dad brought over for my wedding thirteen years ago—in London.

At the ticker-tape parade in Boston, when Larry Bird celebrated his first NBA championship, he leaned into the microphone and got the crowd going by saying, "There's only one place I'd rather be. French Lick." But I wonder if he really meant it at the time, or if it was just one of those things you say about yourself, to make a point. Jews at Passover traditionally say "Next year in Jerusalem," but there's a certain amount of rabbinical commentary around the question of whether you're still supposed to say it if you have no intention of going back. For my mother Jerusalem means the steep-roofed brick cottage her father built on the shores of the Flensburg Fjord after the Second World War. It's not really the house she grew up in, that was farther down the road, but it serves the same purpose. You can see Denmark from the kitchen window—the garden slopes down to the beach. And every summer if she can, she spends a couple of weeks there, entering again the old routines, buying rolls from the baker, digging potatoes if there are any, but my dad is mostly relieved when they go home.

For us, I mean my parents' kids, Jerusalem is Austin, though one of my sisters still lives there and has a much livelier and more honest and up-to-date sense of what the place is actually like. Natives now complain about the traffic, and there's some ridiculous statistic like one in seven Austinites moved to town in the last year, the implications of which dawn on you after a minute. My eighth-grade French teacher, who appeared out of the blue a few weeks ago and invited me to tea at the British Library, told me that being a real Austinite used to mean that you knew the little shortcuts and byroads to get you around the hassles of living there, and now it means that you don't.

KUT, the local Austin affiliate of NPR, recently ran a program about the generational shift in the way people pronounce the city's street names—which involves a funny kind of reverse political correctness, since many of those names are Hispanic and German and the tradition was always to mispronounce them. I grew up off Guadalupe—"Gwada-loop." People called Mueller Airport "Miller," then "Myoo-ler" (which is probably how I grew up saying it), and now I don't know what—it's not an airport anymore, it's a fancy new development. At the really very nice hippie (or rather hipster) food cooperative (the hippies have either evolved or been priced out) behind our house, the bearded guy at the cash register asked me how my day was. I took the kids to the Thinkery at Miller, I told him. That's right, he said, that's how you're supposed to say it, isn't it? We had listened to the same show.

Our local park, which is just a creek running through an overgrown field, is called Hemphill. We called it "Hem-fill" when we were kids, instead of "Hemp-hill." I don't think anyone else ever did, but I guess kids get to make up the rules of their own childhoods. It's where we learned to ride our bikes, and there was an old guy in a run-down house (since torn down and attractively rebuilt) named

Mr. Boyd, who used to give us popsicles on hot days. I don't know that if he were around now I'd let my kids knock on his door. My daughter has an English accent—she hates being called posh, but that's how she sounds—and holds on to the idea of Austin, of Flensburg, as an ace-up-your-sleeve alternative identity. I've promised her that before she graduates high school we'll spend a year in Austin, though whether she'll still want to by the time we get around to it is open to question. But I want to, I think. It's the only place I still play basketball.

—Benjamin Markovits

KERRI ARSENAULT is a writer, editor, and serves on the Board of the National Book Critics Circle and is a founder of the Western Maine Water Alliance. She writes a column for *Literary Hub,* and her work has appeared in the *San Francisco Chronicle, American Book Review,* NBCC's *Critical Mass, Kirkus Reviews,* and *Bookslut.* She is currently working on a book about Maine, from which this piece is excerpted.

Vacationland

KERRI ARSENAULT

Mexico, Maine sits in a valley or "River Valley" as we call the area, because I suppose you can't have one without the other. The hills are low and worn and carved by the waters surrounding them, and trees line the rivers, which confine the town. It's a paper mill town where smokestacks poke holes in the smog they create. *That's money coming out of those smokestacks*, my father used to say about the rotten-smelling upriver drafts that surfaced when the weather shifted. That smell loitered amid the high school softball games I played beneath those stacks and lingered on my father's shirtsleeves when he came home from work, allowing me to forgive the rank odor for what it provided.

From the porch steps of the house where I grew up, to the right, you'll see a street of clapboarded homes, the quiet interrupted every now and then by a braking logging truck. A mile or two out of town, the road narrows and small creeks knit through pastures shadowed by hills, a working farm or two, a long straight road, and smells of cut hay, muddy cow paths, rotting leaves, or black ice, depending on the time of year. The seasons, they calendared our lives.

To the left of the porch, you'll see the end of the road. There, the pavement dips down to reveal the town's only traffic light, a gas station, and the roof of the Family Dollar Store. Behind the store lies the wide, slow-moving Androscoggin River. Just beyond the Androscoggin, on an island in the neighboring town of Rumford, the paper mill's largest smokestack emerges like a giant concrete finger. From anywhere in town you can orient yourself to this stack or the ever-present *ca-chink ca-chink ca-chink* of the mill's conveyor belts and find your way home, even from a pitch-black walk in the woods. When mill shutdowns occur for holidays or layoffs, the smokeless stacks resemble the diseased birch trees dying throughout New England.

Where stack meets sky, the river pivots and heads southeast, under bridges and over rapids, pushing through falls and dams, around islands and along inlets, through Jay, Lewiston, Topsham, Brunswick, and other small towns, until it meets and mingles with five other rivers at Merrymeeting Bay, whereupon it finally and quietly slips into the Atlantic Ocean.

April 2008 and I am home for my grandfather's funeral. My parents' house sighs with winter's leftover lethargy. Spring has arrived in Maine with driveways full of mud and sculled up snow-plow debris; salt stains, shredded earth, and derelict mittens lie in the wake of its embracing path. A few dirty buttresses of snow linger like pocked monoliths, meting out the new season's arrival. The swollen Androscoggin pushes flotsam downriver in the commotion of spring's thaw, and insect hatches will soon begin bursting along its surface until summer opens like an oven. My mother comes out on the porch where I'm standing. *Want to go for a walk?* she asks, her face pinched with the sharpness of her father's death.

We head up Highland Terrace and stop to peek in the windows of an abandoned house, one I always liked, with its wraparound porch, turreted roof, and buttercup-yellow paint. *The owner is sick but refuses to sell the house,* my mother says as we walk across the battered porch. So it sits there, this once elegant home, shedding its brightness, yellow flecking the half-frozen ground. Spray-painted in the road near the driveway: "Fuck you, bitch." The fug of the mill swallows us.

Ahead, we reach the top of the hill, and there, my old high school. To the east, snowmobile trails and abutting them, the mill's decommissioned landfill. To the west, the football field slices the horizon and beyond that, lazy fingers of smoke lick the sky.

We walk inside the school, and my mother stops in the office to chat with the principal. The lobby smells of Band-Aids, warm mashed potatoes, and damp socks. Being there reminds me of Greg, my high school on-again, off-again lumberjackish boyfriend who lived near the town incinerator. I loved him like I would a sorry stuffed animal, one who had lost an eye or whose fur was rubbed raw. Kelly, a girl who wore her black, perfectly feathered hair like a weapon, was in love with him too. When he and I fought—usually because of her—I'd listen to sad songs on my cassette player over and over until he'd call and I'd forgive him in a pattern of everlasting redemption. I only saw Greg once since I graduated. He came to my parents' one Christmas break when I was home from college. He and my mother caught up while I leaned against the kitchen countertop across the room. *Peckerhead,* my father said when he entered the room. He called all boys I dated "Peckerhead" but only if he liked them. If he didn't, my father would sit at our kitchen table like a boulder while the boy fidgeted by the kitchen door in blank-faced silence. Greg eventually married Kelly and got a job at the mill, alongside his sister Janet, who pitched for my high school state championship softball team.

After my mother and I leave, we follow the dirt path behind the football field, past Meroby Elementary where I got into a fistfight with Lisa Blodgett. Lisa and I took turns swinging horizontally at each other's head until a teacher intruded on the brawl. Lisa's strength was tremendous for a sixth grader, her grit shaped by being one of the youngest girls in a family of fifteen kids, most of them boys. When I looked in the mirror that night at home, I was sure I looked different, the way you think you do when you lose your virginity. It was my first and last bare-knuckled fight, except for a few unconvincing swipes at good old Kelly one night at a dance. My best friend, Maureen, who towered over both of us, protected me from Kelly's sharp, red fingernails.

Down Granite Street, an untied dog begins following us, growling. *Just ignore him,* my mother says. But I hear his snarls over the thrum of the mill. As I turn to look at him the dog sniffs my heels, his tail down. I walk faster. My mother continues talking. The dog gives a final bark and sits down in the middle of the road. I look over my shoulder until we are out of his sight and he is out of ours. Down the hill, past the Green Church, the town hall, the library, the fire station, the post office, we walk through the oversized parking lot at the Family Dollar Store. Someone sits inside the only vehicle parked there eating a sandwich with the windows rolled up and the engine running. Nearby, the vacant lot where the Bowl-O-Drome used to be and behind it, St. Theresa's, our shuttered Catholic church where Father Cyr gave me my first communion, confirmed me, and listened to my first confession. *I'm sorry I lied to my parents,* I said to him, though that itself was a lie.

On the corner at the traffic light, a gardening store, a newish shop, to me anyway. Lawn decorations, perennials, stuffed animals, and miniature tchotchkes for terrariums strain the overstocked metal shelves of the store. Most mom-and-pop shops have closed in town, but for a few. In their place, discount stores like Marden's Surplus & Salvage, Wardwell's Used Furniture, the What Not Shop Thrift Store, and other such second-hand outlets and pawn shops appeared over the years, as if the people who live here only deserve leftovers. Walmart with its blinking fluorescent lights and the faint smell of formaldehyde, hijacked the rest of the commerce.

I am inspecting a snow globe when I hear my mother shout, *Kerri, guess who's here? Do you know who this is?* Inevitably, she plays this remembering game, usually in the grocery store, where she will stand next to someone, grab his or her arm as if she were a koala, and ask me, do you remember so-and-so? I will stand there frozen, in the frozen foods, staring at my mother and the person she has grabbed, their eyes like dinner plates, waiting for my answer. *Sure, yes, I remember you!* I had said earlier that same day to Mr. Martineau, the man who lives across the street from my grandfather. After Mr. Martineau left the store my mother told me he has Alzheimer's. *He doesn't remember you,* she said.

Kerri, come see who's here! she shouts again. I walk around the aisle like Gulliver, jiggling the doll-sized plastic floral arrangements, pitching the teeny flowers to and fro. My mother raises her arms upward like a magician. *DO YOU KNOW WHO THIS IS?*

Hi. Long time no see, the woman says. *Yeah, what is it, about twenty years?* I say. Her dry yellow bangs slump over oversized round glasses that hide pink powdered cheeks. On her bulky sweatshirt, something plaid. *Where do you live now?* she asks, leaning on the counter, arms crossed like a fortress. *California,* I say, feeling bad, not knowing why. *San Francisco!* I clarify. *Oh, I went there once. Didn't like it. The people are not very nice. And I never found anything good to eat,* she says.

I look around the store for my mother, for the exit. *It seems quiet around here nowadays. Much less going on than when we were kids*, I say. *No, not really,* she says. *Really?* I say, wondering if she means there is something going on or there isn't. *I went by the Recreation Park yesterday. It's just so . . . so different*, I say, hopeful. I glance at her around the periphery of her glasses, our conversation. She stares at me over the top of her rims, as patient as a road, looks at me without blinking: my leather jacket, my Prada eyeglasses, my fitted jeans. *Nope, you're the one that's different*, she says.

We leave the store and my mother tells me the mill plans to shut down Number 10 paper machine, and others are on a transitional schedule, meaning they too may lumber to a slow hissing halt. In the past few decades, with technology displacing people and digital media overtaking print, the production of coated magazine paper—our mill's primary product—has become as precarious as the livelihoods of the men and women who make it. *We want to sell the house, but nobody wants to live here anymore,* my mother says, panning her hand from one side of the street to the other. Homes sag with ruined lawns—and the families who live in them haven't fared much better.

Around the block, we pass Kimball School where I attended K–4. Weeds root in the tar playground and a plastic bag twirls in the damp breeze. A rusty chain-link fence girdles the property. Dr. Edward Martin gutted the school years ago and transformed it into a medical office, but after he died, the building closed up permanently. Broken glass breaches the milkweed that surrounds the maple tree we had sought shade under during recess. Down the street, my grandfather's house, buttoned up, the furnace long expired. Remnants of crabgrass and soggy leaves flatten his once thriving garden. Mr. Martineau, who my mother and I saw at the grocery store earlier, emerges from the house across the street. He waves. We wave back.

My mother and I walk home in silence. Halfway there, I run my hand along the cool green iron railing that parallels the sidewalk and snag my sweater on it. The rusted, dismembered rail is scattered in bits at the bottom of the banking. On my way from school, I'd roll on my side down that banking, again and again. With grass stains on my clothes, I'd run home, as if my head was made of that same iron rail and my house was magnetic north.

I see the porch of our house from several blocks away, and it looks as it's always looked, only smaller as things often appear when you are older. My mother and I stomp our feet on the front porch to dislodge road grime from our boots. *I can't imagine what will happen if the mill closes*, my mother says, as she opens the door. *So many people are out of work already*, she clarifies. *It will be a ghost town.* I take off my coat while my mother digs out the local newspaper, her forefinger thumping a news article about the mill. *We have to sell the house*, she says. But she has been saying this for years.

The next day, I go for a run through Strathglass Park, a collection of two-family homes by the mill's founder, Hugh J. Chisholm. Brick-by-brick—five million to be exact—Chisholm assembled the houses with long-lasting materials for what he hoped would be a long-lasting industry: slate roofs, granite foundations, handmade headers and balustrades, concrete steps, plaster walls. He even wallpapered the living rooms. Now, broken snowmobiles and other lifeless remnants litter front lawns, and listing, half-baked additions or porches scab the once pristine houses. Sheets shroud leaded glass windows, their bottoms knotted to let in light or keep rooms dark. Garbage lies in heaps alongside scattered woodpiles and abandoned bright plastic toys are half-covered in snow and dog shit. Wind chimes tinkle above the din of a yowling mutt. The road is a glacier. I mince my way along the icy path ahead.

Wandering around in this forlorn landscape, I think later that night, it *is* a ghost town, a place all but vanished but for its dull eggy odor. It complied with my memory of it, yet it also did not, a blend of nostalgia and something else as unrecognizable as the back of my own head. *It's not where we grew up*, a childhood friend said to me years ago. What, then, was it? It was home, that much I knew, and home is the heart of human identity, a blurry backdrop like that fake plastic tree I leaned on during my high school senior photograph.

When I was a kid, my mother stayed home while my father worked: her making pot roast, him making smokestack money. We explored the world through textbooks, Matchbox cars, and made

25

classroom dioramas of what we thought a Mayan village or a Midwestern dairy farm looked like. The rest of the world seemed to be New Hampshire or Canada. Families didn't go on overseas vacations,or hardly even interstate. Our lives were focused inward . . . Red Sox scores, union strikes, and long gas station lines in the 70s, though nobody ever connected the high price of fuel to what was happening in other countries. For us, it was just inconvenient.

Monumental changes were happening in America. However, there were no movements in Mexico and Rumford but for the men walking across the footbridge to work. Blue-collar families like mine were more likely to dry bras on a clothesline than burn them. We lived in a Shrinky-Dink world where everything was there, just smaller. We were lucky in this, felt safe with our doors unlocked at night and ameliorated most of our sins within the latched doors of St. Theresa's confessional. At nighttime football games we watched our high school fire-twirling majorettes toss their batons skyward in a spinning, blazing fan. They caught them dead center every time. Those kerosene-soaked batons in the dusk of autumn, they smelled of permanence.

One year blended into the next with only slight differences in star athletes or town leaders and sometimes one turned into the other. Family businesses occupied Main Street, anchored by the Chicken Coop. "Good Eatin' That's Our Greetin'!" their tagline declared in flat, red paint. On Wednesdays the Bowl-O-Drome hosted my gum-chewing junior high league, and on Fridays it murmured with the sporty jesting of my father's league. I bought penny candy from the variety store next to the bowling alley, as did my mother, as did hers. Up and down the street, businesses opened and closed their doors with the seasons, the economy, and the sun: Lazarou's car dealership, the Dairy Queen, RadioShack, Dick's Restaurant, and our radio station, WRUM. The footbridge to the mill spans the Androscoggin where Main Street tapers off. Three generations of my family and exponential relatives worked there, as did most people who spread *cretons* on their toast before clocking in. We were stamped out like Christmas cookies, as good French Catholics were. We got up, ate, worked, and went to bed, deriving small pleasures between the routine and sometimes because of it.

In the drowsy summertime, when the sun dipped low over the foothills and the humidity of the day invaded kitchens and bedrooms, people in our town flocked to their porches. There, they chatted while dusk knit itself into a tight blanket. The sounds of clinking dishes, faint music, vehicles purring, and light-as-vapor laughter scented the air. Night fell like a bruise. During those school-less days, I often sat on the dusty curb in front of our house and counted the out-of-state license plates as they sped by on their way to somewhere else. When I could finally drive myself I'd cruise around Rumford and Mexico with all the other teenagers, pivoting our used Monte Carlo in the Tourist Information Booth parking lot before another revolution through town. My parents thought the Information Booth was where all the "druggies" hung out, and sometimes the pot smokers did, but really, it was a harmless venue in a small town with nothing else to do but drive around in aimless circles.

My parents shaped their own well-worn paths. While my father walked back and forth across the bridge to work, my mother lugged laundry up and down the cellar stairs, day after day, one skinny arm cradling the laundry basket, her free hand gripping a Viceroy. With a screech and a whack, the screen door would slam shut after she elbowed it open. She would dump clean laundry on the kitchen table, snap each article of clothing three times, fold them sharply into tight wedges of fabric, and stack them like the reams of white paper my father brought home from the mill. When the screen door wore out, my mother replaced it with a new one that came with a squeaky spring. She left it defective, announcing herself into infinity with only my father to hear. His hearing, long dulled by the hum of paper machines, was the perfect match to her perpetual clamor. She'd let her Viceroy expire before finishing it and send me to fetch her a new pack from the corner store. *I'll time you*, she'd say. *Now GO!* And off I went. Go? She didn't need to tell me twice. In Mexico and Rumford, what we needed, we had. Everyone knew everyone and we liked it that way—for what other way was there? *It was quite the place*, my mother says. *There was never any reason to leave.* Things stayed in this balance, with minor adjustments every now and then until small working-class towns started to ebb alongside the industries that nourished them.

I still gag every time I drink a glass of water, a reflex that emerged in my youth when I lived within a football field's reach of the mill and the Androscoggin. At the time, I sweetened the mephitic water with Tang or Zarex or drank no water at all. But as an adult, the memory of our drinking water's brackish and sweetish chemical smell/taste, combined with the sour air above it, precipitates what feels like smothering when I put glass to lips.

By 1970, when I was three, the river's dissolved oxygen level was exactly zero. *Newsweek* named the Androscoggin one of the ten filthiest rivers in the United States. Everything in the river died. *Don't eat the fish*, we were always told, but we couldn't have anyway because we never saw any to catch. There also were no swimmers, fishermen, or boaters in the river William B. Lapham, in his 1890 book, *History of Rumford*, called "beautiful," noting "the scenery bordering upon it is picturesque and often grand." If you squint, the Androscoggin still fits Lapham's description. But if you open your eyes, you'll see what was invisible to me my whole life: the mill's pollutants hovering low over the naturally formed glacial bowl of our valley and in the toxic sludge congregating in landfills and the riverbed. What I did see when I was young, however, was the rainbow-colored foam eddying on the river's edge, which was as enchanting as the gray "mill snow" that floated softly up from the smokestacks and down upon any surface in town. What did we all do? We plugged our noses and placed our drinking glasses upside down in the cupboard so ash wouldn't get in our milk. The pollution was as trapped as we were.

Dioxin, cadmium, benzene, lead, naphthalene, nitrous oxide, sulfur dioxide, arsenic, furans, trichlorobenzene, chloroform, mercury, phthalates: these are some of the byproducts of modern-day papermaking. Non-Hodgkin's lymphoma, lung cancer, prostate cancer, aplastic anemia, esophageal cancer, asbestosis, Ewing's sarcoma, emphysema, cancer of the brain, cancer of the heart: these are some of the illnesses appearing in Rumford and Mexico. Occasionally in suspicious-looking clusters, sometimes in generations of families, often in high percentages. When anyone tried to connect the dots between the mill's pollution with these illnesses, logic was met with justification, personal experience with excuse, stories with statistics, disease with blame.

Between 1980 and 1988, seventy-four cases of aplastic anemia, a rare and serious blood disorder, are recorded in the River Valley. It is the highest rate in the state. A study is ordered to find the cause. Researchers examine potential environmental and occupational sources, such as benzene, a chemical used in papermaking and a known cause of cancer in humans. Each aplastic anemia case gets parsed: some are eliminated from the study because they are referrals from other hospitals; some are eliminated because the stated diagnosis didn't fit into the strict scientific criteria; some are eliminated because certain cancer treatments themselves cause aplastic anemia. In the final report, nobody can determine the exact cause. It is as if nobody ever had the disease at all.

1984-1986. Hospital discharges indicate nine leukemia cases in the Rumford and Mexico area.

1989. The Rumford mill discharges 1.2 million pounds of toxic chemicals into the environment.

1991. In rapid succession, five people in Rumford and Mexico are diagnosed with non-Hodgkin's lymphoma, a rare form of blood cancer associated with exposure to dioxin, a toxic chemical formed in the paper-bleaching process. WCVB, a Boston TV station investigates the flurry of diagnoses in their news series *Chronicle* and calls the episode, "Cancer Valley." During this time, the Dana-Farber Cancer Institute in Boston asks our town physician, "What the hell's going on in Rumford? We're getting all these kids with cancer coming in from your area."

The *Los Angeles Times* talks to our state representative, Ida Luther: "We have a very, very high cancer rate, but we always have lived with that. Nobody can prove anything, but I just can't see how tons and tons of air pollutants going into the air can do you any good. At the same time, I don't want to make [the paper mill] out to be a villain. They're here to make paper and—there's no question about it—this valley depends upon that paper mill." The mill responds by claiming there's "no clear link between mill wastes and cancer or other diseases."

2001. WCVB films "Return to Cancer Valley" in Rumford and Mexico.

2004. Cancer is the leading cause of death in Maine.

2005. Maine's age-adjusted cancer incidence rate is the second highest in the nation and Maine's death rate from cancer surpasses the national average.

2009. Cancer remains the leading cause of death in Maine.

2010. Toxic environmental exposures associated with childhood illnesses cost Maine about $380 million every year, according to the 2010 Economic Assessment of Children's Health and the Environment in Maine.

2012. A headline from Maine's *Kennebec Journal*: "Some Label Toxin Spike as Positive; pulp and paper industry says increase is a good sign, state officials not alarmed." What doesn't alarm state officials and the Maine Pulp and Paper Association are the "9.6 million pounds of chemicals [that] were released by 84 Maine mills between 2009 and 2010, an increase of 1.14 million pounds over the previous year" because the increase in pollution shows an increase in papermaking. Our mill is fingered as the number one pollution producer, releasing over three million pounds of toxic chemicals into the environment for those same years.

2012. Cancer is the leading cause of death in Maine. Dr. Molly Schwenn, director of the Maine Cancer Registry, tenders an explanation. She says contributing to Maine's high cancer rates are "lower levels of education, high rates of poverty, unemployment, and lack of health insurance."

2014. The Cancer Surveillance Report by the Maine Center for Disease Control confirms cancer is still the leading cause of death in Maine.

There's a lag between exposure and diagnosis, experts declared. *People could be exposed from other sources,* scientists explained. *There are uncertainties,* decried the Environmental Protection Agency. *Continued follow-up is needed,* said the mill. While organizations debated who to blame, people in Rumford and Mexico quit jobs or school to care for sick family members; lose health insurance because they lose their jobs; and put canisters on pizza shop countertops to pay for medical bills.

It was often difficult to tell where the mill ended and where Rumford and Mexico began. The mill's employees, in the 1920s, published *The League*, a compendium of work and community related activities. In it, you'd learn "Charlie Gordon was seriously ill Thursday A.M" or in the "Rewinder Gossip" column, you'd find out "Joe Provencher is in his second boyhood for he is wearing short pants again." The newsletter also reported first-aid room statistics, townwide events, movie times, attendance at mill fire drills, or changes in the sulphate mill, the bleach plant, and the finishing room. It changed to the *Oxford Log* in 1952 where someone wrote a story on Labor Day beauty parade "Cutter" girls "dressed in daring ankle-length dresses" and whose "blue bonnets and sashes were made of fine Oxford paper." In that same newsletter, you could also read about Johnny Norris, who worked on the supercalendar machine, who, while on vacation in New York City, found it "hot and confusing." Or Hollis Swett of the "Island Division" who got caught in a lightening storm while fishing at Weld Pond. *The Oxford Log* published profiles of high school basketball stars who were sons of millworkers. Or of Nick DiConzo, a paper tester, who prepared the ski jump for the Black Mountain's Winter Carnival. You'd see vintage photos of the workers adding bleach to vats of pulp, or working in the Kraft mill—gloveless, barefoot, smiling as if there was no end to the prosperity. And it looked to be true; by 1930, our mill was the largest paper mill under one roof and Hugh J. Chisholm, eventually combined twenty paper companies to establish International Paper, then and today, the biggest paper company in the world.

I am home visiting. My parents and I sort through papers, organizing things after their move to a new, one-story house in Rumford. They still haven't sold their old house. It's been on the market for a few years. *If the bank takes our old house, who cares?* my mother says. She flips through a newsletter from 1970. It's thick, printed in color, and features my mother because she helped plan that year's Winter Carnival Ball at Black Mountain on account of her "first-hand knowledge" of the queen's duties; she won the title and a tiara in 1962 when she worked in the mill's personnel department. She was a young mother at the time, wearing a pixie cut and polyester miniskirts that showed off her good legs. In her victory photo, my sisters Kelly and Amy sit in front of her wearing matching blue velvet dresses with white Peter Pan collars, stiff as Communion wafers.

In 1942 when my mother was born, legendary twenty-foot walls of urine-colored foam emerged from canals forty miles downstream in the Androscoggin. By then, almost fifty years of flotsam and effluent had choked the fish. Aeration of the river dimmed. Water temperature rose. Manufacturing and its concomitant pollution reached a stinky zenith. The smell emanating from the river was so appalling people fled town or shuttered themselves in. Coins in men's pockets tarnished. Stores closed. House and car paint peeled like burnt skin. Residents vomited. Laundry hung on clotheslines, blackened with ash.

I was sixteen, my mother says, when the National Geographic Society entered into a fifteen-year contract with our mill. The windfall, while providing steady work, also brought with it a windfall of pollution that exacerbated the toxic load the Androscoggin Rivermaster was already trying to manage. National Geographic demanded white, coated, glossy paper and our mill made it. Making it, however, required using even more chemicals. The town's economy flourished. As the mill modernized and expanded, each year that newsletter, like the town's future, got whiter and brighter. And each year the Androscoggin River and the skies above, seemed dimmer and dimmer. My parents were caught between a stinky past and a hopeful future.

My father, in between the overtime hours or double shifts, along with other millworkers, built Black Mountain on land leased to them by the paper company. The men felled trees, carved up the rocky slopes, and jammed iron ski lift poles in unsympathetic soil so they could have a place to ski. Every winter of my childhood, on weekends, my father piloted our station wagon along the frost-heaved roads winding through the outskirts of town, past the smokestacks, past the Swift River where he learned to swim, past the cemetery where his father was buried, where I lugged my steely equipment uphill through the icy parking lot, collapsed on the snow, and thwacked down the metal buckles on my leather boots pinching my fingers. I was small, the runt in a pack of kids who were already small, and tried to keep up with them and my father, who was probably one of the best skiers on the hill. As I followed them, my leather boots and leather gloves became soaked with sweat and subsequently frozen, in an endless circle of discomfort. We skied until the T-bar stopped clinking and growling, lolling to rest like an iron dinosaur and the last light of dusk would slam shut over the smudged hills. We'd return the following week just as the T-bar purred awake. A video: I am four. My father crouches over me on skis and I stand in front of him on skis too, between his legs, facing forward, gaining speed as we race down the mountain. He warns me to watch what's in front of me, but to also look far enough downhill to see what lay ahead. I think I'm skiing on my own volition. Unbeknownst to me at the time, I couldn't have stood for two seconds without his arms there to carry me.

I ask my mother, *What about the pollution when you were a kid?*
What do you mean? she says.
Didn't it bother you? The pollution? I say.
It was the smell of money, she says. *Plus, we just had a lot of pride.*
Pride.
I heard this word a lot as a child. You were "proud" to be from Rumford and Mexico. You took "pride" in the mill. "Pride" in the paper we made. "Pinto pride" we scrawled on pep rally posters in honor of our mascot. Mill managers instilled a "pride" in their workers. What did it mean, this pride?
I learned from an early age, to be conspicuous was to be coarse. You didn't speak too loudly or too much, *blend in*. This sameness, it turns out, was partially the source of our pride—we were all in it

together, no matter what "it" was. We were a community and like most communities, were proud of what we did, even if it was something we didn't necessarily like. It was part of the same invisible social rules that also felt claustrophobic, so it was difficult to differentiate the two. It was a subtle force, like airplane cabin pressure—massive but invisible. In this togetherness our loyalties to each other and our town were fierce, even if the intimation to conform was benevolent.

This absolute loyalty didn't stop at the edge of town; it extended to hopeless causes like the Boston Red Sox and the New England Patriots who for decades disappointed us with their fruitless company. But we stuck with them because that's what we did despite their unwillingness to love us back. This mix of sameness and loyalty and pride and stubbornness made us tight. We created this shelter for ourselves but it also meant outsiders remained outside. People "from away" weren't allowed into the sanctity of our tribe. And we certainly didn't want to be part of theirs. Solidarity was a matter of safety and comfort, but it was also a matter of hardheadedness that didn't always serve us well.

The mill, the main source of this pride and connectedness, provided us with what seemed like limitless opportunity, the tentacles of its fortune reaching into the county, the region, the state of Maine, America. Our reliance on the mill was like our Catholicism. We were given something to believe in while ignoring our own suffering, all the while waiting for the big afterlife party in the sky. We depended on the mill, as did loggers, whose lopping of the trees was seemingly anathema to the very thing relied upon to earn an income.

Brenda Nickerson walks into the kitchen where my parents and I are still looking through old mill newsletters. My mother and Brenda have been friends since childhood and I went to school with her daughters who were named after Louisa May Alcott's Little Women. My mother says to me, to Brenda, *It was like 'Happy Days.' You*

know the show? That's what we lived. We lived like 'Happy Days.'
Brenda agrees. I ask my mother if this was true for when I was a kid.
*Yes, pretty much . . . but I don't know what happened after that.
It's when our kids had kids that everything changed.*

You mean like me? I ask. *It changed in my generation?*

Yes, she says. *We had our parents' and grandparents' values.
Your generation has different values.*

Brenda says, *Your generation had too many choices.*

When my father retired from the mill after forty-three years,
he received a toolbox (that he used), a Bulova watch (that he
never wore), and asbestosis of the lungs. The toolbox decamped to
our dusty barn and I found the watch years later, in perfect shape,
in the garage on a shelf by the cat litter. Since retiring, asbestos
manufacturers, whose products he came into contact with as a pipe
fitter, compensated him for his scarred lung tissue; sometimes he
received three dollars, sometimes a few hundred. Eventually, the
monies petered out as did his lungs. He was tough, sometimes to a
fault, and I never heard him complain even on the night he died.
He told me a story once about how when he was a kid he walked
around all day with a sharp pebble in his shoe, so that when he took
it out, the relief was even greater than if it were never there at all.

In the summer of 2013, he collapsed on the ninth hole of the
golf course, face up, in the middle of his daily game. After months
of tests, he was diagnosed with esophageal cancer and then a few
months later, lung cancer, which can develop from asbestosis; with
that trifecta, the man simply couldn't breathe. My father asked us
not to speak to him about his prognosis and our family complied in
mute alliance. Weeks of chemotherapy and radiation, a blood clot
in his lung, a catheter, a feeding tube, an oxygen tank, the gloom of
hospice, my father shrank to half his size. *No taste,* he said as he
tussled with a piece of pasta as if it were barbed wire. He lost more

weight and lost interest, too. My mother tried to get him to do his physical therapy, eat a popsicle. He just stared out the living room window while we whispered behind his back.

I went home almost every week that winter. When I did, I drove into Maine from New Hampshire across the Piscataqua River Bridge. One of the first things I'd see was the state-funded welcome sign: "Maine. The Way Life Should Be." *Was there ever such a Maine as this?* I wondered as I sped up the Maine Turnpike. The promise of that phrase just never added up. The silvery creeks, iron gray lakes, red lobsters, rocky beaches, the deluge of trees—they summoned a representation disconnected from my Maine experience. It seemed we had lived on the edge of poverty, anxiety, and illness rather than on the edge of a primeval forest. Practically everyone in our town called the area "Cancer Valley" in a jokey way, yet nobody ever took the nickname seriously, even to this day. *It smells like farts!* kids from other high schools would say about our town because of the foul odor discharged by the mill. And so it did.

Maine's story somehow became so appended over the years, that the story became the story itself. It was like that game you played as a kid where you sat in a circle and one person would whisper a phrase in their neighbor's ear, and that child would whisper it to the next one, and so on. At the end of the circle, the last child would repeat the phrase aloud. Inevitably the murmured telling and retelling distorted the words so the original phrase was no longer recognizable.

I was riding the Metro-North train from New York City to Connecticut one night that same winter, exhausted from my visits home. When I told my seatmate I was from Maine, he said, *I love all that fresh air and woods! Maine is God's country!* I wanted to tell him that behind the photos of birch-lined streams and the lobster logo-ed gifts on the Maine Tourism Bureau website, there is a state perishing under the weight of its own advertisement and where "God" is noticeably absent. Instead I said, *It's a terrific place to grow up*, which was largely true.

But the real contradictions were these: we clear-cut our forests while tourists exalted them; pollution bankrupted the fresh air we advertised; we poured dioxins into our environment, which ended up in lobsters that tourists ate; Henry David Thoreau lauded the "Pine Tree State" but his voice was drowned out by the growl of chainsaws; and what gave our town life could also be what's killing it. As the folksy Maine saying goes, *you can't get they-ahh from hee-yahh*. In other words, the way life should be, the idealized state of Thoreau and tourists, may have never actually existed except in the landscape of our minds.

Slowly, my father began to eat. All he wanted was pistachios, so I bought bags of them. *Those are too expensive for me*, he'd say, as he gobbled them up. We talked about baseball and books so I bought him *The Art of Fielding*, which I read from at his funeral. We watched movies. He made puzzles. By spring, he was able to roll his wheelchair outside to sit in his driveway in the yawning sun.

Always a great athlete, he loathed just sitting around. *You're throwing like a goddamn GIRL!* he'd yell at my throws from third to first if they weren't fast enough, even if I was only ten. He played third base too, the "hot corner" he called it. He was an institution in that position, never relinquishing it to younger guys as he aged. I watched him summer after summer fielding stinging line drives down third base line as he crept in to take away the bunt. He was quick, efficient. I never saw him make an error. Now, he struggled to lift a knee.

Late summer, 2014. I kiss my father hello and after a few minutes, he turns to the TV. My mother shouts something from the kitchen over the clamorous rattle of *Pawn Stars*. I slump in the overstuffed chair.

Over the next couple of days, I learn the new routine of their lives: my mother empties his catheter bag, changes his cannula, washes dishes, makes coffee, turns the heat up, turns the heat down, helps him to bed, tucks him in. One day the "oxygen man," a nurse, Andy (their handyman), on the next a parade of strangers and friends amass then disperse, like a dandelion gone to seed in a quick wind. In the morning, my mother walks my father to the kitchen, her arms wrapped around his waist. I hear them in the hallway.

I slept liked shit, he says. *I just couldn't sleep. I don't know.*

What's the matter!? my mother says.

It ain't much of a life, he says.

My mother procures a voice-activated phone, a walker, the best hearing aids, a hospital bed, bathtub rails, hospice aides, ice cream, Netflix. The days drift. Dinner comes early. The late afternoon winter light hesitates, then crashes, darkening the curtained room. We fold ourselves into the furniture and flip channels.

"Do you or does anyone you know suffer from lung cancer? Give us a call at . . . " The lawyer on the TV beckons.

Maybe I'll call, my mother suggests.

What the hell are you talking about? my father says.

Your lung cancer. Maybe I'll call them about your lung cancer, she says.

I don't have lung cancer, he says. My mother never brings it up again.

My mother tracks his oxygen levels, like volunteers do on the Androscoggin River, judging impairment by percentages, keeping the lower numbers at bay by turning up the O2. The river's oxygen percentages lie somewhere between impaired and threatened, as do my father's. In 1966 the Androscroggin Rivermaster tried to recreate the river's natural aeration by installing "bubblers" in the Androscoggin, which injected air into the water to increase oxygen levels. My father's body, like the Androscoggin, seems to be recycling the toxins discharged by the mill. But he, unlike the river, would never breathe again without a machine to help him.

When I get better . . . he says as he hunches over, his oxygen tank hissing away in the other room, its plastic line leashing him to his chair . . . *I'll visit your new house.* As he keeps trying to live he keeps dying. He is dying at the same exponential rate as the town . . . an unbuilding of a body that had previously built a mountain. His chest working overtime like he often did in the mill.

"Vacationland," our state motto, appears on key chains, tee shirts, coffee mugs, and our license plates but the holidays of my youth were never a seaside fete. As a teenager, my sister and I would sometimes drive to Old Orchard Beach, two hours south, where we'd buy fries on the pier and watch French Canadian men in skimpy bathing trunks cavort in the water. Rather than swim, I'd smother myself with iodine and baby oil and lie on the hot sand, getting the tan that proved I had been somewhere.

We also made yearly visits to my father's mother "Nana" and my step-grandfather "Pop" in Kennebunk, Maine. Despite its sacrosanct location, they lived closer to the town dump than to the beach. For hours, we'd sift through other people's trash with Pop, or play on the broad front lawn with their dog Bijoux, a crabby spoiled Chihuahua. When Pop entered a room, his egg-shaped bald head flirted with the ceiling. His voice was booming and fearsome, yet he was affectionate in his toothless smile, the way an octopus was, embracing his grandchildren with a manic repulsive grip. My grandmother kept her emotions as tightly bound as her arms, which were always crossed over her chest, and she only allowed small giggles through her thin hand, which rose to cover her mouth when she laughed.

The rooms in their house smelled of cigarette smoke and age, a sour, untidy odor I evaded by sleeping in their camping trailer parked in the driveway. Pop, we learned after he died, molested a few of my female cousins. As for the beach, we would sometimes go, but I would rather have been pawing though the trash or the animal-shaped candles in the tourist shops than face a marauding jellyfish sloshing in the lazy waves or meeting up with Pop in an unkempt, upstairs hallway.

E. B. White wrote dispatches for the *New Yorker* from his saltwater farm in Brooklin, Maine. When he drove there from New York, he too crossed the Piscataqua River. In his essay "Home-Coming" he wrote that every time he drove over the river, he "had the sensation of having received a gift from a true love." While he and I may disagree on how we feel traversing the state line or our reasons for doing so, we agree on the reason we are pulled there. "Familiarity is the thing—the sense of belonging," he wrote. "It grants exemption from all evil, all shabbiness." I'm tethered to Maine by this sense of belonging but also by a sometimes paralyzing ambiguity I wrestle to understand—an inexplicable love for Maine and what it represents, even if some of those things are false. I don't think it was ever really a paradise, except maybe for the Abenaki Native Americans who fished the Androscoggin until their lives and the salmon they ate were choked out by disease and settlers.

When we leave home, we leave behind our past and encounter a version of home when we return, built of legends true and false. For me, those legends are so big—Hugh J. Chisholm, Edmund Muskie, Cancer Valley, Henry David Thoreau, Paul Bunyan, Black Mountain, my parents, and trees, endless trees—that it is hard to see beyond their shadows. So when I drive back over the Piscataqua River Bridge with Mexico in my rearview mirror, I may not see "true love," but

I know leaving home can be as complicated as living there and as inescapable as your own DNA.

The night I watched my father die he kept trying to speak, but only a thin awful wail emerged as he thrashed his body against the steel bedrails and wrestled with his sheets. It was the only time I ever saw him make a fuss about anything. What he was trying to say, I'll never know, but I do know I no longer have to keep secrets from him or for him. *What you don't know won't hurt you,* my mother always said offhandedly. She was dead wrong.

I saw in that outline of his body, a lifetime of 7–3 shifts at the mill, where the hot racket of the paper machines would have made me turn into a lifeless cotton ball, a weeping remnant of a human being. I saw in him, too, a lifetime of working for an industry that in the end, led to his end.

You look like your father! People always said to me and still do. Our eyes, in particular, are/were the same blue-gray and one of mine sags a little, as if I am falling asleep, the same as his. In that sameness, I saw what he saw, or at least I imagined I did, or tried to, especially on our walks around town where his telling and retelling of the same stories became more distilled each time he told them. He'd narrate as we went: *This is an historic spot,* he said one time, pointing to the road, as we passed a vacant lot that used to be his high school. *This is where Roger Gallant dropped a jar of mercury.* I imagined the balls of silver pinging along the road in tantric lines. We walked across the frozen soil and scuffed our boots across the thin snow to uncover a plaque of people who donated money for the plaque. He pointed to a Gallant, class of 1951. *That's him,* my father said. *That's the guy that dropped the mercury.*

In the aftermath of his death, two years on, I still can't look at photographs of him, because in them I remember his emaciated body, sacrificed so I could have a new pair of shoes to start school every fall or a new softball glove when I turned sixteen. And in his eyes I see me.

Paul Bunyan looms over the Tourist Information Booth in front of the Androscoggin where Bunyan-sized logs once floated downstream toward the mill. In blue pants, a matching blue watch cap, and a short sleeve red polo shirt exposing his brawny arms, he proffers an equally enormous axe that could clear-cut the Amazon. That statue has been around as long as I remember, although it used to tower above Puiia's Hardware across the street, a catchall shop where I bought charcoals and sketch pads for juvenile renderings of horses. He was donated to the town when Puiia's closed. As a kid, I didn't pay much attention to Bunyan despite his size, and he blended into the background, as improbable as that seems.

I read that Rumford's Paul Bunyan got a facelift between 2000–2002, a body overhaul including a paint job, a new axe, and steel supports secured to a huge block of concrete, which to replace, they had to remove Bunyan's head. After they fastened the supports and before reinstating Bunyan's head, the workmen wriggled out of Bunyan's neck. After Paul's resurrection, Rumford held a festival in his honor featuring a lumberjack breakfast, zip line rides over the waterfalls, a facial hair contest, a flannel shirt dinner dance, and an axe-throwing competition.

Bunyan's origin remains a mystery. Small towns, from Maine to Minnesota, claim him as their own, yet they agree the boy giant was the hero of all woodsmen. Legend maintains when Bunyan's cradle rocked, the motion caused huge waves that sunk ships. He also allegedly whittled a pipe from a hickory tree and could outrun buckshot. Our Bunyan, I found out, was crafted from the mold of the Muffler Man, a giant fiberglass statue who proffered mufflers as advertisement on US byways in the 1970s. Whatever the myth, there our Bunyan stands as a guardian or curiosity for those ambling

43

through the waning mill town of my youth, his shadow sometimes as brooding as the hurtling river beyond. Senator Edmund Sixtus Muskie's smaller, more serious memorial of squat dark gray granite lies just down the riverbank from Bunyan. Muskie was a giant in real life at 6' 4" and the man who penned the Clean Air and Clean Water Acts, though no match for the long shadow cast by Bunyan. Both memorialized in Rumford, their acts equally significant; one deforested the woodlands, the other tried to reclaim them, the rocky pools on the edge of the Androscoggin spanning the gap between the two of them.

My father used to make fun of the Bunyan statue and the ludicrous blue hoofprints painted on the sidewalks in downtown Rumford, made by Babe, Bunyan's blue ox. The town selectmen voted, in 2009, to use $6,500 from their economic development fund to create Babe, figuring that he and his hoofprints would encourage tourists to follow his path. What they forgot to consider was that there's not much left in town to see but Paul Bunyan himself and those garish blue steps that end abruptly at Rite Aid.

Poet and journalist ADISA BAŠIĆ was born in 1979 in Sarajevo. She has a degree in Comparative Literature and Librarianship and a master's degree in Human Rights and Democracy. She has published four poetry collections, *Eve's Sentences* (1999), *Trauma Market* (2004), *A Promo Clip for My Homeland* (2011), and *Motel of Unknown Heroes* (2014). Her poems have been included in all recent anthologies of Bosnian poetry.

UNA TANOVIĆ is a doctoral candidate in the Comparative Literature program at the University of Massachusetts Amherst and has dual focus in comparative literature and translation studies. Her translations of Bosnian literature have been published in the *Massachusetts Review*.

Alipašino

ADISA BAŠIĆ
TRANSLATED FROM THE BOSNIAN BY UNA TANOVIĆ

We're the kids from the neighborhood
that will never end up
on postcards.

To our parts tourists do not venture.

We don't win presidential elections in a run-off.
And no language do we speak better than our mother tongue.
We do not know that our twin brothers live
in all of the cities of the world.

To our parts tourists do not venture.

There is nothing well known here:
an elementary school,
a supermarket, and an old walnut tree long cut down.

To our parts tourists do not venture.

And we have nothing to show them.
Except ourselves.

XIAOLU GUO is a novelist and filmmaker. She was born in China in 1973 and moved to the UK in 2002. She studied at the Beijing Film Academy and the UK's National Film and TV School. Her most notable novels are *A Concise Chinese-English Dictionary for Lovers* (nominated for the Orange Prize for Fiction), *20 Fragments of a Ravenous Youth*, and *I Am China* (longlisted for the Baileys Women's Prize for Fiction). She has also directed several feature films, including *How Is Your Fish Today?* and *Once Upon a Time Proletarian*. They were officially selected by the Venice Film Festival, Sundance, and MoMA in New York. Her fiction feature *She, a Chinese* received the Golden Leopard Award at the Locarno Film Festival in 2009. She divides her time between London, Beijing, and Berlin. Her memoir, *Nine Continents* (in the US) and *Once Upon a Time in the East* (in the UK) is due to be published in 2017.

Fishermen Always Eat Fish Eyes First

XIAOLU GUO

In my adult life, I often hear people say I am a hard-hearted person. They ask me where I came from. I tell them I am from a village called Shitang, literarily, Stone Pond, in Zhejiang province by the East China Sea. They must think that a person's early life forms that person's character. Maybe they are right, maybe I am a hard-hearted person. When I think of my childhood, it occurs to me that it must have been that fishing village, where I spent the first seven years of my life, that killed any tenderness in my heart. It feels to me that my heart was turned into a rock by those steely cornered, jagged stone houses I grew up in. That place made me a hard person, a stoic and even merciless person.

Shitang lies in between mainland China and Taiwan, three hundred kilometers seaway from the Taiwanese coast. Thousands of years ago, this area was a saltwater lagoon next to the sea, and it came to be inhabited by people who built up the land on the seafront, just as Hong Kong and Macau were built from reclaimed marsh and swamp. In my memory, the sea was always yellow-brown. This yellow-brownness was caused by the large kelp beds growing in the shallow water along the shore. The kelp—we called it *haifa*, the hair of the sea—had long and tough stalks with broad palms and long, brown-green stripes. Like a swarm of shapeless sea snakes, the clumps of kelp formed a tangled mass blurring the divide between land and water. Despite its monstrous shape, kelp was a staple in the Shitang diet. We would stew it in eel soup or fry it with pork, along with the tiny fish we found swarming under the kelp fronds.

The soil of Shitang was very salty and largely barren. There were hardly any trees growing in the village, except for the tough gardenias. They grew vigorously between rocks and on the cliffs next to the foamy sea. Their large white flowers would swirl in the salt-laden wind. I loved their strongly scented flowers. Local women often picked the blooming buds to decorate their braided hair. I would do the same with my meager ponytail.

Our family house was a small, moss-covered stone dwelling right on the horn of the peninsula. My grandfather lived upstairs, where he could directly look out onto the sea through a small window by his bed. He was the only one in our house who had a sea view. My grandmother and I lived downstairs. The view from our windows was blocked by the neighbors' washing lines, dried squid and salted ribbonfish hanging on poles. I could see the dishes the neighbors ate through my window. I couldn't say whether I loved or hated that house. I simply treated the house as our house, the village as our village. I lived with my grandparents without my parents present and that was an unquestioned fact for me. I didn't know my father had been punished in a labour camp during the Cultural Revolution, and that my mother was a full-time factory worker who could not raise me. No one told me anything.

Our street was called Anti-Pirates Passage. The name Anti-Pirates Passage came from the Ming Dynasty period, when the area was heavily attacked by pirates from the east Pacific Ocean. The local militias had to arm themselves with homemade guns and bombs and managed, after many fierce battles, to repulse the pirates. That was four hundred years ago. People said nothing much happened in the village after this heroic period, except that after 1949 the local authorities replaced the Buddha posters in their offices with Mao posters. Everyone admitted the village was a backwater. The only dramatic stories came from the sea. We were very close to Taiwan—the evil island that had claimed its independence from Communist China.

During that time, fishermen from nearby regions would often secretly set off in their boats hoping to arrive in Taiwan, where the Nationalist government promised to reward mainlanders with gold and farmland. Some succeeded, but very often we heard about cases of severe punishment: someone's uncle or brothers caught on the edge of international waters and sentenced to death. 'Shot at dawn' and 'life sentence' were regular announcements from our village loudspeakers. In the 1970s, no one had a private radio or television. All news came from giant, high-volume speakers hanging on electricity poles in the streets. My grandparents' house directly faced a pole with two loud-speakers. Every so often, in the early morning, we would be woken up by loud Communist songs, followed by a 'to be shot at dawn in the meat market' death sentence. After hearing such news, villagers would rush to the meat market to watch the execution. I never dared to go and witness a killing. Just hearing a gunshot resound from the market square made me sick in the pit of my stomach.

Given the location of our house in the center of the village, we could always hear talking, crying, arguing, haggling, cocks roosting, kids screaming, pigs oinking all through the day and into the night. There was never a moment of peace and quiet. Now, as I think of it, it was simply the pervading ambient sound environment of China, even in the remote parts of the country. There was untrammelled life everywhere. Nothing seemed to be controlling or directing it. It just flowed like a stream.

My grandparents knew everyone in the village and everyone knew them. They could instantly spot anyone in the street who wasn't a local. My grandmother was a kind, sometimes timid and fearful woman. She barely had a penny in her pocket, but she would still find some small presents for the kids playing in our street: candies, leftover rice, or some colorful seashells. So good-hearted and voiceless, she was the humblest person I have ever known. She couldn't walk fast or even at a normal speed. Obviously, her tiny bound feet, which she never complained about, contributed to that. From as far back as I can remember, she always had this hunchback, even when she wasn't that old. Nasty kids often laughed at me, screaming things like: 'Your grandmother is a giant shrimp, she can only see her toes!' or 'Here comes the upright walking turtle!' She had thin, grey-white hair, bound into a chignon behind her head. With her diseased and twisted spine, she had difficulty washing her hair, which always looked dirty. She also slept poorly. I could hear her long sighs in the night, and the way she moved her bent spine on the bamboo bed, which produced a constant stream of creaking sounds and woke me up in the dark.

No one had photos taken in those days in remote Chinese villages. I have no way of knowing what she looked like when she was young. Perhaps she had been a decent-looking girl, but surely she had always been small and very skinny. Her parents arranged her future marriage when she was still a baby. At age twelve, she was married (or more correctly, she was sold) to my grandfather as a child-bride. My grandfather handed over a bag of rice and eight kilos of yams in exchange. And then, accompanied by her own father, my grandmother walked from her village for three days to get to Shitang for the wedding. I know she came to my grandfather's house to fill her hungry stomach. But she didn't know that her new husband didn't have much rice in his rice jar. That was in the 1930s when China was ravaged by civil war, between the Nationalists and the

Communists. Then there were the Japanese committing atrocities all over the country until 1945. My grandmother had vague memories of Japanese soldiers coming into their house while they were hiding in the mountain temples. The Japs looted everything. When she returned home some weeks later, she saw that almost nothing valuable was left, apart from a wok still sitting on the stove. She lifted the lid, and found a big lump of brown-colored shit inside. She told me about this incident when I was around five, which made me think that the whole Sino-Japanese War had to do with nasty shitting in woks. She had no further comments about the wars, even though she had witnessed almost every conflict in China since the beginning of the twentieth century.

In the 1970s, my grandmother was in her early seventies. In the countryside, peasants and ordinary people were still chained to the feudal system. Many times I saw her crying alone. She would quietly weep in the back of our kitchen or in front of a white porcelain Guanyin statue set inside the kitchen wall. Her eyes were always teary and clouded. Every day she prayed to Guanyin—the Goddess of Mercy—the most popular saint in our region. When I was about six, she told me: 'Xiaolu, I have a dog's life, a life not worthy of living. But I pray for you, and for your parents.'

My grandfather was always grumpy. Even though he knew everyone, he never greeted anyone in the street. It was always the other way around. People would greet him with the standard Chinese question: 'Have you eaten today?' Or something more specific, like: 'How is your boat, Old Guo?' He would never bother to answer. He would just grunt, or silently pass without even raising his eyebrows. My grandfather's silence reigned in our house too. My grandmother would mutter things to me in a small voice. She never talked about my grandfather, at least never in front of me. She was so frightened of him. I saw how her limbs became stiff and she sometimes trembled when he passed in front of us. I never saw them lying on the same bed together, or even staying in the same room for more than half an hour. My grandfather barely ate in the kitchen with us. If he did, my grandmother would retreat, sitting in the corner, usually by the stove—a place that traditionally belonged to the woman. There she would eat the leftovers. My grandfather preferred to take his rice bowl upstairs to his own room, where he could drink liquor by himself and chew on his own unhappiness. I think he despised my grandmother deeply, partly so as to uphold tradition, partly because she came from an inland family and didn't know how to help a fisherman.

I was told that already in their first year of marriage he had decided to despise her. For example, he despised her for not knowing how to eat a fish properly in a fisherman's house. In Shitang, when a fish was being served, the wife would first pick the fish eyes out for her husband with her chopsticks. Eating fish eyes would make a fisherman's eye bright and he would not miss a single fish in the sea. But my grandmother didn't know that custom, she had barely cooked a fish in her inland mountain village. I was told by the villagers that he shouted at her during that meal: 'Stupid woman, don't you know fishermen always eat fish eyes first?!'

After eating the fish eyes, according to Shitang tradition, we would start from the fish tail. Eating the fish head straight away was considered bad luck for a fisherman. But my grandmother thought to show her modesty by choosing the part that her husband was not eating. She ate the fish head. She sucked the bones thoroughly. He grew furious and left the dining table immediately. Perhaps that explained why my grandfather always had such bad luck with his boat. His boat was constantly ravaged by typhoons all those years. Although my grandmother tried hard to learn all the customs of Shitang. Like all women in that area, she never set foot on her husband's boat, or on any boat. To have a woman on your boat brings bad luck, even though my grandmother sewed fishing nets for my grandfather. But it was too late. She never won his heart.

It was an awful partnership. He beat her all the time, for very small things, such as for not fetching a matchbox quickly enough for him to smoke, or for not cooking well enough, or for not being in the kitchen when he was hungry. Or he simply beat her for no reason at all. He kicked her short, skinny legs, and pushed and punched her to the floor. That was the usual activity in the house. She would weep only after he left. When she cried, she didn't even get up from the cold stone floor. Despite my being young, I was numb, witnessing this sort of scene too often. And I would hide myself whenever such a scene was repeated. In 1970s China, in an illiterate peasant house, who could claim that they hadn't encountered such events on a daily basis? I didn't feel close to my grandfather as he never showed any affection or warmth to me, but I didn't think he was in any way a monster. Because where I grew up, every man hit his woman and children. In the morning, in the evening, in the middle of the night, you could hear neighbors howling after an episode—a male voice shouting, furniture being thrown about, then the weeping of a mother or a daughter. That was village life. It was normal.

My grandmother died shortly after I left the village for schooling in my parents' town. Whenever I recall my grandmother, I always have a very sad and loving memory of this old hunchbacked woman using her pitiful savings to buy me an ice stick (a sort of cheap ice cream made with water and sugar). She would wrap the ice stick in her dirty handkerchief upon which she had coughed out her lungs, and would search for me from street to street in the scorching summer afternoons in order to give me that little morsel of sweet ice. She would find me rolling on the ground, playing or fighting with a bunch of kids in some alleyway, and she would unpack her snot-ridden handkerchief and recover what was left of the ice for me. Of course, the ice would have melted, and I would just get a thin little stick with a clot of ice on it. 'Suck it quickly!' she would cry, out of breath from her search to find me. I would suck it thirstily, like a street dog on a steaming day. That was my grandmother's love to me, although I didn't know what 'love' meant then. No one ever taught me that concept in the village, at least not verbally. Later on, after I grew into a teenager, whenever I thought of her I believed she loved me, cared for me greatly. An ice stick cost her five cents, with which you could have bought a vegetable bun in the village. It was a luxurious love by our standards, and for that I should have stood by her, especially whenever my grandfather lost his temper and threw his fist at her face. But I barely defended my grandmother. I was too small and I was also scared of him. I cried often too, but not for my grandmother. I cried because I was born into such a shithole, and I cried with an extreme anger, followed by an overwhelming sense of desolation.

Eventually, my grandfather lost his boat. It was irreparably damaged in a typhoon. He was already in his seventies, and had to become a sea scavenger. Every day, he staggered along the shore with a large but empty sack on his back, his steps heavy and his breath short. He hoped to find something valuable by the water: bits of driftwood, containers, dead crabs, or even dead bodies. If he could find a dead body he could at least harvest the man's clothes and shoes and sell them. I remember one evening my grandmother was worried that her husband would not return, because he had been coughing his head off the last few days. She left home with me and went out looking for him, or in her mind, looking for his dead body along the seashore. But we didn't find him. When we returned home in the pitch black dark, he was upstairs sleeping heavily in his room.

My grandfather scavenged from the shore, until one day he could no longer walk properly. One morning he coughed up blood while drinking a bowl of salty porridge. He had gotten some disease we didn't understand. In the village, there was only one traditional herbal medicine shop, which had a simple clinic. But no one could treat his illness with any modern scientific knowledge. For days, my grandfather limped around our house, coughing and breathing heavily. His eyes were two empty holes, his face grey and lifeless. The acquaintances who passed by on the street would give him one or two cigarettes, and he would just sit on the old threshold of our door, smoking bitterly. Soon the seasonal typhoon arrived, and the violent storms and cold rains shut him back inside the house.

One morning, my grandmother found that her husband didn't come down for breakfast, and he didn't show up at lunchtime either. She climbed the staircase up to his room with her tiny bound feet. I was in the kitchen carving a little boat from a cuttlefish bone, the sort of thing I always did with fish bones. I heard my grandmother scream something upstairs. Then she clambered down, calling her neighbors. She didn't tell me anything in the beginning. The first thing she said to me, in a tone of desperation, was: 'Go get Da Bo, or get anyone next door!' I ran out, pushing open our neighbor Da Bo's door and screaming to everyone inside: 'Come quickly! My grandmother is crying! Come to our house!'

I ran back upstairs, and saw my grandfather lying on the floor. Beside him there was an empty bottle of chemicals and a half-drunk Bai Jiu—a very strong local liquor the fishermen drank in cold weather. My grandfather's eyes were open wide, frozen in their sockets. They looked like the eyes of a dead fish. I fell on my knees and shook my grandfather's arms. But his arms were limp. Then my grandmother came up again, sobbing and speaking hysterically. Da Bo pushed himself in front of her, followed by his wife. With my grandfather's dead eyes still wide open, my grandmother screamed in a pathetic bawling tone: 'I should have called you last night . . . Why did you do this to me? What have I done to deserve this?!'

Then I heard Da Bo say: 'What a sin! He must have poisoned himself by mixing DDT with Bai Jiu.'

At that time, every household had free bottles of DDT as well as other fertilizers distributed by the government, even though Shitang was not the best place for agriculture. Unable to understand what was going on before my eyes, I squatted on the floor, shocked and utterly confused.

My grandmother knelt down, touching my grandfather's body, and howled inchoate half-words.

Half an hour later, a multitude had gathered in front of our house. My grandfather's body was carried down by a few men to the ground floor, where our kitchen was. One of the elderly men tried to close my grandfather's eyes, but the eyes wouldn't close. Then someone screamed to my grandmother: 'Get a warm towel, quick!' My grandmother stood up and grabbed a towel by a washbasin. She poured some hot water from a bottle onto the towel. The man took it and covered my grandfather's eyes. A few seconds later, he removed the towel and everyone could see that the eyes were now shut. The man handed the towel back to my grandmother with satisfaction and began to command the people around him. I looked again at my grandfather's corpse in his black cotton clothes, stiff and motionless. His skinny feet were naked in a pair of broken grass shoes. His mouth was grey and dry, with lips like a dead shark's. Now I began to feel frightened of the stiff body. The villagers first whispered to each other, then they got carried away and spoke louder and louder with excitement: 'Don't you know he drank the DDT?' or 'He didn't get on well with his wife and children, no wonder he went alone!' or 'He must have felt desperate!'

At that age, I couldn't understand a thing about death. But somehow I was tormented by the scene, and felt a deep shame in front of the crowd. My grandmother told me a dead person would become a ghost. But I didn't see any black-clothed ghost flitting around the room. All I felt was a searing anger, an icy cold loneliness somehow emanating from the shriveled dead body towards my own body. I had no one to talk to. Nor did anyone explain the situation to me. Our house was a place for public gossip in front of a poison-filled corpse. And how I hated the feeling of indignity and shame, that afternoon and for days after.

I don't remember much of what happened during the days that followed my grandfather's death. All I remember was that the room upstairs was barely used after he died. We didn't sleep there, nor did we go in there often. I was frightened to enter that room by myself. I thought his ghost might be living there, or might visit us in the night. Any noise occurring upstairs at night would scare me. Since I had always slept with my grandmother on the same bed, I would wake her up and ask her to listen to the scary noise. But she would just open her rheumy eyes and sigh in the dark. Though my grandmother wept for days after the death, and would wear black clothes for the rest of her life, I was a bit numb about the fact that my grandfather was no longer living in this house. Sometimes when my grandmother and I ate our porridge in the kitchen, I felt as if my grandfather was in his room slurping the same porridge and cursing under his breath. He was a shadow in the house when he was alive, and after he had gone it felt like the same shadow was lurking somewhere all the time. I accepted the presence of the shadow without much thought. The room upstairs was the driest room in our house. Sometimes my grandmother climbed up there, hanging ribbonfish on a pole under the ceiling. When the wind came and blew through the windows, the long and pale-colored ribbonfish were like a row of hanging men, swinging weightlessly in the stale air.

I was six and a half. One afternoon I was in the village's auditorium, hiding behind the stage curtains and watching a local opera called *White Snake Lady*. When the opera finished, some kids called me to return home:

'Xiaolu, your grandmother is looking for you! You should go back quickly!'

I ran back home, thinking my grandmother had probably bought me an ice stick, or some exotic candy. But as soon as I arrived at our house, I saw two strangers sitting in the kitchen. A man and a woman. The man looked slender, and was wearing a pair of glasses. The woman was much shorter than the man and had a stern look on her face. She instantly caught my eye once I entered the house. She came straight up to me and took one of my arms. She looked me up and down and stated in a very strange accent:

'Ah, Xiaolu, you are so big now!'

Then I heard my grandmother speaking behind the woman: 'This is your mother, call her Mother!'

I stared at the woman, perplexed.

I sort of understood this woman's lingo, but clearly she didn't speak the dialect we spoke here in the village of Stone Pond. Most of the fishing families here had migrated from the Fujian province long ago and spoke Mingnan dialect. With my grandparents I too spoke Mingnan dialect. So my mother's accent was very alien to me.

Then the man also moved closer, staring at me like I was some curious animal. I was very uneasy to be confronted by these two strangers.

Then my grandmother continued: 'And this is your father. Call him Father!'

The man with the glasses patted my head lightly, with a smile. He had big hands and long fingers. He seemed almost gentle, no fishermen in the village had his kind of look.

I felt anguished, though, and decided not to speak at all. I withdrew myself to the corner of the room. I didn't call them Mother and Father. I could not do it that day.

So that was it. That was the day I remember meeting my parents for the first time. They probably had visited me while I was a small baby, but I didn't have any recollection. Strangely enough, I don't remember much about how I felt in that particular moment. I don't think I had a clear concept of what parents were supposed to mean, since I had never lived with them before. I was aware something had been missing in my life, that I didn't have my parents around like other village kids did. Still, I didn't foresee that it was a significant moment in my life. All I noticed was that there were some new tea bags and rice cakes on the table that the two new people had brought to the house.

My leaving Shitang was an all of a sudden business. I didn't realize that this was actually the day I would leave my poor grandmother behind, that she would now be left alone in the house. There were a few kids I usually played with in the street, but I had no time to say goodbye to them, nor did I realize that I might not see them again. In my confusion, I was told by my parents that they had already packed my stuff: just a few shirts and pants, plus a pair of slippers. We would be leaving Shitang in the next few hours, on the last bus out of the village.

'Where are we going?' I looked at the two adults and asked in distress.

'We are going to where we live, Wenling,' my mother answered with her strange accent. She had a rough peasant manner, and she was not someone you would instantly like. I didn't like her that day, nor did I later on.

'That's where you will go to school,' my father added. He didn't have an accent. He spoke our dialect like my grandparents. At that moment, I understood that he originally came from here. And I felt that he was more friendly than my mother.

I don't remember if I cried when we left my grandparents' house. I didn't really understand what was going on. My grandmother walked all the way to the bus station with us. Because of her bound feet, we walked very slowly through those cobbled alleyways. My grandmother was greeted by many villagers on the street, and each time we would stop as she introduced my parents. 'This is my son, Xiuling,' she pointed to my father. 'He came to take my granddaughter to their town for schooling,' my grandmother would explain to the old women and men, visibly proud. Sometimes my father would recognize someone in the street and go over to pat the man's shoulder and to chat. Eventually, we got to the bus station. The stationmaster, a very respected man in our village, was on duty that day. With a whistle hanging on his chest, he instantly greeted my parents and my grandmother, offering us a handful of sunflower seeds from his pocket. Then he said to me:

'Xiaolu, didn't I tell you that your dad and mom would come to take you to the big city? You will have a great life ahead of you. And your father will give you the best education!'

I nodded my head as my parents chatted with the stationmaster. A great life ahead of me: I was excited to hear this, although I had no idea what it would mean. As we jumped onto the bus, I saw my grandmother's hands grasping the door, her eyes swelling with tears. She then took out her handkerchief from her pocket, the same dirty handkerchief she used to wrap my ice stick. She wiped her eyes with it, but tears were pouring down her cheeks.

My heart felt so heavy. I suddenly realized what was happening, and I was pierced by an indescribable fear and pain. My throat was wrenched from the effort of not crying in front of my parents. Even though I was an unhappy child living with my grandparents in this village, when it came to leaving I felt I was being pushed out of the world I had known. I also felt the weight of my father's hands. He was holding me on the bus seat. I could not move.

As the bus began to pull out, my grandmother followed us outside of the bus window and said with a trembling voice: 'Xiaolu, send me letters and the neighbors will read them to me!'

I nodded my head. Then she yelled in a hoarse voice:

'Always listen to your parents, will you?!'

My grandmother's last words were carried away by a gust of dusty air. The sea blew the salty breeze into the bus, and I smelt the familiar fish scent mixed with the faintest fragrance of the gardenia flowers of Shitang.

VIET THANH NGUYEN was born in Vietnam and raised in America. He is the author of the short story collection *The Refugees* and *The Sympathizer,* which was awarded the 2016 Pulitzer Prize for Fiction, the Andrew Carnegie Medal for Excellence in Fiction, the Center for Fiction First Novel Prize, the Edgar Award for First Novel, the Asian/Pacific American Award for Literature, and the California Book Award for First Fiction. He is also the author of the nonfiction books *Nothing Ever Dies,* which has been shortlisted for the National Book Award, and *Race and Resistance.* He teaches English and American Studies and Ethnicity at the University of Southern California and lives in Los Angeles.

The Committed
Prologue: The Ark

VIET THANH NGUYEN

We were the chosen people, even if the only ones who chose us were ourselves. As we crouched blindly in the unlit belly of our ark, the waves driving us from side to side, we spoke in our native tongues. For some, this meant prayer; for others, curses. We perspired from the heat of our overcrowded cohort, one hundred fifty souls in a space not meant for us but for the fish of the sea, their overwhelming scent soaked into the wood of this, their sarcophagus. When we noticed a change in the manner of the waves, a more forceful shuttling of our vessel, we knew that hours after winding through river, estuary, and canal, we had sailed away from the embrace of our motherland, the only land most of us had ever known and ever wanted to know. One of the few sailors among us whispered, *We're on the ocean now.* This much is true: We did not wait for the flood but sought it.

The navigator opened the hatch and allowed us onto the deck of our ark, which the uncaring world called a boat. Above us floated the crescent moon's lopsided smile, and by its light we saw ourselves alone on the surface of the watery world. For a moment we were happy, until most of us discovered two things. The first was that we had not yet digested our last meal, meager as it was. The second was that we were gyroscopically unequipped for the rippling ocean. All over the deck, and all over each other, those of us neither sailors nor fishermen discharged what we had nurtured in our guts, and even after nothing remained we continued to heave and gasp, wretched with retching and shivering because of the ocean breezes. In this manner we passed our first night on the sea.

Dawn broke, and in every direction we turned, we saw only the infinitely receding horizon. If the night was cold, the day was hot, with no shade and no respite, with nothing to eat but a mouthful and nothing to drink but a spoonful, our rations limited and the length of our journey unknown. But even with having consumed so little, we still left our human traces all over the deck and in the hold, awash by evening in our filth. We could hardly wait for relief, and when we spotted a ship near the horizon at twilight, we screamed ourselves hoarse. The ship kept its distance. On the third day, we crossed into the shipping lanes and came across a freighter breaking through the vast desert of the sea, a dromedary with its bridge rising over its stern, sailors on its deck. Once again we screamed, and waved, and jumped up and down. Worst of all, we hoped. But the freighter sailed on, touching us only with its wake. On the fourth and fifth days, two more cargo ships appeared, each closer than the one before, each under a different flag, the sailors pointing at us. But no matter how much we begged, pleaded, and held up our children, these ships neither swerved nor slowed down.

On the sixth day, the first of the children died, and over her body, before we offered it to the sea, the priest said a prayer. On the seventh day, another child died. Some prayed even more fervently to God, some began doubting His existence, some who did not believe in Him began to believe, and some who defied Him continued not their blasphemy. The father of one of the dead children cried, My God, why are You doing this to us? And only one of us on that ark knew the answer—me—for I was in great sympathy with God, *if* He existed.

If so, then I had been made in God's image, and I understood that God must therefore be a bastard too, just like me. As one bastard to another, I knew the answer to humanity's eternal question of *Why?*

It was, and is, simply this: *Why not?*

On the eighth day, He offered further proof of His existence by sending a cruise liner our way, the vacationers gathered on the railings to stare at us, our spectacle set to the beat of their dance music. We mustered ourselves for one last supplication, but when the cruise liner passed us by, buffeting our dreadful imitation of a yacht with its wake, we knew, at last, how the world saw us—a flotsam of flesh and the refuse of a nation.

Who were we? We were the wretched of the ocean, our hair black, our faces green, our skin blistered by sun and salt, weeping from festering sores. Strangers to each other before we clambered aboard this ark, now we were more intimate than those many lovers who had never seen their beloved wallowing in their own waste and that of others. Among our number were infants and children, for whom no milk remained in either bottle or breast. Among us were men and women, none of whom could be called handsome or beautiful after the sun's treatment. Among us were those originally light-skinned and dark-skinned and every shade in between, but now uniform after being baked by the sun into the same shade. Most of us had fled our motherland because the communists in charge had labeled us puppet, or pseudo-pacifist, or bourgeois-nationalist, or decadent reactionary, or intellectual with a false conscience, or a relative of one of these. There was also a fortune-teller, a geomancer, a monk, the priest, and at least one prostitute whose Chinese neighbor spat on her and said, Why is this whore with us? Even among the unwanted there were unwanted, and I could only laugh. Misunderstanding me, the prostitute scowled and said, What do *you* want?

Let me defer to the question of what *we* wanted, for who cares what I wanted? We, the unwanted, wanted so much. We wanted food, water, and sunscreen. We wanted clean clothes, showers, and toilets. We wanted rain, clouds, and dolphins. We wanted it to be cooler during the hot day, and warmer during the freezing night. We wanted an estimated time of arrival not synchronous with being dead on arrival. We wanted to be rescued, not barbecued under this unrelenting sun. We wanted television, movies, and music, anything with which to pass the time. We wanted love, peace, and justice, except for our enemies, whom we wanted to burn in hell, preferably for eternity. We wanted independence and freedom, except for the communists, who should all be sent to reeducation, preferably for life. We wanted benevolent leaders who represented the people, by which we meant us, and not them, whoever they were. We wanted to live in a society of equality, although if we had to settle for owning more than our neighbor, that would be fine. We wanted a revolution that would overturn the revolution we had just lived through. In sum, we wanted to want for nothing, but somehow, in attempting to communicate all this to my interlocutor, all I managed was to laugh again and say, Nothing.

You're a crazy bastard, aren't you?

At one time in my life, I would have taken offense. But after all I had suffered, after all I had seen, perhaps I actually was a crazy bastard. Perhaps that was just another name for a man with two faces and two minds, whose sole talent was to see things from both sides, whose fate was to live in a world where most people saw things from only one side. At least I knew who I was. That was more than could be said for most. Even when a storm appeared on the horizon the next day, dominating the sky from north to south, my faith in myself could not be shaken. While the believers prayed to God and all others cursed Him, I turned to Bon, my childhood friend and fellow survivor of reeducation, and said, I would rather have a brother like you than a god. And when he blinked his one remaining eye and called me a crazy bastard, I knew he felt exactly the same way.

While the faithful wept and the unfaithful cursed, I tied the plastic sack with my confession around my neck, the 367 pages that I had written during my many months in reeducation and afterward at the navigator's house. Whether I lived or died, the weight of my words would hang on me. Even if the sea seized me, someone might still fish my body from the waters with my waterproofed words intact. I would not be subdued, not even by this storm, massive, dark and brooding, positively cerebral in its appearance, synaptic flashes of electricity lighting its furrows. Oh God, You magnificent bastard! You did exist after all! Nature did not have a sense of humor or irony, but You clearly did. I was in on the joke now, even if my shipmates weren't. When I laughed, they looked at me as if I was out of my mind. Was I the only one who understood that we had nothing to lose?

Even my ghosts had disappeared, unwilling to follow me through this ordeal. There was no way to avoid the storm, surging closer and closer, except to vanish like those spirits of the men I had murdered, who had kept me such good and faithful company throughout my reeducation. But vanishing I would not do myself, knowing who I was. And who was I? I was the man who needed no more fathers, no more uncles, and no more revolutions. I was the man who understood at last that my entire life had destined me to be one among this mass of frightful, filthy wretches, these displaced persons, these refugees, these people who, if they could not be called revolutionaries, could certainly be called rebels. I was the man who no longer accepted questions of whether I was one thing or another, or whether I stood on one side or the other, for I was neither/nor, fated to walk on the solidus, a daring acrobat, sui generis!

As if whipped into a frenzy by my own frenzy, the wind gained momentum, and our ark gained speed and altitude as the waves grew. Lightning illumined the monstrous brain, and thunder overwhelmed the collective groan that arose from the people. It was then I knew what needed to be done. Even as a torrent of rain exploded on us, and as the waves propelled our vessel ever higher, I leapt to the mast. From there, my confession a heavy pendulum around my neck, I called out to these poor devils, I, their messiah, I, their prophet. What did I know that they did not, besides the fact that I could not swim? What was it that I shouted to them as they stared at me with their eyes bulging and mouths agape, our ark perched on the snowcapped crest of a watery precipice, overlooking a deep valley? We will live. Yes, I was sure of it. *We will live!*

And then we plunged, howling, into the abyss.

RABIH ALAMEDDINE is the
author of the novels *The Angel
of History*; *An Unnecessary
Woman*; *I, the Divine*; *Koolaids*;
The Hakawati; and the story collection, *The Perv*.

Hope and Home

RABIH ALAMEDDINE

When I was in grad school, I went to a classmate's apartment for lunch one afternoon, nothing elaborate, just sandwiches and sodas. As I sat at her particleboard dinette table, unfolded for the occasion, I realized that she was the first in our cohort to begin nesting. She had invited me to lunch—the rest of us just dropped in on each other when we didn't want to get drunk or high publicly. More telling, on the coffee table she had placed a glass vase resplendent with poppies and wildflowers she'd picked herself. She was creating home.

I tried the flower trick to make my place feel homier, but it didn't seem to work. In those days, where I lived always felt transitory, like a cheap hotel room. The fact that I had rented a furnished apartment didn't help. I upgraded a couple of times, but the units I lived in still didn't feel homey. They all felt beige.

I was a late bloomer. It took me years and years, till my early forties, before I was finally able to admit that I wasn't leaving my rent-controlled apartment in San Francisco. I wasn't going to live in Paris, Rome, or Kuala Lumpur; I wasn't going to write verse in the Canary Islands, dance flamenco in Seville, or ride a gaucho in Patagonia. My nesting was gradual. I replaced the avocado carpeting with hardwood floors, painted the walls all kinds of bright colors, organized my books alphabetically in more than a dozen book-shelves. I put up paintings. I threw fabulous dinner parties.

One day I bought a small glass vase that could barely hold a single flower. I thought it exquisite. It reminded me of the delightful things I'd seen in Murano on my first trip to Europe, with my mother and sister when I was thirteen. I placed the vase next to where I sit in the den. No one notices it but me.

A few years ago I was in Beirut visiting family—to be more precise, family visiting me. I stay at my mother's apartment, my second home in a manner of speaking, and I rarely leave it. I become a teen-ager again: I don't have to cook, clean, or do dishes, which I don't do in San Francisco either, but there's something more comforting about my mother taking care of me.

I was lounging about doing nothing when my friend Anissa Helou, author of many excellent cookbooks, mentioned that she was writing an article on the changes in diet and cooking among the Syrian refu-gees now that they were in Lebanon, away from home. I thought this was a chance to do something useful. Since I was going to write about the World Cup for a magazine blog, I could tag along, take pictures of some of the children, ask them who they were rooting for and how they were going to watch the games, and publish their responses.

I was unprepared.

That first day, we went to the office of the United Nations High Commissioner for Refugees (UNHCR) in the Jnah neighborhood of Beirut. It was raining, atypical for Beirut in May. Some two hundred refugees sat on molded plastic chairs waiting to officially register with the organization. Anissa, more socially adept than I could ever hope to be, chatted with a few women, asking where they came from and why they had left. I listened, dumbfounded, as they related tales of woe, cities destroyed, relatives killed or tortured, losing everything, losing history.

And I had thought that asking about soccer might be a good idea. I returned to my mother's lovely apartment and hid under the duvet.

Lebanon is home to the largest number of Syrian refugees, and to the largest refugee population per capita in the world. In a country of four million, there are more than a million registered refugees, though the actual number is closer to a million and a half. The operative word here is *registered*, meaning with UNHCR. The official count doesn't include those who choose not to register or who have slipped through the many cracks. Jordan and Turkey have set up camps that allow them to monitor the refugee population as well as control it. Lebanon has no such thing; the country doesn't do control very well. Since their inception, Lebanon and Syria have always had a porous border. Syrians have been living and working here, both legally and not, for as long as anyone can remember. Today the refugees live everywhere, in unofficial tent settlements where they rent a patch of land, in abandoned buildings, storefronts, and warehouses, and in apartments or rooms that only a small percentage of them can afford. Every part of Lebanon has had to deal with the issues arising from the influx. Some Lebanese have been welcoming, others not.

A number of villages and municipalities have put up signs that say, "We ask our Syrian brothers to refrain from any movement in public spaces."

In other words, stay in the homes you don't have.

Americans are up in arms because the United States has promised to admit ten thousand Syrian refugees in 2016.

Terrorists, you know.

After I crawled out from under the duvet, I felt guilty, and guilt is my primary motivator. Not doing anything seemed selfish, maybe even solipsistic. I decided I would talk to refugees, listen to their stories, maybe write something. If nothing else, I could be a witness.

I went south of Beirut first, to a never-finished university building in Sidon where 177 families lived, more than nine hundred people. They had taken over the place, made homes out of classrooms. The building was bald concrete on a mild hill overlooking the Mediterranean. To get to it, I had exited the relatively new seaside highway that connected Beirut to Sidon and South Lebanon, and driven up an unmarked dirt road until I arrived at the end of the line. Laundry and satellite dishes adorned the front of the structure, and children, lots of children, were running around everywhere. The very air smelled of human spoor and a kind of resigned permanency.

Every nook of the five floors was being used, every space peopled. All the families invited me into their homes for tea and a chat—kettles always boiling, always on the ready, doors always open. Noticeable was the higher number of women; it seemed to me that they outnumbered men about four to one. Some husbands and adult sons, afraid of being arrested at the border, had stayed behind in Syria to fend for themselves. Some were out working or looking for work. Most of this compound's refugees were from the rural areas surrounding Hama, from farming and riparian villages.

The rooms I visited were impeccably clean. Colorful mats of woven palm leaves carpeted the floor, intricately patterned textiles covered the walls, both as decoration and to hide the graffiti. For furniture there were one or two cushions and a television, the most important possession—every home had one and it was always turned on. No beds, no chairs, no tables. Rooms with barely enough space for a single person were occupied by families of eight or ten or twelve, sleeping on the ground. Stacks of blankets everywhere.

The Syrian families told their stories, with a cup of tea, of course. All talked about how they left Syria, the routes they took, the journeys lasting days. All told their tales of why they fled, from bombing campaigns and sniper fire to marauding gangs and arbitrary arrests. A common admonishment to misbehaving children was, "Bashar will come take you."

I had the chance to kick around a soccer ball with some kids on the balcony corridor of the third floor. Below us, on the ground floor, the main soccer game was on. More than forty kids moved as one giant amoeba upon the concrete terrace.

I visited a group of women and sat on the floor next to a tall makeshift closet: plywood stacks holding thin mattresses, blankets, and clothes, all covered in fake pink shantung below a red tasseled tablecloth that reached only two-thirds of the way down—a closet and Murphy bed in one. The women told me how they hid when fighting was nearby, leaving their villages, running for cover, ducking into any nearby copse or wooded area.

I said that during the Lebanese civil war we used to rush down to the underground garage for safety. For the seventeen years of the civil war, these garages became more than shelter; they became the hearth of the building, where families congregated for comfort, for entertainment, and, most important, for solace.

One woman said that they had no garages. They'd lived in a poor village with few if any cars. Another said that it would have made no difference even if they did have garages, since the MiGs dropped barrel bombs. "We hid from RPGs," they said, "not from MiGs, which were nothing if not quick death, no hiding, no hope."

Two of the women were pregnant.

"We have to replenish what they took from us," one said.

"Let me bring out my sister's boy," another said.

She returned with the parents and a boy of no more than seven months, wide blue eyes and a scrunched brow that made him look like a young philosopher puzzled by our intellectual infirmities—why oh why did we not understand him? His birth name was Ahmad, but that was not what everyone called him. His mother had experienced complications while pregnant and had given birth prematurely. A Lebanese charity was able to pay for the operation but not for the postnatal care in an incubator. The mother was flown to Turkey, where a second charity was able to keep the baby in an incubator for a month. Upon his return to the compound, everyone, and I mean everyone, called him Erdogan.

The second compound I visited was also in Sidon, in an abandoned underground Pepsi-Cola storage facility that had fallen into disrepair before the Syrians moved in. A long tunnel with rooms on either side and exits at each end reminded me of the hackneyed expression "moving toward the light." Three women were sweeping the cement outside their rooms, and the usual gaggle of kids was playing all over the place, but what differentiated these children from others I'd seen was that a number of them sported kohl around their eyes. I had heard of the long-ago practice of putting kohl around a newborn's eyes to keep away the evil eye, to keep Satan and his jinn at bay, but when I asked the mothers, they said that what kohl kept away was conjunctivitis.

Big sheets of plywood divided each storage space into three or four rooms, and each room, decorated to the hilt, had a minimum of ten people living and sleeping in it. Every room had at least two vases overfilled with fake flowers. Some group, probably UNHCR, had helped clean the place up and drain the sewage when the refugees moved in. The owner of the building now collected $100 monthly rent per room, a new source of income.

"At the beginning of the month," a woman said, "he arrives in his Range Rover, collects the rent from each family, and leaves. He accepts no excuses. You don't pay, you're out."

A young girl wanted me to meet the new bride.

The new bride?

"You must," the girl said. "You must."

She led us along to a dark drawn-back curtain that functioned as a door. The new bride looked a bit startled to see all of us: a stranger, a group of fifteen children and some of their mothers. She refused to be photographed; her right hand, like a stalking cat, lay upon the savannah above her bosom ready to pounce and cover her face if the camera lens so much as tilted in her direction. A bit tentative, somewhat shy, she stood beneath a large sheet of translucent plastic with metal shutters. She seemed more concerned than afraid. She simply did not wish to risk having her picture taken. Her parents were still in Syria.

The modesty of her dress served to highlight her beauty. Many people from that part of Syria had striking light eyes, yet hers were a remarkable griseous blue that grabbed your attention by its lapel. She was seventeen, she said; when she was fourteen, her parents had sent her to Lebanon with her uncles because the army and the shabiha were raping girls as they went through villages. Two days before my visit, she had married her first cousin. There would be no honeymoon.

She called her aunt to come talk to me. A firebrand, the aunt stormed out of her room. I could hear her approach, stomping on the cement, even though she wore soft slippers.

"Why should I talk to him?" she yelled. "Why? I've talked to journalists, to do-gooders, to everyone. Over and over. Told our stories many times. Does anyone do anything? No." With a dismissive wave of her hand and a flick of her left eyebrow, she glared at me. "If I talk to you will anything change?"

"No," I said, "I'm sorry. Nothing will change."

She regarded me askance for a brief moment and told her story.

I have set up my life in such a way that I rarely have to leave my home. It's where I feel most comfortable. I don't handle being around people too well these days, and I avoid them until I get

79

lonely, at which time I either go out on some excursion or invite friends over for dinner. Did I mention that I have fabulous dinner parties?

Home is where I can be most myself.

Talking to refugees drains me, and then I berate myself for being so fearful and weak. What is my discomfort compared to their suffering? I have what I call tennis match conversations in my head. I keep telling myself that someone with my temperament is not meant for this. I'm meant for sitting at my computer and cuddling with my cats, I'm meant for bubble baths and mud baths—oh, and massages, don't forget massages. I'm a spoiled princess by nature. My traumas involve nothing more than a bad pedicure. I end up interviewing refugees because even though I'm useless, even though there's nothing I can do, doing nothing is a crime.

After spending a week with refugees in Lebanon, I needed time off. I took a trip to Botswana all by myself and happened to join a group of Americans for dinner, thinking that some company might be healthy. They were East Coasters, and they wanted to know whether I liked San Francisco. Of course, I said, I'd been living in the city for over thirty years. I should have stopped there, but I'd had a couple of glasses of lovely wine, the night sky was gloriously decked in stars, the fire ablaze in its pit. I didn't think. I was having an outdoor meal in the vast expanse of the Kalahari, for crying out loud. How could I be guarded? I told my interrogators that I was surprised I'd lasted so long because it never felt like home to me—not the city, not America.

One of the men, dressed in high-end Hemingway, dropped his knife. What did I mean? I should have noted his tone, definitely his flushing face, but neither starlight nor firelight is good for color discernment. Okay, okay, I might have had three glasses of wine. I rambled on. I quoted from one of my books, auto-plagiarized so to speak: "In America, I fit but I do not belong. In Lebanon, I belong but I do not fit." Nothing controversial or confrontational.

I was triple-barreled. Three men began to explain to me that America was a great home, the best home ever in the history of humankind. Their wives nodded in concert. Americans were the kindest, warmest people, the most convivial, the most welcoming people. I would have backtracked if I'd been allowed a word. I did not wish to argue, and, most important, I didn't want to lose my most welcome buzz.

Luckily, the only other non-American at the table was a local woman. In a high Brit accent, she asked the men where home was. One of them said he lived in New York and Florida but had to declare New York his home. If he lived in his Upper East Side apartment for less than six months of the year, he would lose his rent control, so he was unable to take advantage of Florida's lack of income tax. He made sure to insist that the unfairness of his situation caused him no little anguish.

In the Bekaa Valley of Lebanon, near Zahlé, I visited a medium-size Syrian settlement. About eighty back-to-back tents ran in a straight line between two agricultural fields—onions, I believe. Almost everyone who lived in that settlement is from the same village near Aleppo or is related to someone in that village. Ahmad M., the man who began the settlement, told me that three-quarters of them are interrelated. A concrete mason, he used to come from Aleppo to Zahlé for a few months each year to work construction jobs in the area. When the bombing of Aleppo began, he brought his family to his small tent in the fields, soon to be followed by his and his wife's relatives. The UNHCR helped make the tents bigger, sturdier, and—though not always successfully—rainproof.

Living on the land was not free. The women had to work the fields for the owner. The deal was this: they worked six hours a day, got paid for five, and the extra hours went toward rent. They were paid 5,000 Lebanese pounds per day, which translates into $3.33, or 55 cents an hour.

The men were paid better if they were lucky enough to find work. One young man had a job as a delivery-truck driver; he left his tent at 4:00 a.m. to deliver yoghurt to Beirut, returning at 6:00 p.m. For fourteen hours a day, he earned $300 a month.

Ahmad M. probably earned a bit more since he had contacts already established, but because of the extra competition, he had less work and his hourly wage had been drastically reduced. He had five children, and one in "the house of fire," a term I had never heard before, meaning a gun chamber—his wife was pregnant with the sixth. Three were in private schools ($600 per child for the year) because he and his wife considered the UN schools not up to par. His wife made sure to mention that her eldest daughter was second in her class, as good as if not better than the local Lebanese.

We sat in their tent drinking sweet tea—unreasonably sweet. Their dwelling consisted of white plastic sheets imprinted with the UNHCR logo, sheets of plywood on the roof, cement floors, one window that was no more than a glassless opening, yet the care and effort that went into making it feel homey was impressive. Knick-knacks and tchotchkes all about, violet textiles draped from the ceiling, matching the ones surrounding the television on a hand-built stand, matching the throw blankets covering cushions and futon mattresses. Violet was the main theme in the mother's headscarf as well as the young daughter's dress.

I mentioned that it was wonderful to see such effort going into decorating. I had visited a tent where a young woman had painted the plastic sheeting bright crimson. Another woman had covered a wall with textile embroidered with mirrors (another ward against the evil eye), only to be outdone by a woman who studded her entire pantry with sequins, with results Liberace would have envied.

"We live here," Ahmad M. said.

I last saw the woman with the besequined pantry in 2014, but I think of her often. What would make someone spend so much time gluing sparkles onto sheets of wood that would become a pantry to store nonperishables? Intricate and delicate, no space left uncovered, so over-the-top that many a drag queen would kill for it.

She looked to be in her mid-twenties, if that, and seemed slightly embarrassed, admitting that it took her a long time to finish it, longer than she'd anticipated, what with caring for her four children, cooking, cleaning, and tending to her husband and in-laws.

"It's good to have something beautiful to come home to," she said. "The children love it."

"I do too," I said. "It's magnificent."

She beamed. "I had so many sequins."

To whoever thought it was a good idea to donate thousands of sequins to Syrian refugees who had nothing left, whose entire lives had been extirpated: Bless your heart.

The tents the Syrians live in are nothing like the flimsy ones used by the homeless in San Francisco. UNHCR donates the wood, the sheets of plastic, everything imprinted with the UN logo, and the refugees build the structure. Some organization donates tents to the homeless of San Francisco, but they are meant for camping. A good gust of wind might send them kite-flying. Tent stakes don't go into concrete.

A few days ago, I walked by a serried group of thirty tents on Folsom Street around 18th Street. None of the homeless talked to me or made eye contact. It seemed to me that they considered it bad form to panhandle where one sleeps.

I should have asked one of them if that was so, but I was frightened.

Years ago while riding the 24 northward, I noticed a homeless woman sitting on an old, bulging Samsonite on the corner of Haight and Divisadero, under the faded green awning of Phuket, a Thai restaurant. The sun was shining. Even though I was in a bus and she was a few feet away, the human aromas emanating from her were stupefying. She had a long blond pigtail that looked like a single dreadlock. Glasses on the tip of her nose, she was reading a hardcover of Alice Munro's *The Love of a Good Woman*.

The World Food Programme had given each registered refugee family in Lebanon a debit MasterCard that they can use to buy food at a number of supermarkets all over the country. In 2014, each account received $30 per family member at the beginning of the month. The amount is quite a bit less now; money is running out. Food in Lebanon is by no means cheap. Every woman I talked to complained that she could not afford any meat or fresh fruit. One used an expression I had never heard before: one piece of coal instead of meat (it rhymes in Levantine Arabic). She explained that she would cook rice and vegetables in a pot, then place a hot coal on a small plate with a layer of olive oil, put that in the pot, and cover it. The meal would end up having a "grilled meat" flavor.

What did the refugees buy most? Not rice or bread, not lentils or olive oil. More than twice as much as anything else, they bought sugar and tea, a specific brand called Horse Head, what they drank back home. The tradition of hospitality must be maintained.

I was surprised the first time I was invited into the makeshift homes of refugees. If someone noticed me passing by, the invitation was instantaneous. In Sidon, in the onion fields, they asked me in for tea.

But there were places where I wasn't invited in.

North of Beirut, in the hills above Tripoli, refugees living in an olive grove did not invite me. Their situation seemed more desperate. Their jerry-rigged tents looked like they wouldn't last the first snowstorm. The ground was nothing more than mud because of the rains. There were no decorations, no tapestries, no tchotchkes, no televisions.

Another camp about half an hour's drive from the onion fields in the Bekaa Valley was in worse shape. Though the tents were of the same materials donated by UNHCR, they were shoddily erected. Smells of sewage everywhere. All the adults were in tatters, all had sagging features. The children looked so miserable, so grimy, that they seemed to be made of clay yet to be fired and glazed.

No one invited me into the tent, but everyone assured me that as soon as the situation was settled in Syria, they were moving back.

I have visited Ahmad M. a number of times, and will probably do so again next time I'm in Lebanon, though I have yet to convince him or his wife that if I drink one more cup of their tea I'll develop type 2 diabetes. On my last visit, there had been a major renovation of the tent. They now had two bedrooms, a kitchen (no sequins on their pantry), and a living room where the family ate all their meals. They had two flat screens.

"Hope?" Ahmad said. "I knew we couldn't return the minute the war started."

"We lost everything," his wife said.

Their latest project, which I have yet to see, is to cover the cement floors with Lebanese stone tiles.

I asked what if the impossible happened and the situation calmed down in Syria and everything went back to normal. Would they return?

"It will never happen," he said.

In January 2016, I was on a small hill in the middle of the Moria refugee camp on the island of Lesbos, Greece. The camp is a military facility and looks like nothing if not a prison, with high concrete walls and razor wire. Ironically, there isn't much space inside Moria. Refugees who are lucky sleep in the barracks, the rest in flimsy tents in the olive groves outside the prison.

I was miserable, the thousands of refugees far more so. It was drizzling. I was not yet soaked. I was supposed to be an interpreter, but I couldn't seem to move from my spot next to the NGO offices. I felt so out of place, so wrong. I wished I were smoking again. I would have been able to do something if I had a cigarette. There was a smell of lard and dampness in the air. The view from the hill made me feel anxious, apprehensive, a much stronger feeling than I'd had in any refugee camp before. At the bottom of the hill, the large squadron of Greek riot police in high butch did not help.

So many people, so many. Families, single men, children. Syrians, Iraqis, Afghanis, Iranians, and more, more. North Africans from Algeria, from Morocco, sub-Saharan Africans from Mali, from Congo. They were running away from so much, the Syrian regime, Daesh, the Taliban, terrorist groups with even sillier monikers. Lines everywhere, for registration, for food, for clothes, for donations. And white people directing pedestrian traffic.

The sun came out. Newly arrived families trudged up the hill carrying their belongings, pulling rolling suitcases, their voices submerged in the hullabaloo of conversations among the volunteers, the *tap-tap* of hard soles on harder concrete, the bustle of movement. A Syrian family walked up the hill toward me, mother, father, three kids, including a boy of perhaps twelve, his face a picture of glacial determination. A large group of young volunteers in neon orange vests walked next to them, more boisterous, less self-conscious. One of them, a blond in her early twenties, screamed. Everyone stopped. She screamed again, pointing at the sky. "Oh my God, oh my God." She screamed once more before she was able to form an actual sentence. "Look, it's a rainbow," she yelled. She tried to engage a little girl, kept pointing at the far sky, spoke louder in English to make herself understood, but the little girl wanted nothing to do with her. The Syrian family reached me before I was able to hear what they were talking about.

"She's excited because she saw a rainbow," the father said.

The mother shook her head. The twelve-year-old boy said in a quiet voice, not realizing that I spoke his language, "She should shove that rainbow up her ass."

The father snickered. The mother smacked the back of his head, not violently, for they were both carrying heavy loads.

DANEZ SMITH is the author of *[insert] boy*, winner of the Kate Tufts Discovery Award and the Lambda Literary Award for Gay Poetry, and *Don't Call Us Dead.* They are a 2014 Ruth Lilly and Dorothy Sargent Rosenberg Fellow, a Cave Canem and VONA alum, and recipient of a McKnight Foundation Fellowship. They are from St. Paul, Minnesota, and are a MFA candidate at the University of Michigan.

what was said on the bus stop

DANEZ SMITH

lately has been a long time

says the girl from Pakistan, Lahore to be specific
on the bus stop when the white man
asks her next where she's from & then
says *oh, you from Lahore?*
it's pretty bad over there.

    lately has been a long time
she says & we look at each other & the look says
yes, i too wish this white dude would stop
asking us about where we from, all these questions
derived from skin
but on the other side of that side eye
is maybe a hand where hands do no good
a look to say, *yes, i know lately has been*
a long time for your people too
& i'm sorry the world is so good at making
us feel like we have to fight for space
to fight for our lives
that might be me projecting
but let me project
i want to say something & this
is the only way i can get in
even half good

solidarity is a word, a lot of people say it
i'm not sure what it means in the flesh
i know i love & have cried for my friends
their browns a different brown than mine
that i have danced their dances when taught
& tasted how their mothers use rice
different than mine. i know sometimes
i can't see beyond my own pain, pass
but black & white, that bullets
love any flesh. i don't know how to write this poem
i want to say something about all of us
without speaking for all of us, i want to
say i know it's foolish to compare.

(what advice do the drowned have for the burned?
what gossip is there between the hung & the buried?)

& i want to reach across that great distance
that is sometimes an ocean & sometimes just a few inches
& say, look. your people, my people, all that has happened
to us & still make love under rusted moons, still pull
children from the mothers & name them,
still we teach them to dance, & your pain is not mine
& is no less, & i pray to my god that your god
blesses you with mercy, & i have tasted your food & understand
how it is a good home, & i don't know your language
but i understand your songs, & i cried when they came
for your uncles, & i wanted revenge when you buried your niece
& i want the world to burn in child's memory
& i have stood by you in the soft shawl of morning
& still, still, still, still, still, still, still, still, somehow, we breathe.

HERTA MÜLLER is the winner
of the 2009 Nobel Prize in Literature, as well as the International IMPAC Dublin Literary
Award and the European Literature Prize. She is the author of,
among other books, *The Hunger
Angel* and *The Fox Was Ever
the Hunter.* Born in Romania in
1953, Müller lost her job as a
translator in a machine factory
and suffered repeated threats
after refusing to cooperate with
Ceauşescu's secret police. She
succeeded in emigrating in 1987
and now lives in Berlin.

PHILIP BOEHM has translated
over thirty books and plays by
German and Polish writers such
as Herta Müller, Franz Kafka,
and Hanna Krall. For these
translations he has received
numerous awards including
fellowships from the National
Endowment for the Arts and
the John Simon Guggenheim
Memorial Foundation. He also
works as a stage director and
playwright and is the founding
Artistic Director of Upstream
Theater in St. Louis.

Germany and Its Exiles

HERTA MÜLLER
TRANSLATED FROM THE GERMAN BY PHILIP BOEHM

First I have to tell you something about leaving Romania and arriving in Germany. Some ten people were sitting in the waiting room of the little train station at the border. The train had long since pulled up and was waiting outside on the tracks. Everyone else had already boarded, everyone except my husband, my mother, and me. We looked at one another and thought: They're not letting us leave after all, this is just a trick, tonight they're going to put us on the wrong train and send us right back. But then where are we supposed to go? We'd been forced to hand over our apartment to the state in "swept and tidy" condition; every object in the house had been sold off, given away, or thrown out. We had nothing except a suitcase. And after years of being harassed by the Securitate my nerves were so shot that laughing and crying had become one and the same to me. There in the waiting room I put on a frozen face. My mother's chin was quivering. Three policemen kept us closely monitored, it was impossible to talk. I nudged my mother with my elbow and whispered: No crying, understood. Then, instead of boarding the train, there was another body search, as if since the first one we'd been able to snatch some contraband out of the waiting room air and stash it away. Finally a policeman escorted us to the train. On the steps of the car he grabbed my arm as though he wanted to help me climb up, and said: Don't forget, we'll get you wherever you go. As the train pulled away we were still looking for our compartment.

It was only when the first Hungarian station appeared in the foggy light of the lanterns that I was convinced we were actually moving, that the train wasn't deceiving us.

But there was something else: it was February 28, 1987, but our passports showed February 29—a day that didn't even exist, since 1987 wasn't a leap year. And just as the Romanians hoped, this parting harassment worked a year and a half later with every German official. No matter what the business, I always first had to explain that this February 29 stamped in my passport wasn't my fault but a farewell gift from the Securitate. Clearing that up sometimes took a whole half hour.

In Austria, we had a stopover where we were interviewed for a TV program about the Ceauşescu dictatorship. The next day we traveled on to Germany. When we arrived in Nürnberg, we were placed in a transitional facility called "Langwasser." And there I underwent a sudden transformation: Whereas in Austria, just the day before, I had been a dissident, now in Nürnberg I was considered an agent. The BND (Federal Intelligence Service) and the Verfassungsschutz (Federal Office for the Protection of the Constitution) interrogated me for several days. The first conversation was surreal. The official asked:

Did you have dealings with the secret police over there?

They had dealings with me, that's different.

I'll be the one who decides what's different. That's what I'm paid to do after all.

When I started to tell him everything I'd been put through in Romania he cut me off.

Naively, I thought the mistake had been cleared up. And then he said: All the same, if they've given you an assignment you can still tell me what it is right now.

I asked him why he didn't first find out what had happened in Romania, instead of immediately treating me as a suspect. Then he uttered the same sentence the Securitate interrogators always used: We're the ones who ask the questions.

After that came further conversations, and the insanity increased. They handed me diagrams with various facial types and asked me to describe the Securitate agents I'd had dealings with. Once again I corrected the official interrogating me: They were the ones who had dealings with me. But the official ignored me. The papers also had descriptive keys for clothing, face, ears, fingernails—for each one there was a list of adjectives in bold type. When I explained that at the time I hadn't been paying attention to the man's ears or fingernails, that I was desperate and afraid he might kill me, the German official kept repeating like a machine: Think hard. How am I supposed to remember something I never noticed, I asked. Have you ever been afraid like that? Once again he ignored me. I also asked if the German secret services would be able to identify a Romanian agent by his ears or fingernails if he came to Germany. Once again came the sentence: We're the ones who ask the questions. I was given one, two hours for "hard thinking" after which it started all over again. This went on for several days, until at last I decided to randomly match a bold-type German adjective to the corresponding Romanian body part of the Securitate agent, just to be done with all the interrogations. For clothing I could choose among: elegant, shabby, sporty, and appropriate. I kept repeating: Just like you have. And with every answer the German interrogator said, with pride in his voice: So then, we'll check "appropriate."

With every other adjective I could picture something. But not with "appropriate." In that particular context, did "appropriate" mean something concealed, something carefully chosen because it was well-suited for a purpose meant to remain undetected?

When it comes to secret services, does "appropriate" mean appropriately devious? In which case it wasn't the clothing that was "appropriate"—it was the person himself. As a result, he forced me to become appropriate as well, so I could finally be done with the facial diagrams, which reminded me of the racial typologies found in my grandfather's old encyclopedia.

I was given a list of bureaus I had to visit and in each one I encountered the same kind of absurdity. I declined nouns and conjugated verbs and passed my language test. Nevertheless, in the next office I was asked whether I was a German or a victim of political persecution. I said I was both. The official said: You can't be both, we don't even have a form for that. You'll have to make up your mind. He asked if I would have been persecuted in Romania if I'd been a Romanian and had done the same things I had done. I said: Yes, it would have been just as risky for a Romanian. To which he said: So there we have it, you're not a German.

My mother had long since acquired all the necessary stamps and seals. She was recognized as a German, having officially declared her desire to reunite with family, and she was granted German citizenship a few weeks later in Berlin with no difficulty whatsoever. I, on the other hand, had to wait one and a half years. Every now and then I would telephone the citizenship office, and the answer was always the same: Don't call anymore, you can't speed things up. An in-depth investigation is necessary. And in the meantime I was receiving death threats from Romania as well as visits from the Verfassungsschutz warning me that my life was in danger. They gave me advice: Never go to certain pubs, never enter a stranger's apartment, never stay on the ground floor while traveling, never accept gifts from strangers, never leave cigarettes lying on a restaurant table unattended, never walk through a park alone, and always carry a blank gun in my purse while in the city. Not to enter or travel through East Germany, because the Stasi could kidnap me on behalf of the Securitate and spirit me off to Romania. Then there'd be nothing we could do for you, the Verfassungsschutz agent explained, since you're not a German citizen. As far as they were concerned, I was being persecuted and my life was in danger, while their counterparts in the BND and the citizenship authorities still treated me like a foreign agent. At one point I turned to the Verfassungsschutz agent, whose ID listed his name as "Fröhlich" or "Happy," and repeated a sentence I knew from Nürnberg: You have to make up your mind whether I'm a victim of political persecution or a foreign agent, I can't be both.

Never again was German citizenship so important to me as when it was being withheld. I was under suspicion because of slanders that were devised by the Securitate and were implemented with the help of the Landsmannschaft der Banater Schwaben, an association of ethnic Germans from the Banat. They had a permanent office inside the transitional facility in Nürnberg. And they were riddled with informants, as I can read today in my file. They had been carrying on a campaign against me for years in their publications, accusing me of "fouling my own nest" and of working for the Securitate. It's likely that the Landsmannschaft fed the West German agencies information at the behest of the Securitate—after all, the agencies and the association were well acquainted, since they had offices in the same facility. The hatred spewed by the "homelanders," the slander campaign of the Securitate, and the suspicions of the West German agencies all converged. The Landsmannschaft could use the German intelligence services and convert their anger at me into an "appropriate" revenge. Evidently the Germans didn't think twice about the fact that this same Landsmannschaft never uttered a single critical word about the dictatorship. Or that they worked hand in hand with the Romanian Embassy to facilitate the reuniting of families.

I hadn't counted on this particular gambit, this complete reversal of facts. The German officials mistook me—not for someone else, but for a person that had been invented by slander. In the meantime, ten thousand people a year left Romania and settled in Germany, officially to be reunited with their families. And among them were hundreds of spies. But they were welcomed as Germans, while I was disgraced because I refused to let the political persecution be blotted out. Because it was a matter of truth—truth I had paid for dearly. I hadn't left to join my uncle: I had gone into exile. This was the proper term, and as far as I was concerned, it was not negotiable. I claimed it because it corresponded with the facts. This bothered the officials because they didn't want to hear about the dictatorship. They cut me off when I tried to explain how this dictatorship had invaded the most private parts of my life. They didn't want to know anything about my life in Romania, so they could maintain their suspicions.

Here in Nürnberg the word "exile" was incompatible with being German. At the same time, the transitional facility was located just across from Hitler's party rally grounds. That was our first shock: We stepped into our room and looked out the little window and there was this Hitlerian monstrosity.

When I tried to take a walk outside to calm down between interrogations, I was overcome with horror: the early winter darkness dotted with snowflakes and here this threatening stone hulk. I made my way onto the former parade grounds. High stairs, a thin coat of snow, gusting wind, scrawny weeds in the cracks between the stones like twitching wigs and moustaches. My head nearly burst. Inside the transitional facility was insanity, and here outside was the epicenter of the Nazi crimes.

How could they build such a facility at such a location? Why were people who were distraught and seeking refuge from dictatorships forced to stay here of all places? Didn't anyone have second thoughts about housing them in this neighborhood? I asked myself how refugees from political persecution, who have known the whole gamut of fear, and who finally managed to make it here—how are they supposed to breathe in these hideous surroundings? Isn't Germany ashamed to greet us new arrivals with this particular view? Was the facility built here possibly because the location was simply deemed "appropriate"—that is, were the authorities so insensitive to the refugees' feelings and so blind to the role that Nürnberg played in the Nazi era? The officials inside and the surroundings outside: actually, everything was doubly "appropriate."

In 1987, I sensed that Germany, a country that had driven hundreds of thousands into exile, still wanted nothing to do with the concept—not with the word, not with the experience of those forced to leave. I had literally turned into a blind alley.

Nevertheless, I realized that compared with the people forced into exile by the Nazis, this blind alley was only a small misfortune. Here I was being put through the wringer, but I spoke German, I had a publisher for my books, I didn't have to cross borders illegally. The transitional facility was nothing like the life-or-death situations experienced by those who fled the Nazis. Back then being allowed to live or forced to die was a matter of luck, good or bad. People experienced chance in a completely different way. We say chance, but actually it was people. Good luck meant people with a little compassion who helped. And bad luck meant unscrupulous zealots who were willing to kill.

In 1942, *Casablanca* opened in New York. It's a film about love and about loss of freedom, about the hardships, tragedies, and despair experienced by people trying to escape Nazi Germany.

Meanwhile, just like in *Casablanca,* artists, teachers, architects, politicians, and others—many of them Jewish—were stranded across Europe, trying to obtain exit visas. It didn't matter where to as long as they could escape Hitler's trap. *Casablanca* tells the story of the Czech resistance fighter Victor László, who along with his wife, Ilsa Lund, needs an exit visa. Other refugees are marooned in Casablanca at the mercy of the corrupt police chief, Renault. The black marketeer, Ugarte, is murdered while attempting to sell some stolen visas ("letters of transit" in the film). In the end, László and his wife acquire the documents and are able to escape the German major, Heinrich Strasser.

The film doesn't only depict the tragedies faced by people in exile. Most of the actors were exiles themselves. Conrad Veidt, for instance, who played the despicable Nazi, Strasser, was one of the best-paid actors of the German film industry. Because his wife was Jewish, he—unlike Heinz Rühmann—left Germany as early as 1933. Once in Hollywood, he regularly played Nazis—a bitter historical irony.

The great Peter Lorre, who played the black marketeer with the visas, had fled Austria. And the croupier at Rick's Café Américain was Marcel Dalio, who had to flee France because he was Jewish. His family died in the concentration camps. Helmut Dantine, the desperate Bulgarian in the film trying to win at the roulette table to pay for exit papers, was interned in a camp for three months before he fled Austria. And Trude Berliner, another roulette player in the film, escaped Germany in 1933 via Prague to the Netherlands, and when the Wehrmacht invaded there, she fled via Lisbon to the United States. One of the officers in Major Strasser's entourage is played by Hans Heinrich von Twardowski, who left Germany in 1933 because he was homosexual. And those are just a few of the émigré actors. The film's composer, Max Steiner, who was Jewish, would have been murdered by the Nazis had he not fled to the United States. In 1938, he was only barely able to help his father, Gabor Steiner, get out of Vienna.

One of the best-known film composers in Hollywood, the Viennese Erich Wolfgang Korngold, had been living in the United States since 1934. He, too, was barely able to help his family get out in 1938. Korngold composed music for nineteen films and received two Oscars. In pre-war Vienna, he was considered a musical wunderkind of modern symphonic music, but in post-war Vienna he was punished with rejection, accused of having sold his soul to Hollywood.

The violinist Daniel Hope has collected and rerecorded music composed by exiled Hollywood composers. In analyzing the mood of this music, he says the pathos characteristic of the Hollywood films stems from the despair and rage of the exile experience. *Casablanca* is a film about the flight from Hitler, but in the film there are no Jews. Nor do we find Jewish names in the big Hollywood studios: Szmuel Gelbfisz called himself Samuel Goldwyn, Hirsch Moses Wonsal chose the name Harry Warner. The director Michael Curtiz was born in Budapest as Manó Kaminer, which he later Hungaricized to Mihály Kertész. He emigrated to the United States in the 1920s. These artists had to Americanize their names because in the Protestant United States they would not have received credit for their work. And in *Casablanca*, the Jews are missing because the film's producers knew the anti-Semitic prejudices of their audience.

Casablanca was first shown in German cinemas in 1952 and was twenty-five minutes shorter than the original. All references to exile had been cut. There was no Major Strasser or any other Nazi. Victor László was now called Victor Larsen and was a Norwegian physicist who had discovered ominous delta rays and was being sought by Interpol. The moving film about exile had turned into kitschy tripe, in the tradition of *Sissi* and the "Heimat" films of the 1950s.

The full version of *Casablanca* was not shown until 1975, when it appeared on German TV.

Casablanca is just one example of how postwar Germany has suppressed the experience of exile. Another is the shamefully late publication of Hermann Ullstein's memoirs—which appeared in Germany some seventy years after they were published in the United States. Ullstein was co-owner of the largest newspaper group in Europe, which published the most important periodicals in Germany and also the first warnings about Adolf Hitler. As soon as Hitler was named Chancellor, the Nazi propaganda machine set to work against Ullstein, infiltrating the publishing company with Nazi party members. Destitute, Ullstein fled to the United States, where he made his living as a night watchman and wrote his memoirs about the family company and the Aryanization of the publishing house. No one in postwar Germany was interested in his recollections of the democratic public sphere that had existed in Germany before 1933.

Nor does hardly anyone today remember Stefan Grossmann, a journalist who wrote for the *Vossische Zeitung,* one of the Ullstein papers. He also edited the weekly *Tage-Buch,* which he cofounded with Ernst Rowohlt. Grossmann, too, was one of the first journalists to openly criticize Hitler and was actually sued by Hitler as early as 1923. In March 1933 orders were sent for Grossmann's arrest, but when the police rang the bell early in the morning, his Swedish wife opened the door and told them her husband was still asleep. Perhaps the police had not yet lost all restraint at that time, or perhaps they were simply unnerved by the tall, blond Swedish woman. In any case, they went away. Grossmann and his wife fled to Vienna with nothing but a suitcase, leaving behind their home and all their possessions. That was 1933 and it was still possible to find fortune in misfortune.

So many coincidences played the role of fate. It's enough to look at one refugee's story to realize how an instant could suddenly turn into an abyss.

In the words of author and playwright Carl Zuckmayer, "The underworld opened its gates and vomited forth the lowest, filthiest, most horrible demons it contained" and "All that makes for human dignity was buried" (from *A Part of Myself*, translated by Richard and Clara Winston.) He was able to save himself in Switzerland because he had a passport that an obliging Austrian official had given him, and because he made an impression on a young border guard near Feldkirch. Zuckmayer explained to the man that he was banned in Germany, that he was neither a member of the Nazi party nor of the Reich Chamber of Literature, and that he was not in agreement with the National Socialist worldview. Consequently, he had to go to London. His frankness fascinated the young soldier who was examining his passport. And his good luck with the young soldier got even better, in an eerie way: The "lean, blond fellow in the uniform of the SS" practically swooned when he saw the WWI medals on Zuckmayer's coat. He praised the older "German man" as a hero and regretted that he was too young to have had a chance to prove himself in war. Zuckmayer consoled him by saying: "There'll be another." "Yes," the man exclaimed enthusiastically, "Let us drink to that."

But how many people did luck abandon? The ones who wound up in despair like Walter Benjamin in the Pyrenees. He had nothing but a briefcase, perhaps full of manuscripts, not even a rucksack, which was a kind of German trademark. When he was told in Portbou that he wouldn't be able to cross into Spain without a French exit visa—perhaps nothing more than a corrupt border guard's attempt to extort some money for issuing the pass—Walter Benjamin poisoned himself. And how many people snapped later on, years after they managed to escape, like Ernst Toller, who hanged himself in a New York hotel? Or Stefan Zweig in Brazil, who could no longer bear the destruction of his "spiritual homeland" in Europe and committed suicide together with his wife, Lotte. Others died shortly after fleeing, sapped of their strength, such as the singer Joseph Schmidt, who after finally reaching Switzerland, suffered a breakdown and was placed in an internment camp, where his heart disease went untreated. He, too, probably encountered "appropriate" officials. Similarly appropriate officials were found in England, where Nazi opponents and Jews who had fled Germany were interned as foreign agents. Else Lasker-Schüler was met with a different type of bad luck when she was denied reentry into Switzerland. The official justification contained the single word "Überfremdung"—implying foreign infiltration. And Nelly Sachs was safe and secure in Stockholm, where fate did not change so quickly from one moment to the next, but the fright had already taken hold of her body, the constant fear of the Nazis had shattered her nerves—Nazis were hiding in the walls, inside the water lines. In addition to

Nelly Sachs's heightened fear in Sweden, there was the fear of the Wehrmacht soldiers in occupied Holland. Konrad Merz, author of the first exile novel to appear after the Hitler takeover, *A Man Drops Out of Germany,* survived exile in Holland hidden in a closet because no one betrayed his hiding place. As an old man he occasionally came to Berlin, and I would sometimes meet him. He cried every time he visited. His homesickness had grown as old as himself.

The painter Felix Nussbaum also had a hiding place, but did not survive the time in exile. Nussbaum painted inside his hideout, a neighbor smelled the oil paints and denounced him. The denunciation cost him his life: He was shipped to Auschwitz on the last transport out of Belgium.

His parents had already fled to Italy in 1934. But homesickness drove them back to Germany in 1935. In 1938 they fled once again, this time to Amsterdam. That proved fatal. From there they were deported to Auschwitz and murdered. No one has counted the number of deaths in exile.

That's how dark it looks in the nooks and crannies of the word "exile."

Today the word has a more alluring luster, good for "confidently stylish furnishings" and "creating a special atmosphere for presenting our furniture"—so say the ads of a furniture store named Exile. Then there is the *"Exil"* restaurant in Frankfurt, where guests "don't have to feel without a homeland," "thanks to warm light and imaginative décor." And where the diners may "enjoy Southern flair in a cozy planted inner courtyard."

This unabashed marketing of the word "exile" makes me think of Gottfried Benn's mocking of those who fled. When Klaus Mann accused him of not distancing himself from the Nazis, he lashed back at the emigrants: "There they are sitting in their resorts and spas and taking us to task because we are joining forces to help build a new state."

In 1945, near midnight between the eighth and ninth of May, the unconditional surrender of the German forces went into force on all fronts. In Germany this is known as "Stunde Null," or "Zero Hour." The military concept came to stand for the new beginning—and the "appropriate" concealing silence. Hermann Lübbe, who can no longer remember having been a member of the NSDAP, has coined the concept of "communicative silence," which he claims was necessary for Germans to become integrated into the new democratic state.

Adenauer, too, felt this "silence" was necessary, because he believed former Nazis were indispensable for the building of the Bundesrepublik, as "people who understood what went before." Unfortunately, the experience he valued was not that of the scientists, artists, entrepreneurs, politicians, artisans, and jurists who had been forced into exile. After the war these people remained unwanted. Their return riled up perpetrators and fellow travelers alike. They disturbed the "silence."

During the election campaign for the Bundestag in 1961, Konrad Adenauer lashed out at the returnee Willy Brandt on account of his years of exile in Norway, and Franz Josef Strauss scribbled: "We really ought to be allowed to ask Herr Brandt: What did you do out there for twelve years? We know what we were doing in here."

What Willy Brandt—like many émigrés—was "doing out there" was resisting the Nazis. He risked his life making illegal trips to the Reich, and in Stockholm he founded a press agency that reported news from Germany. His real name was Herbert Frahm. After 1945 he kept the pseudonym he had adopted—it was that important to him—as homage to the resistance in exile against Nazi Germany. Today, however, this resistance in exile is not appreciated in Germany; even worse, it doesn't play any role whatsoever. What is remembered is the military resistance of officers who followed Hitler far too long.

Exile didn't mean keeping silent. Many authors who were forced to leave actively resisted the Nazi dictatorship through radio broadcasts and newspaper articles and open letters to the governments of England and France protesting the Munich accords. They reported on conditions in Germany for the international press, and in so doing proved that Hitler could expel modernity from Germany but could not fully destroy it. In 1938, Eugen Spiro organized the Association of Free German Artists and mounted an exhibition in Paris entitled *Free German Art* as a response to the destruction of culture in Germany. The German PEN Club in Exile and the German Academy of Arts and Sciences in Exile, founded by Hubertus, Prince of Löwenstein, were important institutions that played an indispensable role in focusing the intellectual resistance.

"Communicative silence" also marked the new German literature, as represented by Gruppe 47, a literary association founded by Hans Werner Richter with the aim of fostering young, unknown authors. He, like many later members, had served in the Wehrmacht. The group ultimately became a leading intellectual marketplace for literary talent. And that only happened because the soldierly pasts of its members were not debated or even discussed. Here, too, the "communicative silence" was "appropriate." Günter Grass kept mum about serving in the 10th SS Panzer Division "Frundsberg"—incidentally, in the same unit as my father. Günter Eich kept quiet about his 1940 radio play, *The Rebellion in Gold Town,* which he wrote in support of Goebbels's propaganda campaign against England. Alfred Andersch hid the fact that he had separated from his Jewish wife in order to join the Reich Chamber of Literature. Others, too, had no desire to recall their membership in the NSDAP. Rather, the former soldiers saw themselves as victims, as a misled and misused generation that went to war in all innocence and returned home chastened and reformed.

Consequently, these "Zero Hour" authors were suspicious of the writers who had gone into exile, for whom the zero hour had struck twelve years earlier. And their zero hour had meant something completely different: the zero point of existence. Perhaps a subliminal anti-Semitism was still making itself felt as well, along with the accusation that the émigrés had run off to safety. In any event, Wolfgang Koeppen had to remind Hans Werner Richter that the exiled writers hadn't just taken off but were "escaping their murderers," and now wanted to contribute the tragedy of their "stolen life" to a new, "Nazi-free" literature.

But they weren't allowed to do this in Gruppe 47.

When, in 1952, Paul Celan first read his poem "Death Fugue" to the group, he was met with malice and contempt. Walter Jens wrote: "The first time Celan read, people said, 'Who on earth can listen to that!' He read with great pathos, we laughed about it. Someone said, 'He reads like Goebbels!'" And Hans Werner Richter sneered that Celan read "in a singsong voice like in a synagogue." Richter also denigrated Albert Vigoleis Thelen's *The Island of Second Sight* as "emigrant German." Today that book, which is about Mallorca as a place of refuge, is largely forgotten in Germany—like so many books and authors of exile.

Richter's diaries prove that he couldn't stand the émigré writers. "Emigration was literature from the 1920s that had been 'canned'—the style, the language, the approach, all canned and preserved . . . the method of the café . . . What was I supposed to do with that?" When Hermann Kesten and Hans Sahl visited the group he felt justified in his assessment; in his opinion, both writers expected "guilt complexes" and were possessed of a "sensitive, fatuous vanity." Evidently the visiting authors disturbed the tacit "silence."

There was no interest in Thomas Mann, Stefan Zweig, Heinrich Mann, Alfred Döblin, Theodor Kramer, or Mascha Kaléko, who declined the Fontane Prize for literature when she learned that the former SS-Mann Egon Holthusen was on the jury. A member of the Berlin Academy appealed to her, saying that she, "as a sensitive woman," couldn't deny "poor Holthusen" her "female sympathy." But Mascha Kaléko refused to discount exodus and exile and did not give in. Whereupon the general secretary of the Academy barked: "If the emigrants don't like the way we handle things here then they should just stay away."

The painter Oscar Zügel, who was friends with Paul Klee, met with similar rejection. The Nazis considered his paintings "degenerate art." They were confiscated and slated to be burned, along with the works of other artists, in the courtyard of the Staatsgalerie Stuttgart. He fled first to Spain, and eventually to Argentina. After the war he returned to Stuttgart, where the caretaker of the Staatsgalerie had saved a few of his pictures from the fire. But the new museum director wanted none of him, because he had ostensibly forsaken Nazi Germany. Like many other painters and sculptors, he was denied a new chance in the new Germany.

Apart from the annihilation of the European Jews, National Socialism had the goal of extinguishing modernism. There was no more room in the Third Reich for modern architecture, painting, or music.

In 1937, Hitler declared a "relentless cleansing war" to be waged with "brute force" against all "elements of cultural degradation"—against books, images, people. The book burnings and campaigns against "degenerate art" and "degenerate music" were not just directed against modernism, but designed to eradicate all memory of modernism. It didn't even help to be a committed Nazi and anti-Semite like Emil Nolde. His paintings, too, were affected by this policy of eradication. The society being brought into line was irreconcilable with modern art and critical science. Many were forced to flee if they wanted to remain true to themselves. For that reason, the exile of hundreds of thousands of Germans during the Nazi era is not a marginal phenomenon. Artists who saw their existence and their art called into question went into exile; even if their lives were not directly threatened, they could no longer live in Germany.

In 1945, Thomas Mann wrote from exile that he considered all books published in Germany during the Nazi era beyond worthless—"they reek of blood and shame." His words were aimed at the opportunism of the "inner emigration."

But those authors defended themselves aggressively. Frank Thiess, later vice president of the German Academy for Language and Literature, justified his staying in Germany with the claim that he had emerged from the period "richer in knowledge and experience" than had he watched the German tragedy "from the balcony boxes and parterre seats of foreign lands." The inner exile was, in his opinion, "much more difficult and painful, compared with the external."

That kind of reframing of definitions of oppression and cowardice played a large role in blocking out the experience of exile. Hans Sahl called this dismissal of the émigré experience the "exile after the exile." And it is still in force today.

For many whose zero hour had struck in 1933, the end of the war did not mean a new start; when they returned they were stuck at the same zero point of existence. They lacked both recognition and the means to live. Their flight into exile was their first expulsion from Germany. And their return became a second, an "exile after the exile," an "appropriate" rejection—one that insured that their banishment back then would continue to affect us today. One could say: Expelled yesterday, and still forgotten.

With the ouster of these writers entire literary traditions were lopped off, for instance the dark, songlike poetry of Theodor Kramer. Or the matter-of-fact prose of Irmgard Keun, who first fled to Holland, and after the Wehrmacht invaded there, returned to Germany where she stayed in hiding. But no one wanted to hear of Irmgard Keun. She drowned her abandonment in alcohol, was declared incompetent, and "appropriately" placed in a psychiatric ward.

To this day, those who were exiled are not recognized in Germany as victims. Not even by the federal government in its National Memorial Sites Concept. Memorial plaques for individual artists do exist, but there is no larger place of remembrance honoring those Germans who were forced to leave starting in 1933 and commemorating their exile. The word "Vertreibung" or "expulsion" is reserved for those expelled from the former German eastern regions. They are known as "Heimatvertriebene"—people driven out of their homeland. Meanwhile, the people who were driven out of Hitler's Germany are called "Emigranten"—which has a very different ring. "Heimatvertriebene" has a warm tinge, the word "emigrant" has nothing but itself. You might say that one word is open-hearted and the other is close-minded. But the question remains: Weren't the "emigrants" also expelled from their homeland?

The Heimatvertriebene, who once even had their own ministry, will soon have a permanent exhibit in Berlin. Hopefully the exhibit won't silence the fact that among the leaders of their representative association were former members of the Leibstandarte SS Adolf Hitler, SS-Panzergrenadiere, and the SA, all pillars of the dictatorship.

It's time that Germany should recognize this exile, this first expulsion from its borders. Because Germany has to answer for it just as it has to answer for the Holocaust. In short, without the first expulsion out of Germany, the second one into Germany would never have happened. But let us please stick with the correct order of events: Before Germany gave one group a new homeland it had forced hundreds of thousands to leave their old one.

There is no place anywhere in this country where the meaning of the word "exile" is fully explored and illustrated with specific life stories. The risk of fleeing, the distresses of life in exile, the otherness, the poverty, the fear, the homesickness. Showing all of this is something Germany still owes its history. Without a suitable place commemorating life in exile there will always be a huge gap in the public remembrance of the Nazi terrors. And this gap is another form of "silence."

An Exile Museum could help younger Germans visualize what this phenomenon really was. It would teach compassion and active concern. In other words, it would be a very "appropriate" museum. And in this way the word "appropriate" would acquire a different and more humane meaning. In 2013, Holocaust survivor Inge Deutschkron gave a speech to the German Bundestag in memory of the victims of National Socialism. She spoke of her father, who had escaped the Nazis and fled to England, and who hoped to be called back to Berlin after the war.

In 1933, they threw him out in the truest sense of the word. So now, he thought, they had to invite him back—after all, he was an educator and a not entirely unknown pedagogue. To be sure, his four siblings and their families were among the murdered victims. Nevertheless, he continued to believe in the Germans who had been his friends and who now felt the same duty he did to construct a new Germany, one whose flags were inscribed with the rights of every single human. But this call, this invitation, never came.

So he went on teaching German in English schools. Every morning he checked his box for mail from Berlin. Instead, he received a letter from an English school board advising him to take British citizenship if he desired to continue teaching in England. He thought about this for days, struggling with himself. Finally he accepted. The mailman delivered the document. My father took it and stood there for hours, holding the paper that made him an English citizen, staring out the window into the distance and not letting anyone near.

What was he thinking, I wonder, in those moments?

EDWIDGE DANTICAT is the author of several books, including *Breath, Eyes, Memory,* an Oprah Book Club selection; *Krik? Krak!,* a National Book Award finalist; and *The Farming of Bones,* an American Book Award winner, and the novel-in-stories, *The Dew Breaker.* She is the editor of *The Butterfly's Way: Voices from the Haitian Diaspora in the United States, Haiti Noir* and *Haiti Noir 2,* and *Best American Essays 2011.* She has written six books for young adults and children, *Anacaona, Behind the Mountains, Eight Days, The Last Mapou, Mama's Nightingale,* and *Untwine,* as well as a travel narrative, *After the Dance: A Walk Through Carnival in Jacmel, Haiti.* Her memoir *Brother, I'm Dying,* was a 2007 finalist for the National Book Award and a 2008 winner of the National Book Critics Circle Award for autobiography. She is a 2009 MacArthur Fellow. Her next book, *The Art of Death: Writing the Final Story,* will be published in July 2017.

All the Home You've Got

EDWIDGE DANTICAT

FAITH

My uncle, the Baptist minister, whom I lived with in Haiti from the time that I was four years old to the time I was twelve, often used the expression, *enfants de la promesse,* children of promise, to refer to children like me. The phrase was not meant to refer to our overall potential, but to the fact that we were born to Christian parents. Being a child of promise, in my particular case, also had to do with being born as a result of many promises.

It took five years from the time my parents were married for them to have me. And between their wedding night and the day I was born, there were a lot of prayers and tears. My father once told me that he'd wondered whether he would have to wait to be a hundred years old to become a father, like Abraham. So there were many promises made before I showed up. My mother had promised that she would consecrate her firstborn to Christ, that she would make sure the child walked no other path, that her first daughter or son would be a servant of the Lord. And my father promised God that he would stop smoking, that he would never so much as look at any other woman but my mother. He promised that he would never leave his children if he could help it. But there were many things that were beyond his and my mother's control.

A few years after my birth, my parents left Haiti to seek a better home and future elsewhere, to escape a brutal dictatorship, to find work, to make money. And for all that to happen they had to leave me and my younger brother behind. So I was a child of promise, born out of pure faith, but a child, and later an adult, whose faith in any kind of home, would, just like my heart, completely break.

WITNESS

When I was ten years old, an older boy moved into my aunt and uncle's house and every night for a few weeks, he would walk into the room where I and several girls slept and he would slip his hands under our nightgowns and touch our private parts. Our bunk beds were lined up near the linen-filled armoire from which he needed to get a set of sheets at night, and before he'd pick up the sheets he would touch us. Sometimes it was one or two of us. Sometimes it was all four of us, all of us too terrified to discuss what was going on even among ourselves, all of us too afraid that he might kill us if we screamed or told anyone else.

In that moment I would pretend that my body was no longer my own and that I had merged with the bed sheet. During the day, I would find certain objects to keep me from thinking about the night: self-made amulets in the form of beautiful black and brown women on toothpaste boxes. I would cut out these faces and their gleaming white teeth and I would think how lucky these women were because, since they neither had homes nor beds, no one could touch them in terrible ways. These ungrounded women could also shield me, I thought, by drawing me into whatever imaginary world they lived in, where people laughed all the time and had no vulnerable flesh.

I was afraid to write openly about these nights while my parents were still alive. I was afraid that it might upset them. My parents had left Haiti in the middle of a thirty-year dictatorship during which most people were being terrorized. A woman or girl being raped, or even killed, was not all that unusual. A girl could be walking down the street, she could even be on her way to school alone, and if one of the dictatorship's henchmen decided he liked her, he could take her away. My aunt and uncle managed to protect me from the street threat. Yet they were not aware that the terror had walked inside their home.

As an adult at family gatherings, at mine or other people's homes, I would sit quietly and listen to story after story of female relatives who had been asked to go to private houses, prisons, police stations, wearing their prettiest dresses to "convince" the colonel, general, foot soldier, or militia man who'd arrested their father, brother, uncle, cousin, not to kill their men. Sometimes the price of a loved one's release was a young female relative's virginity. But no one spoke about any of this until our female heroines had died.

Many of the women in my family covered up being abused with piousness. They wore white clothes and wrapped their hair with white scarves. They wore no jewelry or makeup. They prayed a lot. They tried to make themselves as white as the snow we had not yet seen, as white as light itself. They tried to become invisible.

The less of you that was seen the better, my aunt Denise liked to say. But it was no guarantee of protection, even in the dark, even inside your own home.

"I can't always be where you are, but the more time you spend in church, the more eyes you have on you," my father would say when I joined him and my mother in New York at age twelve.

Having eyes on you made it harder for people to hurt you because there were not only human eyes on you. God and his angels were also watching over you.

PRAYER

When I first wrote about this—as fiction—when I was twenty-three years old, this is some of what I wrote:

> When I was a little girl, I had a small notebook made of a few folded sheets, held together by bamboo syrup. There, I sketched a series of stick figures, which were so closely drawn that they almost bumped each other off the page. My effigies were of a child who woke up in tears every morning to find her panties gone. There were never any bubbles over her scalp. No expressions nor conversations. There was just a burning ache between her thighs and a head that bent down to look and then somehow was never raised again. . . .
>
> I was forced to press my pillow farther against the wall when Aunt Denise's godson Joel moved in. He was a tall, thin fifteen-year-old who looked like a man on account of a shaggy beard. He had just come from the hills of Léogâne and his whole body smelled like the wet clay that was still clinging to the straps of his brown sandals.
>
> After he spent the first night in the far corner of the room, way over on the boys' side, I woke up and found my panties gone.
>
> I couldn't string together the words to tell. ("Lost Shadows and Stick Figures," *The Caribbean Writer,* Volume 6, 1992.)

I asked that this be published as fiction, but I am not sure it was. I find it interesting that in my fictional version, I put him in the same room with me and the other girls, "way over on the boys' side." I also gave myself a notebook to write and draw images in. Reading this now, I wonder whether worse things happened to me than my protective childhood mind has allowed me to remember. But what I most want to hold onto now is the fact that words and images had become an alternate home, my safest place. My imagination had rescued me. My prayers had saved me too—I consider writing a kind of prayer—even though they had not been answered in the way I'd yearned for or expected.

A few years ago, I ran into Joel at my aunt and uncle's house in Haiti after my aunt had died. I stood away from him, and though I had both dreaded and rehearsed this encounter over and over in my mind for years, I did not publicly blurt out what he had done to me. I did not cry or run away either. I did not even cringe. I answered his hello and looked into his eyes, and though I saw no visible sign of remorse or soul-searching there, it was the first time in my life that I stopped praying for his death. He was now a shadow to me. I had escaped his grasp, and strangely enough, my imperfect faith in God, which had led me to supplement my prayers with my own protective visions of those bodiless women, had been a big part of my being able to stand in the same room as Joel and mourn the same loved one.

I am still waiting to experience both perfect forgiveness and perfect faith, though. I am not yet able to love my enemies the same way I love my friends. I am unable to pray for those who persecute me beyond praying for them to stop persecuting me. But I am still praying that this particular persecution will not follow me all the days of my life.

GRACE

I have always had low religious self-esteem. Whenever I am in a church, be it my home church or a church I am visiting, there is always a moment when I expect someone to walk over and escort me out, saying, "This is not your place. You don't belong here. We are kicking you out."

The feeling that God let me down by allowing Joel to touch me sometimes makes my faith plummet in a way that is as clear to me as a special-effects meteorite in a movie. But it is much harder for me to express how my survival of this ordeal is what keeps making my faith rebound—not just my being alive, but being able to love my husband, and my two daughters, being able to write my stories, and also to contribute some things, both tangible and intangible, to the world we all live in.

Many of the people I grew up with, some of whom are now pastors and choir directors and other functionaries in different types of churches, are very happy to see me in church. But others, armed with public revelations that writers directly or indirectly make in their work, are hell-bent on seeing me draw a line in the sand and make a clear declaration of "pure and absolute faith," as one friend put it.

For a long time, a childhood friend would email me accounts of dreams that she'd had about me and my family. Her most consistent dream about me involve my having sold my soul to the devil, unwillingly, in my sleep. She could tell by the things I had been writing, she said, and by the fact that I refused to write Christian stories.

"You might have strayed too far from home," she once wrote me, "a little or a lot from the path your uncle and parents taught you. Jesus does not do in-between or lukewarm. You're either inside his kingdom or out in the cold."

I felt condemned by this person because she had very accurately described my often wavering faith, which could be lukewarm or sometimes cold. At times it was because of gatekeepers like her, whose level of certainty I could never match. But most of the time it was because my imagination would not allow me to constrain myself to one set of beliefs, one set of people, and one set of "certainties." As a writer, I told myself, I had to live in other spaces, in other bodies, in other homes, in other minds, in order to convincingly create my characters, which, if I am lucky, represent a whole range of beliefs, lifestyles, moralities, and hopes and dreams.

"This kind of thinking is a certain road to hell," another *enfant de la promesse,* who actually fulfilled her religious promise and was attending a theological seminary, told me.

None of this shocks or offends me; I grew up with a minister after all. Hell was not just other people, but even deviant thoughts, which is a minefield for fiction. I understand drawing lines and unambiguity. I understand not compromising. I understand you're either with us or against us. But that is just not me. Besides, I'm not always sure who "us" is. Is it the gatekeepers to our celestial home? Is it God? Might "us" not also be a group of wounded people whose faith often wavers but who are still seeking a home in God?

Whenever my faith wavers, I try to stick to the basics. I am not expecting any cookies for it, but I still believe in prayer and I still believe in God. I understand, as my minister uncle used to say, that the Bible has many contradictions. I am still struggling with the way these contradictions are often used by human beings to hurt, and even assault, others. Yet I want to respect other people's religions. I want—need—to seek inspiration in the stories of strong people from a whole range of faiths and religious paths.

In the strict religious environment in which I grew up, that makes me a heretic, and a messy one at that. A heretic who refuses to wonder off too far, to not believe at all, yet still continues to walk around with a messy and incomplete faith that sometimes feels like living in a half-finished house.

One thing trauma and the resulting restlessness keeps reminding me is that we are all born vulnerable. Unlike an actual house we are not made of wood, stone, concrete, mortar, or cement. We are easily broken, and we might end up spending the rest of our lives trying to find some way to fix that brokenness. One can still learn, though, from other wounded people—real or fictional—whose faith seems complete, "finished," people whose faith is—or feels—actually like home. One of those folks for me is the lay preacher Baby Suggs in Toni Morrison's novel *Beloved*.

I sometimes find myself prayerfully muttering a few lines from one of her outdoor sermons.

"Here," she said, "in this here place, we flesh; flesh that weeps, laughs; flesh that dances on bare feet in grass. Love it. Love it hard."

Reading this, I always imagine her meaning that sometimes our bodies are all the home we've got.

Then I whisper, *Amen, Sister, Amen.*

NIR BARAM was born into a political family in Jerusalem in 1976. His grandfather and father were both ministers in Israeli Labor Party governments. He has worked as a journalist, an editor, and an advocate for equal rights for Palestinians. He is the author of five novels, including *Good People*, which was translated into English in 2016. His novels have been translated into more than ten languages and received critical acclaim around the world. He has been short-listed several times for the Sapir Prize and in 2010 he received the Prime Minister's Award for Hebrew Literature. His book of reportage, *A Land Without Borders*, will be published in English by Text Publishing in 2017.

JESSICA COHEN is a freelance translator born in England, raised in Israel, and living in Denver. She translates contemporary Israeli prose, poetry, and other creative work. Her translations of critically acclaimed works by major Israeli writers include David Grossman, Etgar Keret, Rutu Modan, Dorit Rabinyan, Ronit Matalon, Amir Gutfreund, and Tom Segev.

A Land Without Borders
They Yelled *Allahu Akbar*: Balata Refugee Camp

NIR BARAM
TRANSLATED FROM THE HEBREW BY JESSICA COHEN

A young boy in an undershirt kneels on a patch of dirt by the side of the road. He is blindfolded with a handkerchief, his back is arched, head bowed, hands tied behind his back. His arms look strong and muscular. The sky above him is a crisp blue, with Mount Gerizim and the Palestinian village of Burin in the background and sunlit green mountains on the horizon. Young soldiers with cocked rifles surround the boy. None of the passing vehicles stops, and no sound comes from our car. It's a peculiar tableau: the boy, the soldiers, everyone motionless.

The minute we get out of the car, the soldiers rush at us, yelling, "Military zone! Get the hell out of here now!" We ask them repeatedly why the boy is tied up, but they just keep yelling. When our photographer runs past and snaps a few shots of the boy, the soldiers lunge at him, but then they abruptly relent and switch from barking commands to a friendly request that he back off. They seem unclear on the procedures—or perhaps there aren't any. I can see another young boy tied up behind the army jeep with his body hunched over.

The sides of his head are shaved, a style popular among soccer fans in these FIFA World Cup days.

The soldiers gradually relax. "They came up to us and shouted something in Arabic," the one with black hair and glasses tells us excitedly. "Then they pulled knives and ran at me!" Another adds, "They yelled *Allahu akbar* and were about to stab us!" We ask when this happened. "Fifteen minutes ago," explain the soldiers, who are serving in the Kfir Infantry Brigade.

I notice two new-looking sharpened assault knives on the jeep's hood, laid out neatly alongside cigarette packs, identity cards, wallets and cell phones.

The soldiers stand the kids up and walk them to the jeep parked on the shoulder. "Where are you taking them?" we ask. A short soldier with a smiling face and a large yarmulke replies, "To the nearest pit. Babi Yar." His friend steps in. "Don't listen to him, he's kidding." The boys are sitting on small benches inside the jeep now. One of the soldiers arranges their legs more comfortably. We ask the kids where they live but they don't answer.

When we speak with a long-time local activist named Zekharia, who works to get Palestinian detainees released, he says stabbing soldiers is a serious offense and he can't help these boys. He's heard they're from Askar, one of a group of refugee camps in the Nablus area that includes Ein Beit al-Ma' and Balata. The black-haired soldier who said he was the first one the boys tried to stab insists: "They came at us with knives and a crazed look in their eyes."

The door slams shut and the jeeps pull away. We drive in the opposite direction, to Balata. Only a few other cars are on the road. We pass heaps of vehicle parts, green tree-lined hills, and clusters of single-story houses. The Israeli radio channel Reshet Bet reports: "Near the village of Burin, south of Nablus, soldiers have arrested two Palestinians who approached them and aroused their suspicion. The Palestinians were found in possession of knives." We get to a hilly range populated by wealthy Nablus families and drive past a lavish estate, on the edge of Mount Gerizim, owned by businessman Munib al-Masri, Sprawling across almost seventy-five acres, it is considered the most luxurious estate in Palestine.

The alleyways of Balata Refugee Camp are crowded, the roads dotted with potholes, trash, piles of dirt and sewage. The alleys branch off into long, narrow lanes, just wide enough for one person, and children start to emerge from every lane. Lots of children. "How are you?" they ask in English, over and over again, laughing. The walls are covered with graffiti: a rifle with crosshairs, and not ten yards away two peace doves taking flight. On the main street, the Kasbah, there are clothing shops, produce stands, a small meat restaurant and a few grocery stores. Two little girls in white dresses, one of them holding a queen's scepter, wave hello. In the United Nations Relief and Works Agency (UNRWA) building, where staff oversee the refugee camp's daily affairs, the offices are abuzz. The building will soon be taken over by doctors from the NGO Physicians for Human Rights, which is holding a temporary clinic here today. The medical care they provide is useful, but the main attraction is the containers full of pharmaceuticals they deliver. More than 40,000 people live in Balata and there is only one medical center here, run by UNRWA, which operates five days a week until 3:00 p.m. After that time residents can seek medical care elsewhere, in Nablus for instance, but most people here can't afford a private doctor.

The doctors are chatting with directors of the local committee about a topic they are all familiar with: a training course in Tel Hashomer Hospital, near Tel Aviv, to which doctors from Gaza were invited, but which they ultimately decided to boycott under pressure from the BDS (Boycott, Divestment and Sanctions) movement. Participating in the course would have meant collaborating with the Israeli establishment. Some of the Palestinians support the boycott, others object. A young Palestinian nurse told me: "These enticing offers for medical or economic co-operation are part of the normalization of the occupation. The Israelis know we need co-operation to improve our lives, and it's good for their image in Israel and around the world. It happens everywhere, all the time. We face a constant dilemma: collaborate or not."

Now they're discussing the Palestinian minister Ziad Abu Ein, who died in December 2014 after a confrontation with Israeli soldiers. Abu Ein's acquaintances say he used to call them back when he was being held in Israeli prisons to report on the detainees' conditions. I meet with Ghassan, who chairs a committee set up to resist settler violence in the northern West Bank. He used to work with the late minister. Ghassan says he visits villages that have been attacked by settlers every day, mainly in the Nablus region. "There are twelve settlements around Nablus, with about 2,500 residents, and it's mostly people from Yitzhar settlement who keep attacking the villages. We protect them as best we can."

I tell Ghassan that I recently spoke with West Bank Palestinians who complained about the fecklessness of the Palestinian Authority (PA) in the face of the settlers' "price-tag" operations—burning mosques, smashing windshields, attacking Palestinians, uprooting olive trees. They feel the PA's response isn't forceful enough, that it seems a little fatigued, indifferent even, perhaps wary of confronting the Israeli Defense Forces (IDF). They claim that ad-hoc initiatives like one in the village of Qusra, where a local force has been set up to protect residents from the settlers, are far more efficient. "What kind of talk is that?" Ghassan responds. "We don't have any real power or authority, and the IDF works for the settlers. We document everything, we talk, we take action, we file reports, but complaining to the IDF is useless, and if we respond with violence the army will quickly act against us, which is exactly what the settlers are waiting for. I'm working under impossible circumstances."

We are surrounded by a dozen teenagers wearing orange bandanas and grey vests embroidered with the word "Yafa." They stand quietly listening to the adults. After a while, I sit down outside with them. They don't speak any Hebrew, so their twenty-something counselor translates. They belong to a youth group, part of the World Organization of the Scout Movement, which has about 150 members in Balata. Their movement has a political consciousness, they explain. "We volunteer and we go on demonstrations," says a boy named Salakh. "The emphasis in our movement is on volunteering. Our goal is to serve the people in the camp. There is a lot of distress in the camp, a lot of unemployment. We help the poor and needy, we clean streets and pathways, and on holidays we have activities and plays." Today they have come to prepare the building for the doctors and help carry containers of medication to the top floor, where an improvised pharmacy has been set up.

"Where are you from?" I ask the boys.

"From Yafa," says one. "Yafa," repeats another. One says Kafr Saaba—the Arab village that lies east of what is now a booming city in Israel's central region and bears the Hebrew name of "Kfar Saba." One boy is from Gaza. The vast majority give the names of towns or villages from which their grandparents were displaced in 1948. Salakh tells us that when the Israelis occupied Kafr Saaba, his family fled to the town of Qalqilya, then to a village near Salfit, assuming they would be able to go home after a few weeks. His grandfather was a farmer who owned lands near Kafr Saaba.

"Have you ever been there?"

"No," they all say. None of them has been to Tel Aviv either.

"What political solution do you believe in?"

"We don't think anything bad about anyone, only good things, and so there will be peace," one boy offers and everyone laughs. "For us, Israelis are the occupation. We all have brothers or cousins who've been killed by your army or are in prison," says a boy with glasses;

he puts arms around two of his friends. "We believe in a Palestinian state and living with the Israelis. But you have to understand: there is a difference between an Israeli and a Zionist. Jewish Israelis are people who believe in a certain religion and they have a God. Zionism is a terrorist organization."

Dozens of people are gathered on the second floor of the UNRWA building. They are not waiting for a doctor but for an audience with Ahmad Thouqan, who directs the Department for Refugee Affairs, which is part of the People's Committee in Balata. The Committee is affiliated with the Palestinian Liberation Organization (PLO)'s Department of Refugees and was founded in 1995, after the PA established its base in the West Bank. There were always similar committees in refugee camps in Jordan and Lebanon, but until the Oslo Accords they were not permitted in the West Bank. Thouqan sits at a large desk in his smoke-filled office, with a group of people who purchased a plot of land near the camp where they want to build a playground. The main issue is money: there isn't enough. The camp sits on a small area and is extremely crowded. Children have nowhere to play, families have nowhere to stroll.

Thouqan, a chain-smoker in his fifties who is always delivering terse answers over the phone or to his staff, is visibly impatient with his loquacious visitors. Clerks regularly appear on either side of him to show him various documents. Health issues are a major concern for him, he says. The camp is overcrowded, there isn't much sunlight, the air is "not good," and many residents suffer from respiratory disease, high blood pressure and, most prevalently, diabetes. There are roughly 1,200 diabetics in the camp, many of them children. The problem is that sometimes they need to be checked several times a day, but the UNRWA clinic closes early and the children have no choice but to see a private doctor. This costs money, as does medication. Residents with jobs might earn fifty to eighty shekels a day (roughly $13 to $20), and even if a visit to the doctor in Nablus is cheap—roughly twenty shekels, or about $5—they still can't afford it.

Unemployment is another worry. Thouqan estimates a jobless rate of roughly 35 percent. In recent years many Palestinians who were imprisoned during the Second Intifada have been getting out and coming home to the camp. Most are uneducated and struggle to find work. They want to be part of the PA's security apparatus, but they are usually rejected because they are too old or there aren't any positions or they're simply not wanted. When a man walks out of prison at age thirty-five with no family, no job and no education, the camp must help him, in recognition of his contribution to the Palestinian struggle. "Relatively speaking," Thouqan adds proudly, "we have a lot more prisoners and casualties than they do in Nablus."

Some three hundred residents of Balata were killed in the Second Intifada. Recently, however, confrontations with Israel and the IDF's raids are not the only cause of unrest in the camp. One of the women waiting in line to see a doctor explains: "It's tense here, there are loud noises at night, sometimes gunfire." The PA suspects that some of the armed men in the camp, supposedly members of the organization Fatah, are in fact working for Mohammed Dahlan, their financial backer. Dahlan, who was a senior Fatah figure and head of the Preventive Security Force in Gaza, was expelled from the PA's jurisdiction by President Mahmoud Abbas (Abu Mazen) after the latter suspected Dahlan of attempting to remove him from office. Dahlan now spends a fortune in the West Bank and Gaza in an effort to unseat Abbas. In February there were reports of bloody confrontations in the northern West Bank, particularly in Balata, between PA security forces and Dahlan loyalists, after the latter opened fire while the PA was carrying out arrests.

I ask Thouqan where he gets resources for running the camp. After all, it can't be from taxes.

"We have a good relationship with the PA," he replies, "mainly with the Prime Minister and with Abu Mazen, who help us. We also get a lot of donations, and there's UNRWA and the PLO of course. But I'll give you an example of something that's been preoccupying me lately, and can be really frustrating. We have more than five hundred students at universities like An-Najah and Birzeit. Pay here is around 2,500 shekels ($650) a month. If a family has two kids at college, that means each kid needs about 10,000 shekels ($2,600) a year for tuition. How can they manage that? Now, the only way for people here to get out of their predicament is to study. Because these are people who don't own land or property, and anyway, there's no commerce here. So this is the reasoning: you study and then move to Ramallah or Saudi Arabia or Dubai, you work there and support your family in the camp until your little siblings grow up, then they go to university and support the family. And then you're free to support your new family."

He shows me a document displaying the number 28,000 with a series of columns next to it. They had requested aid to enable families to send their kids to university, and the PLO had sent 28,000 shekels, which is enough to give small subsidies to fifteen students. Thouqan has roughly two hundred requests, and he spent weeks trying to decide how to distribute the funds. He knows that a university degree allows a graduate to support an entire family for several years. He decided to give the money only to students who have more than three siblings, none of whom is currently at university. This narrowed it down only slightly, as the average family has six children.

Beyond the daily troubles, the question of refugees is at the root of political consciousness in the camp. Everywhere in Balata one can see old maps of pre–1948 Palestine, paintings and pencil drawings, pictures of houses and vistas that signify the world that existed before the Nakba, the Arabic term for the catastrophe of expulsion. When you ask people where they are from, they will often mention the family house from before 1948. Thouqan's own story is a good example.

His family lived in Yafa—he means the Yafa District, he emphasizes, which until '48 was a thriving center of Arab life in Palestine, with some 120,000 residents. His village was called Al-Sawalima, and the family owned about twelve acres of land and a large modern house they'd built in the 1940s. They grew oranges, watermelons and other fruit. They had up-to-date equipment, including an engine that pumped water. They were deported in the 1948 war, and roamed for a while, eventually settling in the Balata Refugee Camp in the early fifties. Thouqan's father struggled to recover, constantly comparing his existence in the camp to his previous life. A man with lands, money and social status, whose name was known throughout Yafa, now found himself competing for the same low-paying jobs with a laborer he had brought from Egypt to work his fields. "A mixture of humiliation, anger and shame," says Thouqan. One day a friend found Thouqan's father a job as a guard. When he was driven to his new workplace the next morning, he was shocked to find himself standing on his very own land. Everything was destroyed except the water pump. "This is my land," he told his new employers. He showed them the pump, pointed to trees he had planted himself. He was in such emotional distress that he had to be hospitalized. Ever since that day, he never wanted to set eyes on the place again. He died in 1990. Thouqan's mother had grown up in the village of Jayyous. After the 1967 war, the land around Jayyous became part of the West Bank, and she received almost two acres from her father. The hopes the family pinned on this inheritance were dashed when, in the early 2000s, Israel built the separation wall, which hit the village of Jayyous especially hard. Sixty percent of its agricultural lands are within the seam zone (the limbo area located between the Green Line and the separation wall), which means Israel controls access to those lands by means of a "permit regime." Residents frequently discover that they are not permitted access to their lands. Since the construction of the wall, the villagers' agricultural output has declined by half to roughly four thousand tons of olives a year. Thouqan says his family's plot isn't worth much anymore. Now he can't even visit it.

I ask him about the two-state vision advocated by his organization, Fatah, and about Abu Mazen's negotiations, which do not address the Palestinian right of return to their land and property.

"There are Palestinians who live in Israel, inside the Green Line, right?" he asks. "So why shouldn't Palestinians who used to live there and were deported not go back to their homes? I'm certainly willing to live in the State of Israel."

"So is there no resolution without the right of return for the refugees? You must see," I point out, "that you are asking to completely alter the state of Israel."

"Our lands, our home—that is not something I can give up. I don't even have the right to. My home is Arab al'Awsat. This is not my home here."

"You've lived here in Balata your whole life."

"Yes, but it's not my home, and it's not the home of anyone who lives here. This is where many people live who were kicked out of their homes and their lands, and those of their parents and grandparents. No one has the right to give those up."

In Chile, home to one of the world's largest Palestinian communities, I heard similar talk recently, when I took part in an event with the Palestinian-Chilean writer Diamela Eltit. After the talk, a young woman whose parents lived in Balata but who was born in Chile came up to me. "There's something you people don't understand," she said. "You talked about time—1967 or 1948—but you didn't talk about space. Our spatial perception is different. For Israelis, Palestinians are in Gaza and the West Bank, but our spatial perception also includes refugee camps in Jordan and Lebanon, and large Palestinian communities around the world. It's a non-linear, truncated space, but it is the space of Palestinian consciousness."

A while ago I read Yehouda Shenhav-Shaharabani's Hebrew translation of *The Meaning of the Nakba*, a formative account by the Arab intellectual Constantine Zurayk, written in 1948, right after the Nakba. Zurayk writes:

> In my opinion, it is our right and our obligation to recognize the enemy's vast power and to thereby not impose excessive guilt on ourselves. But at the same time, it is our right and obligation to recognize our mistakes and the sources of our weakness [...] Worst of all would be to evade this responsibility and shut our eyes to our limitations, and to point the finger at an external factor without seeing our own weakness, flaws, corruption and deficiencies.

Before I part with Thouqan, I ask him one more question. "Do you think that self-reckoning has taken place?"

"I'm not entirely sure," he replies candidly. "There was a reckoning about the Nakba, our failures, our fears, our lack of organization. But sometimes I wonder if we made the changes that were necessary after the Nakba, if we weren't too rigid, whether we wouldn't have become much stronger if we'd had the courage to dig into our wounds with our bare hands."

At midday, the Kasbah in Balata is bustling. Ahead of me, a small family—a handsome young mother and father with two children dressed in white—takes a leisurely stroll while sewage flows in the gutters beside them. I sit down for a conversation with Dr. Fathi Darwish, a short older man who has had an interesting career in the PLO. He asks if I speak Arabic. I stammer and say I took two courses, and manage to string together a couple of sentences. He laughs. I assume he speaks Hebrew, but like many others he chooses to talk to me in English. In the 1970s he spent time in refugee camps in Lebanon, Syria and Jordan, working on healthcare policies. In the eighties he moved to Tunis and worked in Yasser Arafat's office, and in 1994, after a thirty-year exile, he returned to Palestine with Arafat. He recalls how the Palestinians lined the streets for days to welcome their leader: "We were full of optimism then, for us it was the end of exile. There was hope for the end of the occupation, that our children would have a better future. It was clear to all of us that the end of the occupation was very near."

Darwish was born in 1944 in the Haifa neighborhood of Wadi Nisnas. His family lived on Kings Road (today named Independence Road), on the first floor of a building that had a bakery in the basement. He remembers how, one day during the war in 1948, the smell of bread baking gave way to burning: the bakery was on fire, and his father carried him and his sister outside, where they stood watching the building burn. They moved to the village of Ya'bad, west of Jenin, and then wandered on to other places. There are eleven children in Darwish's family, four born in Haifa and the rest in the West Bank and Kuwait. "We're a classic example of the dismantled post–1948 Palestinian family. Like a grenade that explodes and the shrapnel flies everywhere, my siblings are scattered around the world. I have brothers and sisters in Kuwait, in Saudi Arabia, in Serbia, in America, in Jordan. I haven't seen some of them for more than twenty-five years."

Darwish is a veteran PLO man. When he talks about the future, he gives the official PA line: "I believe the government of Israel must reinstate its agreements with the Palestinians and go back to the two-state vision. That means a Palestinian state within the 1967 borders with Jerusalem as its capital, and perhaps minor exchanges of territories. Meanwhile, the settlements are threatening to put an end to it all."

"Are you a two-state advocate?" I ask.

"I don't care if there are two states or one state, the important thing for the Palestinians is that the occupation end and they be given the same rights as Jews."

"It seems fair to say that Abu Mazen gave up on the right of return during negotiations. Do you accept that?"

"All over the world, refugees have the right to return. The refugees—they are a fundamental question in any resolution."

"And the answer?"

"How can I explain to refugees in Syria and Lebanon that a Jew from anywhere in the world can go back to Israel because two thousand years ago he had roots here, but they can't go back to their homes? Most of the Palestinians who were born here and then exiled have homes and land—don't they have the right to come back?"

"So the future you see is two states and the return of refugees to their homes in Israel? Because that is very different from the plan that was under discussion: it's not exactly the familiar two-state solution, but more like one state."

"Ask the kids in Balata where they're from and you'll see they'll tell you: I'm from Acre, I'm from Haifa. All those people must be given an answer. I believe that, if there is goodwill and serious negotiation between the Israelis and the Palestinians, we can reach a solution on the refugee issue."

Darwish's arguments raise an interesting point. Two distinct groups are emerging among Israelis, Palestinians and the international community, with divergent views of the past and conclusions for the future. The factions in each group do not share a common purpose but rather a similar historical perspective. The first group might be labeled "the '67 group," and it includes Israel's center-left and some of its right-wing blocs, the international community, and parts of Fatah. For them, the defining event was the 1967 war and, accordingly, they work towards a two-state solution. This group also includes, of course, Palestinians who do not believe that the 1967 war was the defining event but who nonetheless recognize that it is the international parameter for solving the conflict.

The second and more complex group comprises most of the Israeli right wing, primarily the settlers, as well as Israel's far left, and large parts of Palestinian society; these constituents believe that the defining event was 1948 and the expulsion of the Palestinians from their lands. This is also the root of the settlers' claim that Ramat Aviv (a generally left-leaning Tel Aviv suburb built on the ruins of the Palestinian village Sheikh Munis) is one and the same as Ofra or any other West Bank settlement. Members of this group do not believe that the conflict can be truly resolved, although they may support ideas such as the annexation of parts of the West Bank, a single state, the Palestinians' return as part of a two-state agreement, or, like some Palestinians I spoke with, a notion along the lines of "peace, freedom of movement and equal rights within the framework of an agreement." To them, the key to the solution is contending with 1948. Furthermore, most of the PA representatives who speak of 1967 and the international parameters would agree with Fathi Darwish about the return of the refugees, namely, that "they have the right to return." There are those in this camp who do voice reservations, sometimes extremely significant ones (such as an intent not to "change the character of Israel"), but they will not concede on the principle of return, and so the debate with them is a pendulum that swings between '67 and '48. One thing is clear: most Israelis, including those in the peace camp, are unwilling to acknowledge the Palestinian view of 1948.

Darwish says that if Israelis were to read Palestinian writers and poets such as Ghassan Kanafani, Emile Habibi and Muhammad Ali Taa, who wrote about the expulsion, they would gain an understanding of the Palestinian soul, of the moment when a person loses his home and instantly becomes dispossessed. Taa, for example, describes the expulsion of the residents of Mi'ar (which sat just over ten miles east of Acre), including his family, in the '48 war:

> The people left the village taking few possessions: a blanket or two, pillows, some flour, jugs of olive oil, a pot and a few dishes. My father hoisted a blanket and mattress on his shoulders and carried my brother Mahmoud in his arms. My mother perched a half-full sack of flour on her head, and held my little sister Alia and a jug of olive oil. I hurried behind her […] The men began loading things onto donkeys and mules. The families who had beasts of burden were the fortunate ones. The Jews were entering the village. Sounds of gunshot echoed everywhere. The mosque's dome blew off into the sky. There was a loud thundering. Stones flew in the air and there were thick clouds of smoke. And people set off on their way.(from *Time of Lost Childhood*, translated into English from Yehouda Shenhav-Shaharabani's Hebrew translation.)

Darwish has been fighting against the Israeli occupation for fifty years, yet he is still optimistic. He has long worked cooperatively with Israel and is now troubled, not to say insulted, by Israel's indifference to the Palestinian issue. "After all the killing, the land grabs, the imprisonments, the checkpoints, we keep explaining to our people that we can live in peace with the Israelis. But they don't believe us anymore. We see the elections in Israel, with not a word about the occupation, about the Palestinians, about our rights. Your elections might as well be taking place in Europe. The Palestinians are constantly engaged with Israelis because we have no choice, the Israelis interfere with every aspect of our lives. But we just seem to bore you now, don't we?" After a pause, he adds, "I was in Tunis on the day Arafat and Rabin signed the accord. But the extreme right murdered Rabin. And in fact they destroyed everything."

I ask whether he thinks the impending—to his mind—Palestinian state will result from negotiations, or only through the strategy of the Hague and BDS.

"We have to use any tool that might end the occupation. We must remember the lessons learned from South Africa: the boycott was a critical tool in that struggle. We're not about to spend another twenty years in negotiations so that a hundred more settlements can be built in the meantime. It appears that going to the UN, the international treaties, BDS, those are the only things that affect the Israelis, who are obsessed with their standing in every other place in the world but don't care what their neighbors think of them. If we don't kick up a fuss around the world and there's no terrorism—we might as well be air for the Israelis."

On Al-Quds Street between Nablus and Balata, there is heavy traffic. A Palestinian policeman in uniform stands on the side of the road. Two teenaged boys sit in the back seat of his car. One of them looks straight ahead with a stern expression, while the other smiles and lights a cigarette from a red pack of Marlboro. A few hours ago, when they were blindfolded, they probably did not see me but might have heard my voice. They wear jeans and T-shirts. The policeman was recently summoned to the checkpoint, where the Israelis handed him the two boys who earlier that day had been suspected of attempting to stab soldiers. It seems improbable that Israel would simply set free two assault suspects, so why were they let go?

I ask the boys themselves, but they have been instructed by the policeman not to talk, so they just wave and smile. I ask the officer; he doesn't know. Zekharia says that, judging by the findings, the kids were not planning to stab anyone; if they really had attacked the soldiers with knives, there is no chance they'd be sitting here now. The soldiers probably exaggerated or misunderstood or perhaps even fabricated. But we saw the knives, I remind him. He asks the Palestinian officer about the knives. No answer. He asks the boys again; they say nothing. Lots of organizations and people here— the IDF, human rights organizations, the settlers, the PA, various officials—spread rumors and conflicting accounts of every event, particularly those that get little attention in the media. Every story has a competing—or contradictory—version and, in the absence of one fact-checking authority that is acceptable to everyone, each side clings to its own version. These sorts of incidents happen frequently, and in a few days no one will remember these two kids anyway. I ask if they're going home now, to Askar. The answer, as I understand it, is affirmative albeit evasive. I repeat my question but the second answer is even more oblique. The Palestinian policeman says goodbye and drives away. It's drizzling, and the wind is getting cold. It'll be evening soon. Zekharia is talking to someone on the phone about some olive trees that the settlers cut down, and a house on the edge of the village that was stoned.

It's been two months since my visit to Balata. In a little café in Hawara—a serene village south of Nablus full of auto shops, restaurants and confectionaries—I meet Attorney Zidan. A young man of twenty-five, he wears a black sweater-vest and a tight-fitting blazer, with a fashionable goatee and sideburns. His voice is gentle and he has a shy, winning smile. We speak in English. He studied law in Jordan and started a small practice in Nablus two years ago, which takes different types of cases. This week he is in court in Nablus defending a Palestinian charged with selling hashish: a trifling affair, since he only sold to his friends.

At the end of 2014, Zidan was contacted by the parents of one of the two boys from Askar—the younger was seventeen and the other just eighteen—who asked him to represent them against the PA. As it turns out, the car they were in that Saturday did not take them back to Askar but to the PA's prison in Nablus. They were charged with illegal possession of a weapon. Zidan was denied a request to visit his new clients. When I describe for him the scene I saw near Burin a few minutes after they had allegedly tried to stab the soldiers, he smiles dismissively. "They got to the checkpoint and said to the soldiers, 'We have knives, we want you to arrest us.'"

I tell him the soldiers claimed they'd yelled *Allahu akbar*.

Now he laughs. "Maybe they did also yell *Allahu akbar*."

"Why did they want to get arrested?"

"All sorts of reasons," Zidan explains. "Sometimes Palestinians turn up at a checkpoint with knives without any intention of stabbing soldiers. They want to be arrested so that their families will get money, or to earn a matriculation certificate, or because someone in their family is being accused of collaborating with Israel."

"But I'm talking about these particular boys," I insist. "Do you know why your clients did it?"

"They're poor, they had no jobs, no nothing, they wanted to be arrested to get money from the PA. The PA gives money to prisoners in Israeli prisons. That's the whole story, it happens all the time."

I tell him I heard they were in prison for thirty-six days. "How did they get out?"

"I filed a petition to drop the charges because they didn't have any weapon or anything really dangerous, just knives," he answers, "but the petition was denied. I filed another one and it was denied. I persisted and kept filing petitions to drop the charges. On the fourth petition they suddenly notified me that the investigation was over and there was no evidence against my clients and they let them go. I didn't understand the whole procedure, it was the first time I'd worked on a case like this. When they got out of prison I met them for the first time."

Zidan says the boys were only in prison for twenty-two days; later he claims it was just over two weeks. I ask if the PA kept the kids in prison to scare them, and he gives a circuitous response. Attorney Zidan is wary of criticizing the PA, the courts or the police. He is demonstratively courteous but gives brief answers. According to him, one of the two kids has found a construction job in the Jenin area, which makes his parents happy, and the other is at home but his father makes sure he doesn't get into trouble. Zidan prefers that we not photograph him. He's in a hurry to get back to Nablus. Competition among lawyers is stiff, he says, everyone wants cases, doesn't matter what kind—criminal, civilian, commercial, big, small—as long as you get clients. Fortunately, he's very busy these days.

LEILA ABOULELA was the first winner of the Caine Prize for African Writing. She is the author of four novels, *The Kindness of Enemies*; *The Translator*, a *New York Times* 100 Notable Books of the Year; *Minaret*; and *Lyrics Alley*, Fiction Winner of the Scottish Book Awards. Her collection of short stories, *Coloured Lights*, was shortlisted for the MacMillan Silver PEN Award. Leila grew up in Sudan and moved, in her mid-twenties, to Scotland.

Pages of Fruit

LEILA ABOULELA

The first time I met you, not face-to-face, but through your words, was when I read "The Wedding Pistol" in an anthology of short stories written by women. This was back in the 1990s. To me, your voice was the most compelling, your story the only one transparent and in 3-D. I remember the armchair I was sitting on that day, the one that had belonged to my mother-in-law in London. We moved it to Aberdeen and it was still in good condition. Green leaves, a spring look which softened the dark afternoons I was getting used to. We no longer have this armchair. The children wore it out even though I removed the cushion covers regularly and washed them but the base of the chair sunk and having shipped it all the way to Abu Dhabi, I gave it away to charity and upgraded to leather. So I was sitting on that armchair reading your story and around me the house would not have been quiet. The boys would have been rummaging in the kitchen or watching *Thomas the Tank Engine* or they would have been out in the garden, the sound of their football hitting against the rotary dryer and the fence. But it did not matter because you had my full attention and I was deep in your world which in its settings, webs and cadences was also mine but made by you, enchanting.

I remember I had my period while I was reading. It must have been the second or third day, after the tension and the cramps had subsided and what was left was the gentle steady flow. It relaxed me almost to the point of sleepiness. But I was not sleepy at all, I was fully alert to your voice, pulled down and immersed in the here and now of the pages in my hand. I gave in to the serene sense of my reproductive organs existing in passive mode, my days off, the secret celebration that I was not pregnant; another month's reprieve. I sank into the armchair, into myself, and I took your story, understanding every reference, getting every joke. I hummed the tunes of songs you mentioned, I saw maps of the streets you pointed out. I was your perfect reader and I was too rapt to even stop and think that I don't want this to end.

This was the first time I recognized myself in fiction. Not my inner self, I was able to do that between the most unlikely covers, novels written by men from other centuries or set in places I didn't even know existed. But in your work I recognized my country, my values and the social circles I grew up in. Of course I had read African literature before, the classics in which I recognized the people, weather, the landscape, the great panorama of life. But your story was different. Unashamedly you wrote about the top ten percent. A privileged childhood similar to mine. A highly educated family who could afford to travel to London for holidays and degrees. A family in which the children were brought up to dress, eat and speak differently (i.e., more Westernized) than their elders. I knew all about the outcome of this, the mixture of pride and opportunism; the growing impatience with needing to explain, the compulsion to stop and assign value.

I was in my twenties when I first read you, a decade younger than you. I was voluble and impressionable. Immediately I wanted to be your friend. We had so much in common, both of us here and both of us from there. I was eager to talk to you about your story; about what I recognized and what was exciting. I felt that I already knew you and that sooner or later we would meet and the conversation would sparkle between us. Looking back now, I can see that I was lonely, cut off from my old friends and country. Your story was a bridge to a world I had left behind after marriage and migration. A world I was losing but through your words it became vivid again. I could inhabit it.

Did I read your novel first or write you a letter? I wrote my first letter to you by hand and I do not have a copy. People, I am sure, had said to you "I devoured your novel," but your novel devoured me. The pain of the heroine became my pain, her conflicts more vivid than my existence. For days I neglected my children and husband. I saw them through glazed eyes, I sleepwalked through the housework. I was with you, not with them.

I dreamt of you (or your heroines, I am not sure, you were interchangeable) happy dreams in which we sat side by side on stairs, like little girls. We talked and looked at pictures together, pictures of your heroines, hand-drawn scenes from your novels. Of course in real life your books, apart from the covers and your photo, did not have any drawings. But in my dreams, your words became visuals; top actresses vied to dramatize them on the silver screen. You and I didn't always speak about fiction, sometimes we swapped day-to-day experiences too—the school run, grumpy shop assistants, newspaper headlines—and your observations on life in the West chimed with mine. I was not shy or in awe of you. I shared freely my own digs and frustrations. You did not patronize or talk down to me, we were equals in spirit, our friendship based on shared experiences and ideas.

Us sitting side by side, indoors or outdoors. Or the two of us on a seesaw, going up and down, both of us the same height, the same weight. I continued to have variations of the same dream. The easy laughter between us, the words tumbling out of me. Telling you this and that. Repeating what I had already said in my letters or adding more. And you understanding every word without need for background explanation or elaboration. I would talk to you about my school friends, children and cousins and you knew them all already. They interested you for you hung on every word I said, threading in your own observations, details and insights specially formulated for me. You never needed me to introduce or to present, our conversations were an infinite continuation, a stream of goodwill. Sometimes the dream would last all night and even when I woke up, the happiness and warmth remained with me, infusing the day as if it were healing it.

But you never replied to my letters. A year passed. After the novel a collection of short stories was published. It included "The Wedding Pistol." And just reading in the Acknowledgements that "The Wedding Pistol" was previously published in the anthology of women writers that was on my shelf, made me want to say out loud, "Yes, I have it. Yes, this was my first time to read her and I would never forget it."

Your second novel made more of a splash. I cut out the reviews from the newspapers. But I noticed that even the good ones were patronizing; few gave you your due. One did say "a landmark" and I agreed. Even more exciting for me than the reviews were the interviews with you. A photo of you and your little girl on the beach. Your candid answers. Details of where you went to school and where you went to university—even your parents' careers. Such abundance, as generous as your prose. I now had so much to piece together, to match biography with fiction, to speculate, to double guess. In my plain, limited life you provided me with colour and adventure. I superimposed your life on films I had watched, I held you up as the epitome of intellect and glamor. The activity of reading and thinking about your work brought me hours of joy. Thank you.

I spoke about you often to my husband and friends, who did not read your work, who would be (were, actually, the times I went over plots) shocked by your progressive take and explicitness. To be honest,

(*continued on page 147*)

Home, the Real Thing of an Image

VELIBOR BOŽOVIĆ

Presented here is a small selection of photographs taken during my visits to Sarajevo, the city that had been my home for some thirty years, before my wife, our son and I left in 1998. We resettled in Montreal, which quickly became our new home. It took five years before I went back to Sarajevo, and another three before I visited again. Since 2008, I have returned at least once every year. With each visit, bewilderment overwhelms me, for what I foresee there, in Sarajevo and Bosnia, is what I remember.

We learn at a young age that photographs are images of *real* things. But *real* things of images continue to live on, for some time, at least. In Montreal, I live with images of Sarajevo at all times: Some are just a tap away on my phone, some stare back at me from prints I have scattered around our home and in my studio, and some are neatly arranged in family photo albums. Some pretend to be memories, and some have nested themselves deep in my subliminal self only to awaken and take hold at unexpected moments. So when I disembark from a plane that has carried me across the ocean, and find myself in Sarajevo, I feel as if I've just inserted myself into the *real* thing of those images that haunt me when in Montreal. And with each visit that feeling gets more agreeable and thoughts of living, once again, in the *real* thing become increasingly seductive.

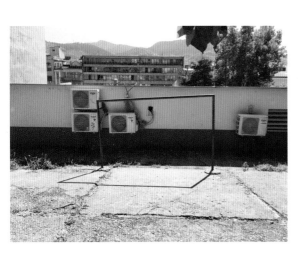

the people around me were more conservative than the families in your books and your own family by extension. I had said that I thrilled to the familiarity of your characters and social circles, I had claimed them for myself. In truth, though, you and your characters inhabited the liberal fringes while I remained with the sedate majority. Theoretically, in an abstract imaginary situation, my parents and your parents would be acquaintances but never friends. True, they would have been members of the same club and been invited to the same parties, but they would sit at different tables. My father would have heard of your father, the celebrated journalist. And your father would have bought his car from my father's Toyota agency. But your parents married for love, while mine had an arranged marriage. You studied in Britain as a child, while I came here as an adult. I have never smoked, drank alcohol or worn a bikini. If Westernization was a linear progression (and that is debatable of course and not politically correct, in public to maintain your wide readership you would understandably refute it) but if it were true, then you were ahead of me by several steps, more sophisticated, more progressive, and if assimilation was our ultimate goal (and that is debatable in itself and your great love and loyalty for our homeland is well documented), then you were more blended, more diluted. You belonged in Britain better than I did.

In my imaginary conversations with you and in my fan letters which were not purely doting, I took you sometimes to task for your risqué scenes and the sinful behaviour of your heroines. Hopefully you didn't misunderstand me, I was neither aggressive nor didactic. My tone was gently mocking, more of a tut-tut than outright condemnation. It would be dishonest not to admit that your explicit love scenes added to the allure of your work, made it somewhat dangerous, altogether satisfying. Besides, I enjoyed the bristle in my mind in accommodating your more liberal stance. But in my day-to-day life, in my own personal views I was as restrained and conventional as the people around me.

Now that I am older, now that I am looking back, I ask myself whether I envied you. Was yours and your characters' lives the one I longed for? More daring than mine, livelier if not more fulfilling. Certainly in school, I had known outgoing girls similar to your younger heroines, girls who were brimming with confidence, unencumbered by shyness. They had boyfriends who rode motorcycles and with them they dabbled in weed and unchaperoned meetings. This cool club glittered out of reach and yet I was avidly curious about its members. At times I even ached for recognition from them—one of my diary entries at the age of thirteen reads, "What I want is that when they are asked who this girl (me) is, their answer would be this is so and so, she is quite nice but I don't know her very well. This is not what is happening now. They don't even know my name!" That last sentence is the wail of a teenager. I can hear her and remember the angst. Your heroines are a resurrection of those sparkling girls for whom I was invisible. The ones whose approval I craved. So you see, your writing did not transport me to another world but instead welcomed me into conversations and outings that had been barred to me. It was as if, in the reading, I were mixing with people who had at one time brushed past me but never had the patience to stop and engage. Thank you for this access.

And for being there for me when I came out of hospital—when the painkillers wore off your paperback was the alternative drug. When we moved house—putting your hardback up on the new shelves from John Lewis. When I had the miscarriage—one of the nurses was also called Selma. When I got my first laptop and typed you a letter. When my father passed away—his funeral exactly like the one you described. When I enrolled in the Open University and told you about it in a letter. When we went on holiday to Barcelona and I came across *Frutos de Loto* in a bookshop near the hotel. I had written about *Fruit Lotus*, my favourite of all your novels, to the Richard and Judy Book Club when they first started asking for viewer recommendations. Today the newspapers call for more diverse literature, but in those years you were often unfairly overlooked, consistently underrated. Bear this in mind, that I was one of your early champions, long before you became mainstream.

When the World Wide Web entered my home, I searched for you. Even before Google, I put your name in AltaVista and Ask Jeeves. I revelled in the results—photos, interviews, reviews. Links to other members of your family, your ex-husband, your artist brother and even your friends. It was like raking through a treasure. Was that snooping? Or lurking. Or that other word my growing children later started to use, to explain to me, with a mixture of exasperation and indulgence, the etiquette of the internet—"stalking"?

The first email I sent you, I remember signing it "your fan from Aberdeen." I always used this signature so that I would stand out and be remembered. "Ah," I imagined you saying with fondness, "that lady again from North Scotland." Perhaps you would also be proud that you were read so far north, though, over the years and with your growing success, you might have started taking a larger readership for granted. I wrote to you about my parents' divorce. I cringe now when I reread this email and intend to delete it. (I will delete them all.) When I wrote that first email my husband was away on business, my youngest child was ill with fever and it was a public holiday so I couldn't get him to the doctor. My period was late and I was holding my breath, anxious that I was pregnant again. To make matters worse, I was also getting obscene anonymous phone calls so upsetting that every time the phone rang my blood ran cold. Because I couldn't sleep, I wrote to you about my mother.

The toddler with the rasping hot breath tossing next to me, the phone off the hook, my body on high alert for the first sign of my late period—the women in your novels don't go through these things. They are not always in control, but still their will is strong and their confidence high. They triumph and they surge forward climbing mountains, confronting riot police, filming a lioness giving birth. My mother resembled your heroines. I elaborated on that in the email. She was outspoken and vibrant, the kind of person everyone agreed was ahead of her time. She left my father because he stifled her. She walked out on us and struck out on her own, supporting herself and fulfilling her potential. My mother's story would not have shocked you. You understood that the West's image of "the Muslim woman" was a reduced, simplified cliché. My mother was neither more nor less Muslim than others, she was different because of her personality, education and more significantly her independent means. In my email, I showed off about her because I couldn't show off about myself. I couldn't write down how fervently I was praying for my period to come, for my husband to return, for my son's fever to break. Instead I spoke of my mother standing up to society and how pioneering she was. I glossed over the actual abandonment, the child (me) running after the moving car, the father vomiting all night, the torturous phone calls, the scathing things people said. I told you that I was close to her, that she, like you, was an inspiration to me. That night I dreamt of a woman who was my mother and who was you at the same time. She hugged me and I wept with relief.

Your feminism and that of my mother's was of a similar kind, birthed in one city with the same influences. It meant birth control, work outside the home; it meant ability, self-sufficiency and a refusal to be bogged down by either convention or religion. This particular kind of feminism could not accommodate sisterhood, other women were to be climbed upon to get to the top and it did not mean compassion because that was a weakness. It meant moving forward, wearing success like a cape and getting things done. I was a disappointment to my mother while at the same time fulfilling her prophecy that without her upbringing I was doomed. She sacrificed me. These were her words, not mine. She was content to have a daughter who was lesser than her. Now that is an oddity especially in our part of the world, where every generation strives for better education for their offspring and a higher standard of living. You might want to write about my mother. Her anguish (or not) at having to leave her child. Knowing that she had no choice. It was either us or her. We were the noose that hung around her neck—her words, not mine. Would that not make a great scene? The tearful mother gazing down at the sleeping daughter, whispering, "Forgive me." I doubt this ever happened. My memory is that she left in a burst of self-righteousness, in the middle of a blazing afternoon, but your readers would be delightfully torn. They would demand that she take the child with her and you would need to explain to them all our laws and customs. They would bristle at the injustice of it all. Except that I did, once, ask my mother why she did not take me with her. And she smiled sadly because my question betrayed my stupidity. She had wanted to leave me as much as she had wanted to leave my father.

If you do go ahead and write about my mother, I am afraid I might not side with your heroine. As much as I enjoyed your novels, I often saw things differently than your protagonists. If you don't mind me criticising them! One thing infuriates me. They often take things at face value—one after the other seduced by the charismatic lawyer or enthralled by the sophisticated art collector. They have no time for the diamond in the dust, the gentle boy next door or the fool with the heart of gold. I often wanted to shake them and say, "Look deeper. Look with your heart." But then they have no patience for breastfeeding on demand and the husband who is setting up from scratch. They are heroines, they are not me.

The first time I met you. Oh, it was a big thing just to get myself to Edinburgh. I had never travelled alone, ever. Would you believe it? I was twenty-eight and I had never travelled alone. He asked me, why do you really want to go? What are you going to do there? What are you going to gain? I had to answer these questions in order to get the necessary green light. Weeks of preparing babysitters and meals, sorting out all the logistics. I bought a new outfit, I went on a crash diet, I splurged on a facial. The finances were an issue all to themselves. There was the return train ticket, the ticket to your event, the cost of your new hardback which I would surely buy and stand proudly in the queue to get it signed. Why proudly? Because I had been your fan for years and because it would be my first ever time to speak to a writer. I would only queue for you and no one else, believe me.

Naturally I didn't sleep the night before. All the growing excitement, the false alarms that flared up to threaten my outing. At the station, seeing an ad for the Edinburgh International Book Festival with your name on it made my palms turn cold. And I hadn't prepared myself for missing the children. The ache hit me as soon as I sat on the train. My wrong empty lap, the KitKat I couldn't share and all the sights that rolled past my window—but it would have been intolerable to have you in Scotland and not be there to welcome you.

Charlotte Square was busy with sun, wind, tents and people of all ages. Having traversed such a wide distance (metaphorically speaking), I was suddenly filled with a sense of urgency. No need to waste time, I had to immediately find you. I walked into the Authors Tent, my eyes adjusting to the dimmer light. You were moving the first time I saw you, you were not sitting or standing still. A buffet was laid out and you whisked through it, stabbing your choices, knowing exactly what you wanted, filling your plate with efficiency. You were as beautiful as I had imagined except for that extra energy, a fire that didn't show in photographs, almost a jerkiness. I went up to you as you were twisting away from the table, greeted you like a friend. You stopped as if I were blocking you, you stiffened at my familiarity, my presumption. "Do I know you? Are you a writer?" Before I could answer, your eyes scanned my face, flickered over my clothes. It had seemed to me a miracle that I managed to get myself out of the house without a child's grubby hands leaving a mark on my new skirt or a splatter of Ribena. But faced with your effortless elegance, my new Marks & Spencer outfit suddenly felt clunky. And all too soon you had already judged me, sussed me but it was not where I wanted to be placed. I said, "I am your fan from Aberdeen. I wrote to you. I write to you . . ." But it was too late, you noted my accent, your novelist's eyes picked up the signs of early marriage, abandoned university degree, rampant fertility. "This is the Authors Tent," you said, moving away not to join a group or to be claimed by someone else; you were even more independent than I had imagined. You did not need an entourage.

And you were right, I did not belong. There was even a sign that politely and clearly said so. This tent with its cushioned seats and free copies of the newspapers, with its journalists and chairpersons, biographers, poets and photographers was reserved for those participating in the festival. I should not have entered this tent. In another country, let us be frank, in our own home country, I would have been stopped at the door or you could have called security and had me thrown out. (This might be an exaggeration, but you know what I mean.) Yet that wasn't what was troubling me. I was shaken by only one thought—all the letters I had written to you over the years, all the emails, meant nothing to you. You've never read a single word I'd written.

I walked out to the deck chairs and ice creams, the good-natured crowd who knew how to behave. They had read more books than me and met more writers. And here I was callow and overdressed. I almost headed to the train station but common sense prevailed. I decided to stay and attend your talk as planned.

During the event you were how I wanted you to be, making me proud, speaking with intelligence and a vulnerability I had not expected. I clapped with everyone else. The audience were mainly woman. As you were being led outside, I heard one of them say, "This was a treat. She's very attractive." I immediately wanted to tell you about this. I imagined us sitting at one of the tables that were scattered over the grass, our coffees between us. I imagined your relief that your session was over and I going over what the woman in the row behind me had said. But I knew even as the fantasy formed clearly in my mind that it wouldn't happen. You would not sit with me and you would not hear me out. I bought your new novel but I did not queue for the book signing. I was afraid that you would hurt me again.

I took the train back to Aberdeen. No one would guess my feelings. My pain was exaggerated but real. No heroine of yours would travel, as I did, back by train and into the arms of her husband and children, abashed and broken, regretful that she had ventured out. In terms of the unwritten rules of the housewife, I had taken a "day off." An expensive one at that. The expectation was that I would resume my duties refreshed and in good spirits. Instead I moped around the house analysing the failure of our meeting. Were you haughty and undeserving? Or was I truly beneath you, unworthy of your attention? Did I approach you the wrong way?

The answers were in your work, where else would they be? I had nothing else, no friend of a friend you had previously snubbed, no fellow fan. I combed your novels. There were the digs at the women who wore hijab. Such women were never, God forbid, the heroines or even friends or relatives of the heroines but only jolly servants or passersby, members of the population. I had never taken these digs seriously. Perhaps I was wrong and they were a lot more than dismissive digs. They were reflections of a composite, definable rejection. You didn't like the hijab, you didn't believe it was necessary, you were even opposed to it so naturally you would not welcome being approached by a fan who was wearing it. But we have so much in common, I wailed to your receding back. Could you not look beyond it? And if you—a Muslim and an African—couldn't, then how could Western, Christian women, those whom I met at the parents' evenings, my midwife, my son's speech therapist, my neighbour? Surely you would not want me to despair, you who believe in our shared humanity, in love between East and West, surely you would not promote more entrenched positions, more ghettos, more each to their own kind. Surely not.

So you were haughty then? A bit of a diva. It had all gone to your head—the prize nomination, all those white people queuing to hear you talk, the four-star reviews of your latest paperback. It had given you delusions of grandeur and made you look down on your own kind. We had become mere fodder for your fiction, you would use our lives but not grant us your company. Cruella de Vil. Yes, I should laugh the whole thing off. Or, as a modern consumer, deprive you of my custom because of your poor client treatment. Sticks and stones will break my bones, etc. And there were other writers waiting to be read.

Weeks later I still buzzed occasionally with injustice but the hurt diminished with each passing day. A new pregnancy (twins this time, believe it or not) pushed you completely to the back of my mind. A new school for the children, my husband's promotion. A year passed and then more. My family were growing and I took pride and care in the children's lives. My sons, taller than me now, engaged me more as semi-independent adults than needy children. Their company was a joy. My two little girls, alike but not alike, were absorbing. I delighted in their closeness to each other, their intimate infinite friendship. Sometimes seeing them sitting on the stairs side by side whispering or perfectly balanced on either side of a seesaw, I would remember, fleetingly, my dreams of us. But I no longer wrote to you.

Once in a while, though, I googled your name as if checking up on an old friend. Your career had taken another direction. You started to write for children. You teamed up with your brother, the artist, and wrote picture books in which you upgraded the *One Thousand and One Nights* for a modern, technologically savvy global readership. I admired you for working with your brother. It showed how authentic you were, still tied to our family values. Actually, I only bought one of your new books, the one modelled on *Ali Baba and the Forty Thieves*. By then my sons were too old and my daughters preferred the Powerpuff Girls. (This was long before you wrote *Sindy, the Sailor*, the modern female incarnation of Sindbad.) When the twins were very young they rejected anything that had a whiff of African or Muslim culture about it—including your books. This disappointed me because I wanted them to have pride in their heritage. Thankfully, it was a phase and they got over it as they became older and more conscious.

All this goes to explain why when you first started writing for children I was not reading you. I drifted away and started to regard you as a passing craze. My mind was now preoccupied with other things. The birth of the twins had been a watershed for me. I was determined not to have any more children and to complete my distance learning degree. To be honest, I still raised the radio's volume when you were interviewed on *Woman's Hour*, I still admired your new hairstyle in that photo in the *Telegraph* but my interest had lost its edge and I never had imaginary conversations with you.

The second time I met you was fifteen years later, in Abu Dhabi. We had moved because of my husband's work and after settling in, I too found a job. I became first an assistant, then a coordinator in an educational non-profit foundation which promoted a love of reading among children. My life changed when I started to earn my own money. I could now afford a part-time maid and to pay for the children's school bus. Freed from the weight of the school run and the bulk of the housework, I poured myself into my new job. And during the public holidays (such a joy to live again in a country where Eid was celebrated!) I began to enjoy myself. To take delight in the malls and the beach; my wardrobe improved, as did my confidence. I relaxed in this family-oriented environment, where children stayed up late and the pace of life was slower.

Your name came up often in the course of my work. People have short memories. Your taboo-breaking novels were now forgotten— some of them were even out of print and not available on Kindle. Instead, you were now famous for your wholesome children's books. Her Highness, Sheikha Hadia, the CEO of our foundation, spoke of them highly. I liked Sheikha Hadia for her direct warmth and her unself-consciousness. In her black abaya and designer sunglasses, she possessed a "can-do" attitude that was combined with infor-mality. During meetings, she would fiddle with her phone, wipe her fingers with Wet Ones or slide her feet out of her sandals and rub them against the carpet. Once I came across her in the prayer room, indistinguishable among the bowing staff and the cleaners. Her movements were heavy and she fidgeted with the folds of her veil which always exuded the smell of incense.

An invitation was issued for you to visit the emirate. Sheikha Hadia wanted you to visit seven schools, to whom we would, if you accepted the invitation, distribute free copies of your books. I remember that the week it took you to reply coincided with my mother's visit. After years of not seeing her, I strained for approval and spent considerable time, effort and expense in showing off. Her opinion of me had never been positive and she had in the past openly expressed her disapproval of the core elements of my life—my lacklustre choice of husband, number of children and lack of career. So I was overjoyed when our life in Abu Dhabi appealed to her. She admired the children's international school, she was impressed with the compound we were living in and by extension my husband and his work for providing such excellent housing. Best of all, though, was how pleasantly surprised and admiring she was of my job. "It took you ages," she said, "but you've finally made something of yourself! I had written you off." Such praise threaded in scorn did hurt and once or twice I hid in the bathroom and cried. But I was relieved that I had risen in her estimation and that our relationship was warmer than it had ever been. Outwardly, I handled the visit well, without a single mishap or argument. By this I mean that I did not reproach her for the past or even mention it, I controlled myself. This control must have taken its toll, though, because when she left, I took the afternoon off and spent the rest of the day in bed too fatigued to even get up and cook.

The children ordered pizza and when the delivery man rang the doorbell I continued lying under the covers, not even turning my head to see which child was the one rummaging in my handbag for money. The sounds of him/her bounding down the stairs and of his/her brothers and sisters grabbing their slices were remote from the darkness around me. I did not feel sad or depressed. Only like a machine temporarily switched off. I rarely spoke of my mother. Not even to close friends. Loyalty stopped me—respect for parents is deeply ingrained in our culture, is it not?

I had written to you, hadn't I, long ago about my mother? I was not whinging but trying to understand. I thought that you would perhaps write back to me with some wisdom or insight. I didn't want "to come to terms" with the fact that she had abandoned me as a child. I didn't necessarily want help to heal the wound. I believed I was capable of doing that by myself. What I wanted was simply to understand why. And after having my own children, how on earth could she? This always perplexed me, the answers flickering close but then evading me. Perhaps I read your novels in order to fill in the gaps. That day, after I drove her to the airport, I got into bed even though it was the middle of the afternoon. I went over things she had said in passing, framed as general comments. For example,

"Divorced mothers are lying when they say that their feelings for their ex-husbands don't influence their feelings for their children. How can it be when the child is made up of that hated spouse! The child is not the mother's clone; the child is also an extension of the disappointing husband." Women in your novels are not that blunt. "Saccharine," a nasty reviewer once said; he was unfairly exaggerating. But to go back to my mother, it suddenly dawned on me, as I lay with the bright sun blasting through the closed blinds and curtains, that my mother believed herself eternally and organically superior to me. I was lesser than her because I took after my father and he had been the biggest mistake her parents had arranged. A mistake she had spent the better part of her life putting to rights and, in her eyes, it was further proof of my deficiency that I had not credited her for this accomplishment. She would have wanted me to understand and applaud her from a distance. Instead of sulking, which is what I did. My mother left us because we were less that her, a millstone around her neck. She left us in order to survive and to flourish.

These words felt like dried rusk in my mouth. Like the broad outlines of a tedious lesson I must learn. If only I were one of your feisty heroines! I would have leapt out of bed. I heard my dear man come home and ask the children about me. His instinct that something was wrong. I heard his footsteps on the stairs and then he sat by my side. Are you ill? Do you need anything? Was the drive to the airport okay? In *Fruit Lotus*, your most poignant novel in my opinion, a husband stops loving his wife. Just like that. It is fascinating, I agree, how love can come to an end, how it can just stop like the gush of a tap ceasing, like a long night surfacing up to a dawn, like sweetness lingering on the tongue then vanishing. The fictional husband does not leave his wife for someone else but we know that by the end of the novel, he will. You spare us the details, you are subtle but we know that the treachery is round the corner. No longer loving the heroine, he is open and primed for a fresh adventure while she soldiers on with the children and the blow to her femininity. Of course, I assumed all this was autobiographical, a fictional rendering of your own divorce. And I admit, I felt a little smug that my own husband still loved me. See, it paid to go for the steady, reliable bloke rather than the firebrand and the dashing. My man slid into bed next to me and listened while I rambled. He said I had every right to begrudge my mother for her selfishness but it would be better for me to ask Allah to forgive her. It would be better for me to become a little more selfish myself. And perhaps, he suggested, I should think of what she had given me instead of what she had withheld. The first important, formative years of my life. Some people don't even have that. He held me and soothed me. We talked with the sounds of the children coming from the sitting room and the bedrooms—the television, a friend leaving through the kitchen door, the patter of the shower—until I felt well enough to go with him downstairs and eat the rest of the pizza.

Thank you. You pulled me completely out of this temporary setback with an email saying how delighted you would be to visit Abu Dhabi and how fervently you supported the foundation's aim. I found myself approving the Business Class tickets on Etihad, the booking of the five-star hotel and the chauffeur-driven car. I personally answered your email queries on the availability of free Wi-Fi in your room. In addition to the school visits, we were also holding a one-day seminar on writing for children, in which you would give the opening speech. We also scheduled for you a special dinner with the Sheikha. All other meals were, of course, provided for you at the magnificent Emirates Palace Hotel.

You did not remember me or the fan mail I had long ago sent. I didn't expect you to. Besides, I was a different woman now, older and more confident. Not the callow fan ingratiating herself in Edinburgh. You, too, were heavier looking. Despite your dyed hair, there were tender bags under your eyes and your deep smoker's voice aged you.

But you were still beautiful and vibrant. In no time at all the whole foundation was eating out of your hands. Compared to Edinburgh, there was a relaxed goodwill about you. Abu Dhabi pleased you—this desert miracle, a futuristic world of optimism and lavish expansion. You singled me out as the only one in the foundation who was from your home country. Years ago I had longed for this connection. And now here it was.

Privately, we spoke in our dialect; a few times we exchanged knowing glances and inside jokes. All mild and relating to work—but it was enough for me. That old wish to be your friend flickered. I remembered with fondness my dreams of the two girls sitting side by side on the stairs talking and talking. And holding all this together was my pride in how much I had achieved since that day in Edinburgh. When I spoke of my admiration for your early novels, I did so without belittling myself. I never referred to my gushing letters and emails of long ago. I was mature and professional. Too senior in the foundation to accompany you on every school visit, I met you in the more official events including the dinners. Privately, I chaffed a little at this. Sitting in the car, negotiating the heavy traffic from one school to the next, would certainly have meant spending more time with you, but Sheikha Hadia was demanding my full attention. The success of your visit had long-term consequences for the foundation; the favourable response of our company sponsors, the local media and the Ministry of Education were our primary focus. I was scheduling separate press interviews for Sheikha Hadia and for yourself, though at times I would much have preferred to be the one in close attendance, taking orders for your coffee.

I admit that as a foundation, we did spring upon you the children's writing workshop. I must apologize. Yes, you were right, it was not something we had agreed on beforehand. You see, the Sheikha's niece, who was studying in Harvard, phoned on the eve of your visit and gave her that idea. Yes, that's how things can be set in motion—a leisurely

Skype conversation in the middle of the night! And the rich do use Skype, they can be more frugal than we think! Once Sheikha Hadia set her mind on the idea of a children's workshop, there was no going back. I was used to this way of doing things. It was part of my job to be flexible, to understand that, from my employer's point of view, everything was doable. I am sorry that despite your objections, I insisted on going ahead. To quell your rebellion I invited your publisher's Middle East sales representative, who was based in Dubai, to come to the workshop and threw in an overnight stay for him, his wife and toddler at the Beach Rotana. His role would be to remind you of how your visit was impacting on the sales of your books to the extent that your delighted publishers in London were reprinting. I also brought in a young upcoming local writer who had recently written his first graphic novel for teens. His role would be to massage your ego and, if need be, do the actual hard work of giving feedback to the children.

My strategy worked. But only just. After huffing and puffing, you seated yourself in front of the children. The young local writer charmed them with his familiarity and charmed you (only a little, judging by your grudging smile) by praising you to the skies. You made a few general comments about writing and the importance of books. All excellent points that pleased Sheikha Hadia. Then it was time for the children to read out their stories to you. Head bowed over an open notebook, you doodled dark angular lines; you drew prison bars, broken wings and shaded faces. I could see them because I was sitting next to you, as if symbolically hemming you in so you would not abscond! You drew knotted wool and crooked wire; steel scourer and patterned grids. You doodled with rage, flinching from what you were hearing. You did not, once, look up at the stuttering child struggling to read what he had written, the one swaying side to side chanting a rhyme she had made up, the serious boy who had no concept of grammar.

Worst was to come when the children lined up for you to sign their books—the ones the foundation had distributed to them for free. To be honest, they didn't really line up, they were all over the place, pretty noisy, shoving the books under your nose, elbowing each other out of the way. When one of them pushed a copy of *The Very Hungry Caterpillar* under your nose, you lost your temper. "That's not my book," you lashed out. "I won't sign a book that's not mine!"

With an agility I thought I had lost, I rose from my seat, grabbed a copy of *Ali and the Forty Baddies* and placed it instead into the girl's hand. I removed the offending *Hungry Caterpillar* from under your nose. Things went more or less smoothly after that.

It was your last night in Abu Dhabi, the special dinner with Sheikha Hadia that had taken so long to organize. I sat next to her with you on the other side. The atmosphere was relaxed and so were you. You spoke at length about your brother, the artist who collaborated on your books. It occurred to me that you might have been under family pressure to help him with his career. Could you have started writing for children motivated by the urge to provide an outlet for his talent? I admired you for promoting him in front of the Sheikha. She was accustomed to people asking favours of her. Some needed jobs, residence visas or referrals. She was primed for this and though you were not at all forthcoming in making any specific requests, the ground was set for the future. Next time, we as a foundation would most likely invite your brother as well.

Sheikha Hadia, as was her habit, wiped her fingers with Wet Ones in between courses and more often. She would open her handbag, take out the packet, peel it open and slowly remove a scented wet cloth. The scent used to be amber but now, it seemed, she had switched to an alcohol-free, antibacterial. I was used to her habit and sometimes even concerned that it implied an obsessive-compulsive disorder. So I was taken aback when, after she left the dinner, you made a slight dig about it. It was a whisper aside, aimed only at

163

me, said in our dialect, and a part of me was flattered that we were sharing a joke (and that you trusted me) but still. It crossed my mind that your disdain of the hijab, less obvious to me now than it had been that time in Edinburgh, extended to the Sheikha's flowing, black abaya. I smiled at your witty remark but my heart wasn't in it.

"I need a cigarette," you said as the rest of us got up from the table. "Anyone care to join me outside?"

I volunteered to go with you. We walked out of the hotel through a side door that opened out onto a slip road and further ahead was the busy motorway. In contrast to the cold air conditioner inside, it was humid and still. The air was full of car fumes. They shimmered suspended over the gleaming cars waiting for the valet parking. The hotel porters walked back and forth wearing a heavy, theatrical uniform unsuitable for the weather. I felt sorry for them.

You looked relieved that you were flying back home tomorrow. Jaunty as you took your cigarette box out of your handbag. "You don't smoke? I can tell you're not the type."

I shook my head. You were already lighting up. True, I was not the type. But still your words had the flicker of a put down, a gratuitous insistence that we were different. I had been slow to understand what you intuited that first day in Edinburgh. That we would never become friends.

It was my turn now to look at you with eyes that were not a novelist's eyes. I saw that you were beautiful but not sexy, more talented than blessed, brittle but not weighty. And I was your opposite. Perhaps all I had ever wanted was a sense of equality, the two little girls balanced on either side of the seesaw. I said, "I hope you enjoyed your time here."

Your reply was the same one I had heard this morning on the local radio. The exact wording. Except that you now added how your mother, a gynaecologist, worked here in the 1970s and delivered a prince. This was not new to me either. I had read about it in your piece in *O, The Oprah Magazine*—part of an inspirational series in which each month a writer, male or female, wrote about their mother's work.

I asked only because I could. "Do you ever read your fan mail?"

"From the children?"

"From readers in general."

You shrugged. "I'm not an agony aunt. And I don't want to be told 'write about me' either."

It still hurt a little bit, but I had it under control. You had said these exact words before in an interview, "I'm not an agony aunt." Although you were lifting the cigarette to your lips, although you were flesh and blood, I felt as if I were in the presence of a statute, one that was opaque and unyielding. It made me suddenly miss the voice on the page, the fluid lives you had written down.

There was nothing more that I could take from you. Nothing in addition to what I already had on my shelves.

Later, I went home and instead of checking up on the children, instead of tackling the kitchen or setting the table for tomorrow's breakfast, I got into bed and started to read, again, my favourite novel.

BARRY LOPEZ, a winner of the National Book Award, is the author of *Arctic Dreams* as well as nine works of fiction and six other works of nonfiction. His stories and essays appear regularly in *Harper's*, the *Paris Review*, *Orion*, and the *Georgia Review*. He is the recipient of an Award in Literature from the American Academy of Arts and Letters, as well as fellowships from the Guggenheim, Lannan, and National Science Foundations. His new book, *Horizon*, will be published by Knopf. He lives in western Oregon.

The San Joaquin

BARRY LOPEZ

M y late mother, Betsy Krall van der Meer, grew up on a farm in
the Transvaal, after the Boer War, near the town of Beestekraal.
She met my father, Edward van der Meer, in boarding school in
Pretoria, a city they later returned to as a couple after he finished
medical school in Cape Town. He began practicing as a family doctor
there but quickly developed a specialty in the treatment of malaria.
In the summer of 1939, just before Hitler invaded Poland, he and
my mother and their two oldest daughters moved to Rotterdam.
He'd been invited to join a staff of doctors at the Port Hospital there
famous for their work with tropical diseases. I was born in the Netherlands after the war ended, as was a younger sister. In 1956, my
father fell out of favor with the director of the hospital over political differences and, rather abruptly, he moved the six of us to San
Francisco, another seaport city. He continued his work in tropical
disease across the bay at Highland General Hospital in Oakland.
In 1967, my oldest sister returned to Rotterdam with her German
husband, and I entered law school at UC Berkeley.

Perhaps it was the tenor of all the stories my parents told us
about growing up happily in an agricultural district in South Africa,
the neighborliness and camaraderie that prevailed, that fueled my
determination to move to the San Joaquin Valley in 1973, with

167

David. After finishing his law degree at the University of Virginia, David had immediately come west to Silicon Valley. I urged him to imagine how much happier we'd both be living in the San Joaquin together, instead of working with two different law firms in San Jose. Obliging man that he was, he agreed to make the jump. We set up a practice together in Modesto, Van der Meer and Severe, and put money down on a small two-story house near Hickman, on the Tuolumne River. Our primary interest at the time was labor law, but we soon incorporated immigration law. We also helped farm families deal with medical and workers' compensation claims, and guided them through the layers of injustice embedded in all the government bureaucracies they had to contend with, from county social services to the Internal Revenue Service.

My sisters in Oakland hounded David and me from the beginning to adopt, but there was too much on our plates for us to take a chance on raising children responsibly. We couldn't imagine how that was ever going to be possible, not if we were truly intent on providing for our clients. My sisters in Oakland had both married and had their own children, and David and I loved having them visit us on weekends. Some summers all six nieces and nephews were with us for two weeks. I thought our arrangement was a good way to keep the Van der Meer family intact. The arrangement seemed to meet everyone's needs—David's and mine, to express our affection for the kids and demonstrate support for their future plans; my sisters' needs for rest, and time with their husbands; and the real need we thought the kids had for an alternative home, a safe place to hang out as they entered their teens.

Our house, in a nearly constant state of remodeling, sat in a windbreak grove of eucalyptus trees, about a hundred feet from the river. After a while David and I gave in and added a two-bedroom extension to ease the crowding, especially in summer. The kids were thrilled.

I really don't know what they got out of staying with us. They loved to water and weed and harvest in the garden, and the four girls were always excited about cooking with David. They arranged cut flowers around the house most afternoons, gladiolas, snapdragons, tulips. I like to think that, as they grew older, they understood what compelled David and me to do the work we did. We told them about marching with César Chávez, and about when the writer Peter Matthiessen stayed with us for a few weeks while he was working on *Sal Si Puedes*, his book about the United Farm Workers movement. We introduced them to John Steinbeck's books and explained why all the California papers attacked him for publishing *The Grapes of Wrath*.

David, whose family went back five or six generations in Charleston, was an only child, so a houseful of kids was sometimes a little harder on him than me. The polite way to convey what happened to him in South Carolina is to say that his family and relatives simply distanced themselves after he came out. A fallen angel. The kids and I became a surrogate family, and I know he loved the way the kids threw their arms around him, though sometimes he said he didn't.

In 1980, my father died of cerebrospinal meningitis. Mother sold their San Francisco house and moved into an apartment in Gilroy. She began showing symptoms of dementia in her early seventies and my sisters and I decided to move her into assisted living. She hated every place we found for her. My sisters, I knew, their homes full of teenagers, couldn't help any more than they already had. David graciously agreed to have her move in with us, at least for a while. She stayed in one of the kids' bedrooms for three years, until she didn't know anymore who she was, or who we were. We moved her into assisted living after that, in Modesto, where she passed away in 1985.

David died of metastatic prostate cancer in 2006, and in 2009 I closed the law firm. I spent my time looking after the house we'd spent so many beautiful years creating together. I thought I would see more of my nieces and nephews when I retired, but by then they'd developed busy lives elsewhere, and I didn't want to travel alone to see them. I hardly heard a word from them anymore. The two boys moved to Hong Kong, where they're thriving in an import-export operation they bought. We lost the youngest girl in Afghanistan, a combat death. The oldest one owns four or five Carl's Jr. fast-food franchises, all in the San Joaquin, but she rarely drops by. The other girls have moved away, to Chicago and Miami.

I've grown more reflective since retiring, and wonder, of course, what my life has actually come to. David and I did good work in the community and I believe we provided well for each other. We made a comfortable home, which was for years a cherished playground for my nieces and nephews. I want to think David and I were perceived as neighborly, both in the community where we chose to live and in the way we practiced law. That we were good men. David was far better in the kitchen than I was, but it turned out I had a gift for working in the garden. After he passed, I was at a loss, though, trying to prepare the vegetables I grew. I couldn't do justice to them, and, of course, there was simply too much food. I gave most of what I grew away—the produce and berries, the spices, the fruit from trees I'd planted as saplings.

For a period of about a year after I retired, I reread a lot of Steinbeck, especially the lesser-known books like *Sweet Thursday* and *In Dubious Battle,* his assessments and reflections on farm labor and socialism. I enjoyed them all over again, I suppose, but they didn't affect me as powerfully as they had when I first read them as an adolescent. This morning, though, I happened to pick up a contemporary book with similar themes, *Right Out of California: The 1930s and the Big Business Roots of Modern Conservatism,* by Kathryn Olmsted. The title gives you the gist of it. I am intimately acquainted with the history she writes about, as was Steinbeck, and

Peter Matthiessen for that matter. With the rise of the United Farm Workers in the sixties I'd felt compelled to become a litigator. Once I learned to redirect my outrage over inequity in the farm labor system, however, I did better work as a mediator.

I hoped reading the Olmsted book wouldn't rekindle the anger and frustration I felt so often in those years, emotions David and I tried to free each other of nearly every day. I remember a county commissioner once denouncing me as naïve and "pathologically misguided," but I don't think so.

I recall hearing stories my father told about practicing medicine in rural South Africa in the days leading up to the worst of apartheid, and I have wondered at the curious ways in which you can presume you're actually starting out on your own course as someone's son, only to understand, years later, that you grew up in a family, and that buried in all those years-ago conversations were, often, the very models that made you believe so fiercely in the way you chose to live your life.

A few years after David and I moved to the San Joaquin, I planted sixteen fruit trees in a corner of our property, away from the eucalypts, which are thirsty trees. Oranges, lemons, plums, and two pomegranate trees. We always brought fruit baskets to my parents when we visited and to my sisters' homes at Christmas. Frequently we gave a neighbor, Ernesto Rulfo, much of the rest, which he sold along with his own fruit and eggs at a roadside stand. After David passed I saw more of Ernesto. The house needed repairs I couldn't manage alone, and he could use the vegetables. Around that same time, his wife, Louisa, started bringing me meals once or twice a week. Just yesterday, Ernesto stopped by to repair the doors to my root cellar and to help me pick lemons. When we finished I made coffee, and we sat in the shade of the trees with some cheddar cheese and the last of a loaf of sourdough bread I'd baked and we ate a few ripe greengage plums. Ernesto is a little younger than I am. I think he's worked here all his life, though he was born in Mexico, somewhere in Guerrero. I'd handled several things for him over the years, the fallout around an automobile accident one of his sons had had, a problem with Ernesto's father's railroad pension.

Ernesto reads a good deal and we trade books regularly. He brought me Juan Rulfo's *The Burning Plain* a few days ago, and I hope to recommend the Olmsted book to him after I read it. He talks a lot about his children, how they're getting on. I've wanted to tell him that my sisters urged David and me to adopt but that we chose not to, that instead we chose to serve the community as lawyers. But as I considered the story yesterday, it seemed too complicated to explain. I gave up trying. And it was too beautiful an afternoon for disappointments—balmy winds rattling dry leaves in the eucalyptus trees, a fragile, Delft blue that suggested the sky was old. Or maybe napping. It was also too lovely a day to talk about what, in fact, was really on both our minds. Water. Where was irrigation water going to come from this year? I'd just read that the federal government had plans to raise the height of Shasta Dam on the Sacramento by eighteen and a half feet, in order to provide more water storage for irrigation in the Sacramento basin. If they carry through with this intention, the increased size of the reservoir behind the dam will flood the very last Winnemem Wintu ceremonial and ancestral sites there. The Bureau of Reclamation says it's the price of progress, but they don't say where this kind of progress is going to take us.

Ernesto says I should plant peaches, so that in a few years we'll have peaches to savor. Before he leaves, he tells me Louisa wants me to come over for supper the next day. He says he wishes to be respectful of my time, but, really, he has to go home and tell Louisa yes.

I tell him before he drives off that I've been reading the poems of W. S. Merwin, that the lines of the poems are so perfectly joined there is no need for punctuation. A marvel. I ask Ernesto whether

there is a phrase for this in Spanish, where the lines of a poem are
bound together so perfectly that this alone communicates something
important. "Yes," he says. "We say *hacer versos en conjunto,* to
make the lines nestle together like braided hair."

I have set this morning aside to read the Olmsted book, but I'm also
thinking about supper tonight. When David was alive, we would
sometimes take a couple of weeks and go somewhere like the Gulf
Coast, swim in the sunshine and collect shells, eat fish fresh from
the water. If we could afford it, we'd go to the South Pacific, to Bora
Bora or Palau. When we got home we'd create elaborate displays of
exotic shells. Ernesto's kids were fascinated by the shapes and the
fluting when they visited, the pale colors. Yesterday, Ernesto told me
his kids and his grandkids would probably be there for supper and
this started me thinking. It occurred to me that I could start there,
start by giving the shells away. It's that time in my life now when
I'm considering giving away things that, before, I could not imagine
living without. I'll save out a few of the most beautiful ones for Louisa, and take enough to give one each to the grandchildren. I'll tell
them about searching for shells with David in Tahiti and wading in
the South China Sea. And this afternoon I'll begin reading a few of
the Juan Rulfo stories. Then maybe this evening I'll be able to ask
Ernesto for some amplification.

LAWRENCE JOSEPH's sixth book of poems, *So Where Are We?*, will be published by Farrar, Straus and Giroux in 2017. He is also the author of two books of prose, *Lawyerland* and *The Game Changed: Essays and Other Prose*. He is Tinnelly Professor of Law at St. John's University School of Law and lives in New York City.

What More Is There to Say?

LAWRENCE JOSEPH

December mild, deep January cold,
sunlight filtered through blue haze,

yellow the grass closely pressed,
patches of dirt, in red-and-lavender

twilight, a tugboat in the harbor
clearing the ice. In those circles

in which all heaven breaks loose,
touched by who she is, by what

she wills; in the envisioned heart
inmost issues take the form

of a credo. The God to whom
an account must be rendered,

my dead to whom I pray,
as I, in turn, pray the life once theirs

is transfigured. What a story
to tell, violence from the terror felt,

violence in the suffering, violence
in the mind, collectively modified,

escalated to maximum speed.
So what more is there to say? Many times

the mass of the sun, solar masses
spiraling into space time, radiating

energy in gravitational waves, the edges
of the islands soft in the black-gray sky,

on this side of the Battery, near the ferry,
a small bird's footprints, here, in the snow.

New moon, mauve cloud, sea level
higher than normal, the harbor again,

green and gray, punctuated by waves
lashing about. Thickening, the mists,

this early morning; repeated, sounds
of foghorns we hear from afar.

AMIRA HASS is a correspondent for *Haaretz*, an Israeli daily, in the Occupied Palestinian territory, and author of *Drinking the Sea at Gaza.*

TAL HARAN is a bilingual Israeli activist who translates occupation-related materials. Her translation work includes *The One-State Condition* by Ariella Azoulay and Adi Ophir, *The Girl Who Stole My Holocaust* by Noam Chayut, and numerous reports and testimonies for journalists and organizations such as Breaking the Silence, Zochrot, and Machsomwatch.

Stone Houses

AMIRA HASS
TRANSLATED FROM THE HEBREW BY TAL HARAN

Clear, warm ripples fill my chest whenever I pass by an old stone house in Ramallah/Al Bireh in the West Bank—where I have been living for nearly twenty years. The number of stone houses, homes of the indigenous inhabitants of these neighbor towns, has dwindled over time—I wish I could mean this only relatively, in view of the increase in new concrete buildings whose thin stone-slab coating cannot mislead us. Sadly, real stone buildings—they don't build like this anymore—are gradually disappearing as well, for the ground under them is lucrative, and it is so much easier to divide the inheritance among one's grandchildren, and even great-great-grandchildren, once the house is torn down and replaced by a tall apartment building which accommodates some of the many new city dwellers.

And yet many of the houses stand strong. At times they hide in the shadow of apartment and office towers constructed nonstop in the unofficial, forced capital of the obscure and fragmented Palestinian entity. At other times they are noticeable because of the pomegranate tree branching out from the garden and onto the sidewalk or thorny plot next door, where goats graze among the rocks. Usually they stand out because they are such a pleasant sight—an ode to the duet played by the architecture and its builders with nature and with the history of their first inhabitants and their families. They are handsome and elegant even when they have not been lived in for many years or even when neglected and half-ruined—but it is not their beauty that drives those clear ripples of mine.

These stone houses have brothers and cousins throughout Israel, but let us focus just on Jerusalem for the moment, the western part of the city that became the Israeli capital in 1948. The city is full of them. Inhabited and well-tended or neglected and half-ruined—these houses are memorials of the Palestinian lives that we, Israelis, erased back then and since then. Jews live in them now and call them "home," and their beauty is a plunged sword. The very same aesthetics and that same duet—every time I pass them by I feel a noose tightening around my neck, and instead of clear ripples there is a choking sensation.

In the West Bank—not only in Ramallah and Al Bireh—stone buildings 80, 100, or 150 years old resonate with the enviable innocence of their builders who never imagined mass expulsion, depopulated and demolished villages and neighborhoods, the loss of home in every sense of the word. With pre-Nakba innocence, this massive stone quarried in the hills and hewn by artisans speaks of time: the easygoing time that was at hand to build a house, the unlimited time that was imagined and planned for a house so that it could serve its purpose: the gathering and nurturing place of a primal, protective human unit. The place that guarantees continuity. The stone speaks of stability, rootedness, belonging, security. In short—the obvious. Home.

Mute but talkative, this limestone evokes ripples of relief, of gratitude that it was spared the fate of being hacked off and displaced like its twin on the other side of the "green line." But that relief is precisely the inverse twin of the choking sensation.

I grew familiar with stone from the moment I came into the world. From my birth until I was eight years old I lived in an apartment in a real stone house in Jerusalem. It was there that my constituting material image of "home" took shape: walls 80 to 120 centimeters thick, high ceilings, a red-tile roof (as it sometimes snows in Jerusalem), the climbing bougainvillea bush in the yard, an arched niche in the wall and a broad windowsill, of stone as well, for my first books, and its extension into a wide desk with a reading lamp. No wonder those ripples are warm. Happily this childhood house was originally built for a Jewish family long before 1948. Yes, Jews lived there in the Holy Land before the catastrophes. Notwithstanding the Palestinian architecture style, our apartment walls did not hold memories of an expelled Palestinian family. From that apartment we eventually moved to another, and then another—and growing up, my idea of home expanded. Childhood songs, the language, slang, and yet again the slang and the language, the fragrance of watermelon on the beach, the humor, names of trees as we learned them in the first and second grades, friendships, a favorite bookshop, unchanging bus lines and all the things that exasperate us and seem changeable only if more people join social-political struggles: exploiting contractor companies, the deterioration of public health care and other welfare services, gardens becoming car parks, the ever-widening social gaps. As we said: home means belonging, and thus—caring.

In that first real-stone home my Sarajevo-born mother, who had been expelled from her own home, told me how amazed she was, coming to Jerusalem when she immigrated to Israel in 1949, to discover that all the houses were built of stone. And I—six or seven years old then—was amazed at her amazement. How would one build houses if not in stone? I wondered. Wood? Mud? Baked clay bricks? Mortar and concrete? All were still beyond the limits of my imagination as building materials. I did not yet know that already during the British Mandate in Palestine/Eretz Yisrael both a commandment and its deception were invented: all Jerusalem houses had to be built of stone, decreed the legislators/rulers, and if not the real thing, then concrete must be coated with stone. In my childhood, the other stone houses in Jerusalem, in neighborhoods that had been purely Palestinian and then no longer so, were not yet a plunged sword. More precisely, I had not yet realized that their existence and meaning go far beyond the definition of "exasperating things that are changeable."

Imagination is limited, unlike the methods of destruction and the capacity of our state to destroy. My profession has shown me so much destruction in the past twenty-five years that my automatic identification of "stone" and "home" has toppled down along with it. I have documented numberless demolitions of all sorts—mostly of homes made of concrete but also of stone and many tents and other similar shacks—in the territory that Israel occupied in 1967: in Gaza, in East Jerusalem, in the West Bank. And even if I cannot recall all the names of the families and communities—the sights are all etched, as well as the pretexts for demolition: They were built without permits, they housed a senior Hamas member, they housed a minor Hamas member, they stood in the way of Israeli tanks, a wanted man living in them did not give himself up, we thought they contained a weapons stash and apparently we were wrong, they interfered with our field of vision, they had a tunnel underneath, a lookout post on the roof, future stabbers must be deterred, as well as simply—"no comment." The demolitions were carried out in wars called "military operations," in military operations called simply "activity," assaults that are called "defensive actions," and in routine workdays of bureaucrats and inspectors of the occupation authorities throughout the West Bank (including East Jerusalem), in daytime, nighttime, with the pressing of a button and a photo of the billowing smoke by drone, by the Corps of Engineers equipped with explosives, or by silent contractor employees and a bulldozer. And always escorted by dozens of enthusiastic soldiers or policemen.

Documented destruction rescues from its physical description the abstract meaning of the word "home." No less than thick stone walls blasted with dynamite, the ripped tarpaulin, the crushed corrugated iron, and the twisted metal rods in a Bedouin encampment were signifiers of a primal protective human unit until a minute before the bulldozer shovel hit them. A concrete structure, whether a single story housing one family, or twelve stories high—blasted by a missile or a bomb (whose inhabitants were ordered out, or, to our horror, at times with all of their inhabitants inside), in the refugee camp in Rafah, Gaza, or in Jenin in the northern West Bank, a dwelling cave or tent in a hamlet east of Nablus or south of Hebron demolished by a bulldozer while a woman-soldier kept their inhabitants from disturbing the peace, Italian marble or bare gray concrete, with a blooming bougainvillea bush or merely a mint plant in a pot: all those piles of rubble line up in my head, all of them sites of belonging that remain so in memory, creating an obstinate, logical, but unbearable continuity from the sites of belonging that were robbed and destroyed in 1948.

All of the houses, stone or others, that Israeli bulldozers and—no less Israeli—bombs have and will destroy, rescue from the Israeli national ethos of return to the homeland the naked essence of our state. And this is how I meant to continue the sentence and write: that essence is the erasure of the other's existence for the sake of our own existence. We make the Palestinian disappear so that we Jews can prosper. But I have changed my mind and am writing: the real essence of our state is *an ongoing attempt* to erase the existence of the other for the sake of our own existence. An attempt to make the Palestinian disappear so that we Jews can prosper.

The houses no longer stand. But the majority of their dwellers and carriers of their memory—down to the second and third and fourth generations—are alive and kicking, alive and resilient. In exile or in refugee camps a walking distance from their demolished homes, in rented apartments, in Palestinian enclaves in the West Bank and in villages inside Israel, whose land has been stolen from them. Displaced, but very much alive, they never cease to belong to The Home. The Israeli attempt at erasure succeeded only in part, happily. But the partiality of that "success" does not halt the conveyor belt moving the state's essence in its repeated act of destruction and attempts to depopulate. Every additional demolition, every takeover of land is another knife plunged, and the unceasing continuity since 1948 only grows heavier. And with every knife, another question mark is raised about the "home-ness" of home and the reasons that I have to remain in it.

Only a few of us Jewish-Israelis feel those plunged knives. This feeling does not disentangle us, few, from our actual, biographical belonging to the collective that builds for itself and demolishes the other. Does our ethical and political rejection of state policy—which sometimes finds its voice in dissident activism—rescue us from our emotional belonging to the place, from our attachment to it as the home we never chose for ourselves? Or is rather the opposite true: activism expresses our emotional belonging, caring, and concern, for this is home.

Akram, of Jalazone refugee camp north of Ramallah, son of a family expelled from Al-Lydd put it in the bluntest way: "Why, when you realized what this state really is, did you not leave and move to another country?" In short, why did I not make my home elsewhere; why did I not divorce this place? He did say this was not his own question but that of a Palestinian acquaintance. He also said: On principle, all Palestinians have the right to return to their homes and lands, and it is not our problem where you Jews would go after we reclaim the homes (both existing and metaphoric) which you stole. Then he added that he knew it was unrealistic to think we would all leave. But the emotional principle is what interests us here. I imagined him envisioning his grandparents' house in Al-Lydd, now inhabited by a Jewish family, or the housing project erected on the plot of land that used to belong to his family. His claim to return to what should have been his home is but natural.

His question did not surprise me. I have heard it asked by quite a few Palestinians, and the longer I live among them, the less aggressive it sounds to me, and all the more sensible. More than Akram could imagine, it corresponded to questions I ask myself. But the logic and rationality of the question do not assure a satisfying answer, or one answer only or any at all.

The geo-historical layer—rational, scholastic, and argumentative—offers a counterquestion that is an answer of sorts: if so, would all people in the world who acknowledge that their states/homelands are based on the displacement and even annihilation of indigenous peoples cease to feel at home and seek it elsewhere? True, dispossession processes undertaken by Israel, ongoing at present in full force and arrogance, give this question extra legitimacy, but subtler dispossession processes have not ceased in countries such as Canada, the United States, Brazil, Australia. Why should the subtlety of a crime alleviate its punishment?

The comparison is not relevant to Akram, the person asking, and not because of the relative subtlety of current dispossession means. Unlike those other regions of displacement and settler colonialism, we did not nearly annihilate the Palestinians—Oh, what relief!—and they are not a minority in the region. Even in the entire country itself—from the Jordan River to the Mediterranean Sea—their number will soon equal that of the Jews. Exile and displacement are not annihilation, despite the loss, the pain, the ruin. When we speak of a numerical nonminority that is part of the greater majority in our part of the world, it is easier to imagine a demography-based political assertiveness translated into legal (not theological) constructs of crime and punishment. Therefore, history's tribunal of justice is more likely to connect the sentence/prophecy of the Jews' leaving as the solution rather than that of white-Canadians leaving. Speaking only in terms of a theoretical verdict and sentence, this is not the judges' concern that the sure means of making the Jews leave is regional war whose steep price is overall barbarity and unlimited brutality.

On the immediate political level, Akram's question is psychologically expected because for the past two decades Israel has cynically exploited the political process (Madrid and Oslo Accords) in order to deepen the social and territorial fragmentation of Palestine—by means of military assaults, colonies, laws of ethnic separation, and a proliferation of master-race bureaucracy. Akram belongs to the post-hope generation, after the First Intifada that had given many people hope that change was possible, based on the mutual acceptance of the two peoples, and Israel's dissociation from its colonialist characteristics. The twenty-five years since then have proven that Israel not only rejects the Palestinians' national right to exist in their own homeland, in their home—it continues to harass that existence and sabotage it. So it is only natural—even if to me it seems escapist—that Akram and others would not accept that this is home for us (Jewish-Israelis) too.

On the personal dialogue level between us, imagining the return to Akram's family home, which was once a fact on the ground, is stronger than the reality of its erasure. The dispossessor's belonging (mine, for example) to the sites of destruction now coated with construction for others is regarded by him as impossible, improbable, improper. On this personal level, radical dissident positions, political involvement, and the choice to live among Palestinians *are not extenuating circumstances*. Quite the contrary: Akram and others like him find that my awareness—and that of my friends in the Israeli left—of our own complicity only makes the crime worse.

That was why there was no point in answering him, that it was important for those struggling for change to remain, those who use their hegemonic privilege to subvert it. I did answer Akram that Israeli settler-colonialism is not an individual problem and will therefore not be solved individually, by the leaving and disappearance of a few dissidents.

And what answer do I give myself? About ten years ago I drove a friend of mine from Ramallah to the giant Ikea branch near Netanya (in central Israel). I believe I was "smuggling" her in, since she had no permit to enter Israel. I wish I had dared to do this more often. But the penalty for driving an "illegal alien" (Palestinian) if caught is heavy. She and her family were moving, and the large, inexpensive variety offered by the Swedish firm suited her needs. She wandered among the stacks and halls like a fish in water. I went to have coffee. In the huge dining area I sipped the black liquid, and around me dozens of people talked and talked. In Hebrew, of course. Ordinary Israelis. Typical Israeli conversations. Suddenly I found myself wondering: "How is it that I understand every word?" Meaning, I felt in a strange land.

With the seventy-year-old father of that same friend (he insisted on coming only when he had a permit, and only with me), I drove to what had been his native village, on the coastal plain. His grandson came along. The schoolhouse at the edge of the village, functional concrete British Mandate–type architecture, remained as it was, and a giant sycamore tree enabled the seventy-year-old refugee to reenvision the location of the obliterated houses. Again I realized to what extent a single, old building, talkative in its muteness, and an ancient tree nearby are a natural part of my own childhood landscape. They are familiar and painful just like a home. It was there that I realized why I so easily chose Ramallah as my residence: at least in the West Bank I am spared the sights of mass ethnic depopulation.

In summer 2016, at the end of the Ramadan month, I attended the funeral of fifteen-year old Mahmoud Badran, from a village southwest of Ramallah. Soldiers had fired at the car he was riding in—happy and lighthearted along with his cousins—back from a cheerful night swim in a village pool nearby. The excuse for the shooting: stone throwing along a road that is built on Palestinian villages' land but which serves only Israelis. The soldiers—who functioned as false witnesses, prosecutors, judges, and executioners all at once—fired madly at the car with the excuse that it was carrying the stone throwers. After the funeral I said to Mahmoud's father, a former political prisoner, that I was there not just as a journalist (who even at such a tragic time had to interview him) but on my own personal behalf. And he warmly replied: "But of course, this is your homeland."

ALEKSANDAR HEMON is the
author of *The Question of Bruno*,
Nowhere Man, and *The Lazarus
Project*. His latest short story
collection, *Love and Obstacles*,
was published in May 2009. His
collection of autobiographical
essays, *The Book of My Lives*,
was published by Farrar, Straus
and Giroux in March 2013. He
was awarded a Guggenheim Fellowship in 2003 and a "genius"
grant from the MacArthur Foundation in 2004. His latest novel,
The Making of Zombie Wars,
was published by FSG in 2015.
His book on the United Nations,
Behind the Glass Wall, is forthcoming from FSG Originals.
From 2010 to 2013 he served
as editor of the *Best European
Fiction* anthologies, published
by Dalkey Archive Press. He
is currently the Distinguished
Writer-in-Residence at Columbia College Chicago. He lives
in Chicago with his wife and
daughters.

The Sound of Hemon

ALEKSANDAR HEMON

HEMONS

Traditional Ukrainian Folk Songs

Українські Народні Пісньі

As far as I know, there are no songs that could be sung about the Congress of Berlin, yet the 1878 gathering of European power-heads, orchestrated by the great Otto von Bismarck, greatly influenced the way my family experiences music. For it was in Berlin that the Ottoman Empire, defeated in a war against Russia, agreed to cede the province of Bosnia and Herzegovina to the Austro-Hungarian forces. The occupation was supposed to be a temporary arrangement, but pretty much everyone involved knew it would last. After the Austro-Hungarian troops entered Bosnia and Herzegovina, the Crown started importing its subjects from other provinces into the new territory in order to colonize it. In 1908, the Habsburgs used the Young Turks' rebellion against the Sultan and the subsequent dissolution of the monarchy as an excuse to annex Bosnia to the domain, which accelerated colonization efforts. This is where we enter: My family on my grandfather's side—the Hemons—became part of that acceleration as they, slowly, traveled to Bosnia from Galicia (now western Ukraine). Hauling their meager possessions, including a hive or two of bees, they arrived in 1912, my grandfather Ivan as old as the twentieth century. Just about the same time, my grandmother's family arrived from Bukovina, the province to the south of Galicia. The migration preceded the political formulation of Ukrainian identity, so the new arrivals, stumbling unwittingly into the perpetual trouble of Bosnia, became known as the Galicians. Less than a century later, in a census taken a year before the most recent war, there were about five thousand Ukrainians in Bosnia and Herzegovina. In one way or another, I was related to at least half of them. After a couple of generations, the war would push many of the original colonists' descendants to emigrate again.

So it was because of von Bismarck's Prussian pushiness that I was in the audience gathered in a school courtyard in Prnjavor, Bosnia and Herzegovina, on a summer day in 1990 to celebrate the centennial of the Ukrainians' arrival. A Polish-Ukrainian choir, *Zhuravli* (the Cranes), was to perform as part of the celebration, and I could see them, conspicuously tall and improbably handsome, brandishing their Cossack mustaches, high boots and white Ukrainian shirts with patterned collars, flirting with the weak-kneed local maidens. The Cranes looked like a big deal: On a very big bus they came all the way from Poland to the small town of Prnjavor to help us recall our foreparents. After the grand centennial celebration, the Cranes would tour all over the not-yet-former Yugoslavia, including Sarajevo, where my then-girlfriend and I heard them singing Rachmaninoff's Vespers at the cathedral. I was unduly proud, as though I were genetically entitled to belonging in the Cranes' flock, and she was duly impressed; I do believe that afterward we had sex. In Prnjavor, however, the Cranes would sing different tunes, though just as impressively. Sitting in the front row, I was as eager as everyone else for them to step on the stage and unleash their testosterone-heavy voices.

But before they did, we had to hear the opening acts, including the Vocal Octet Vučijak, which exclusively featured men from my family: my father, Petar, and his brothers, Štefan, Bogdan and Teodor, my cousins, Ivan and Vlado, plus Kosta, the husband of my cousin Slavica, who was visiting from Belfort, France. The name Vučijak refered to the hill outside Prnjavor, where our family had originally settled, where my father and his brothers had been born, and where the Octet had rehearsed for the performance in the preceding days. My mother claims that Vučijak is to my father's world what the sun is to the solar system, and I would have to concur.

The ascent of the Vocal Octet onto the stage is one of the strongest memories I have from my previous, prewar life: I can recall them climbing the stairs to the stage, my blind uncle Teodor holding on to Kosta, nearly falling as he tripped over the last step. They lined up before the microphones, bumping into one another like discombobulated cattle, wearing the same traditional Ukrainian shirts as the Cranes, except theirs were considerably less glamorous, what with being stretched at the belly, while their Cossack pants appeared baggy enough to conceal a diaper. They glanced at one another to communicate a need for a synchronized opening note; their hands rolled up into fists as if to prevent sweat from nervously dripping off their palms; they nodded and burst into song, their voices somewhat uncertain, no doubt due to stage fright—they had never performed before such a large, *international* audience.

The clearest detail in that memory is of the moment when my father's hand, theretofore an anxious fist, unrolled just as the Octet reached the point in their first song when they realized they could no longer fuck it up. They unleashed their voices, their ease and confidence rising, not least because the audience started clapping to the rhythm. On they went, belting away the greatest hits of the Ukrainian diaspora: "Rospriahaite Hloptsy Konyi," "Chom Ty Ne Prishov," "Ivanku Ta Y Ivanku," "Poviyav Viter Stepoviy" and so on. At the end of the performance, the audience promptly stood up to applaud and provide ovation. As far as the Vocal Octet was concerned, they never quite sat back down. It was a triumph, one of those instances in family history that is often remembered and misremembered, and at great length too. Yet even the greatest and sharpest memories contain a hole—no one can quite remember who the eighth member of the Octet was; it is possible that it was, in fact, a Septet.

The audience also included a delegation from Rukh, the Ukrainian nationalist movement that had emerged in western Ukraine during the perestroika years. They wore their Ukrainian shirts, and obligingly clapped with great excitement, cheering the singers on. I suspected the Rukh delegates had come to Bosnia to seek out and meet the long-forgotten and neglected diaspora, which by virtue of its absence from the homeland had remained pristine and uncontaminated by Soviet ideology. I guessed that for them the songs my family sang had a fly-in-amber quality, that they might have heard them as perfect records of a time gone, of a culture nearly extinct. They must have been affected by the quaintly obsolescent Ukrainian dialect, unspoiled by the sovietization of the language (even if infested by ukrainianized Bosnian words), that the singers so confidently used. For the Rukh people the Vocal Octet (or Septet) encapsulated a national essence, thus remaining an abstraction, a symbol useful for their nationalist refashioning. To me, on the other hand, they were my flesh and blood, as concrete as any bodies can ever be, as real as the sweat dripping off their foreheads. Before I saw the Octet/Septet on stage, I'd admired and loved the singing, but with a measure of condescension, finding their musical enthusiasm lovably exotic with its connect-to-the-roots romanticism. I was a city boy, born in Sarajevo, not in the countryside; I did not speak Ukrainian; and I regularly listened to the kind of music my father summarily dismissed as "scraping." (The word he used was correct: I was into Sonic Youth and Einstürzende Neubauten.) But I was swollen with pride as the Octet/Septet sang, and more important, I was overwhelmed with love: I loved them for their voices, for their courage and anxiety, for their un-Crane-like awkwardness, for their faith in the song and its protections, in the knowledge that, as long as they kept singing, everything might turn out all right.

Back in those days, I freelanced for a Sarajevo radio station, and therefore had the idea of doing an audio reportage about the centennial celebration. So I'd brought along a portable Uher, a radio reporter's magnetophone, and a stack of tapes to record interviews with my family and the other Ukrainians who came to Prnjavor to recollect the mythical original settlement. But, in fact, what I would do most of the time was record the Octet/Septet's pre-performance rehearsal in order to play it back to them so they could correct their harmonies and adjust their tempos. Occasionally, my uncle Teodor, unimpressed by the presence of the professional equipment, perhaps because he couldn't see it, would arbitrarily assume the authority of a conductor and admonish one of the voices for falling behind or missing a note, and then someone else would snap back at him for talking instead of singing, and the vocal harmony would quickly disintegrate into discordant bickering, and then another take was required and I would rewind the tape to start from the beginning. In the end, I fully taped only two songs, but even in those recordings Uncle Teodor's encouragement could be heard—"Pick it up!" he would say, or "That's it!" I may have recorded parts of their stage performance too, possibly the background noise, the din of the audience, maybe some applause, the cheers of the Rukh delegation. Honestly, I don't remember, and those tapes were never cut into any kind of reportage. They eventually disappeared during the war, like most of my other recordings. Contrary to the common misconception in our foolishly digital society, technology is perishable, while even weak, incorrect or incomplete memories persist, because they live in, and are passed on among, bodies. And the bodies can sing too.

Throughout my childhood, and youth, and life, the Hemons sang. I have no doubt they'll continue singing in the great beyond, as they have at weddings and memorial services, in the church and in the field, or wherever there have been enough of them—which really means more than zero—in the same place. They sing like they breathe, their need irrepressible and not contingent upon any kind of external stimuli. Alcohol, for example, has never been involved, the serotonin high always achieved by way of music. Indeed, my father insists that alcohol (a common, crucial ingredient in standard-issue Slavic nostalgia) should have nothing to do with it, for it would not be the soul singing in a drunk person, but the *rakija*—the booze. My family's love of music is partly rooted in the culture of poverty familiar to all Slavs: Singing together was the easiest, cheapest and most comforting entertainment while working the land or dying in a war.

My grandparents, for example, were poor peasants, subsistence farmers ever struggling to feed the ten children; they endured much of their life without electricity and running water, let alone television or any kind of electronic entertainment. So they sang, with their six daughters and four sons, in various combinations, on various occasions. They sang when their neighbors and musicians stopped by on the way to a dance (*igranka*). They sang sitting in a circle while ripping husks off ears of corn for storage or threading wool, the common peasant tasks. They sang *kolyade*—carols—at Christmastime. They sang teasing songs during that part of the wedding when all the guests approach the groom and bride to give them money in exchange for a piece of cake.

And in the new land, they learned new songs. Prnjavor and the surrounding area used to be known as Little Europe, as the Empire added to the standard Bosnian mix of Serbs, Croats and Muslims colonists from all over: Hungary, Italy, Poland, Bohemia, Austria proper, and, of course, Galicia and Bukovina. Which is to say that diverse songs were passed around and shared among the peoples in the area—music, like language, cannot be kept within the stuffy confines of what is known as identity. One of my grandfather's favorite songs, which he would sing to himself while working, no doubt with his Galician accent, was "Tamburalo momče u tambure," a classic *sevdalinka,* sung originally by Bosnian Muslims, whom he casually referred to as the Turks, which was (and still is) a derogatory term. My adolescent father once fell in love with a Croat girl solely, he says, because of the beautiful way she sang Macedonian songs. He's still very fond of Macedonian songs and thinks they are similar to Ukrainian ones in that they're all about "leaving for the world" (*odlazak u svijet*)—or, if you wish, about displacement. "The people who don't love music, the tone-deaf people, are damaged," my father says. "I feel sorry for such people."

Never has my family sung exclusively Ukrainian songs, yet those were the only kind they felt a need to keep alive—the perpetual singing was a way to remember and never lose those songs. As far as Father is concerned, singing (*pjesma*) is in the Ukrainian blood; suffice it to say that a common family name among Bosnian Ukrainians is Muzeka—music. And I do remember being awestruck in 2003 before a spontaneous choir of Ukrainians—old men and ladies, young people and children—at the Rynok, the main square in Lviv, who gathered in the afternoon to sing, sometimes for hours. I knew many of the songs, and instantly recognized the same kind of deep devotion as in my family. In all my travels, it was only in Galicia that I saw that kind of heartfelt grassroots singing. I am not prone to identifying with groups of strangers—to what one would call nationalism or patriotism—but listening to the singers at the Rynok, I couldn't help thinking: "These are my people."

It is likely that singing acquires a greater value in diaspora, and there is no shortage of diasporic experiences among Ukrainians or Bosnians. The songs my family sings invoke mythological memories of the life before the original displacement; the longing for what has been long inaccessible could in singing detach itself from its original object and enfold entire new realities, all that using minor scales. My father's singing face looks nothing like his non-singing self—he becomes someone in a different key, someone I have no access to, unless, perhaps, I sing with him, which I seldom do. "Singing makes everything easier to bear," Father says. "There is an unburdening in the soul." It is therefore not uncommon that people in my family tear up while singing. "It is possible to cry and sing at the same time," he says, as if anyone who knows him would think otherwise. "How can you stop the tears," he told me not so long ago, "when you hear these lines?"—and he recited, with a trembling voice:

"If you knew, mother, how poor and unlucky I am
You would send me a sparrow with some bread,
And a tit bird with some salt."

Apart from all the animals summoned to ease poverty, displacement and pain, the cast of characters in the Ukrainian songs in the standard Hemon repertoire is fairly limited: Cossack/soldier, maiden, horse, mother, or any combination thereof, except maybe a solo horse. Many songs contain Cossacks flirting with or

seducing girls carrying buckets of water, yet somehow never help-
ing them. Others are about a soldier dying on the battlefield, his
mother mourning him, his girl longing and/or crying for him, his
metaphorical resurrection fueled by his love of freedom. In those
songs, water has special significance, there is an abundance of war
and steppe, the Cossacks ride their horses, play the bandura, die
and dig said water wells, not necessarily in that order. The maiden is
frequently Halya—the name of one of my aunts (dead) and of another
cousin (Edmonton, Canada). The trees, particularly the sturdy oak,
tend to have symbolic value, as do wheat and buckwheat, while the
kalyna—cranberry—is practically holy. These songs came not only
from the far-off homeland, but also from an entirely different century and attendant economy, now obsolescent even in my family.
The songs were originally sung by rural, oral people whose minds
were mythological, untroubled by modernity. There are no cities
in them, no governments, no cars or airplanes, no running water.
They feature equestrian Cossack landscapes thoroughly devoid of
horseflies or shit, nevermind sheep or cows. Neither is there any
record of endless toil required for mere survival, nor of any illness
that cannot be cured by love, be it for freedom or for Halya. The
songs operate at a level of abstraction: my father and his brothers
have seldom ridden horses or had any interest in them, probably
because even if my grandparents ever owned one, it was used for
plowing and tilling; they have never played the bandura; they would
get lost or bored in the actual steppe; they don't particularly care
about the *kalyna*, let alone the cranberry plant, not even when it's
in bloom. (They can dig a good well, though.) While the dying soldiers in the songs commonly extol the values of courage, freedom
and Ukraine, few Hemons have been eager to give their lives for any
country, let alone the distant Ukraine, where we have only distant
family, the descendants of those who had not migrated. The musical vessels of nostalgia in the repertoire—some patriotic, some not

quite—invoke the kind of feelings that orbit the lived experience, and cannot therefore be simply described or defined; they can only be (re)imagined as a refracted utopian past. In my family, whose history of ignoble wars and displacements contains no heroes or horses, we prefer vocalizing songs to discussing feelings.

The biggest concentration of my family anywhere in the world, Bosnia and Ukraine included, is in the greater Toronto area. There are more than a hundred of them, sorted out in three generations, including many young ones whose names, or parents, I cannot begin to remember. Twenty-five years ago, when my parents landed in Hamilton, Ontario, at the height of the Bosnian war, the closest family was in Edmonton, where my cousin Halya and her family had disembarked in the late eighties. Little by little, the other Hemons landed in Hamilton—first Štefan, and then Bogdan, with their families. The fourth brother, Teodor, had been blinded by a hand grenade when he was six, at the end of World War II, losing his right hand as well; his disability disqualified him from immigration. He stayed in Bosnia, where a few years ago he died of a heart attack. But his son, Ivan (*not* the one who was in the Octet/Septet in 1990), came with his family to Canada by way of Croatia, carrying two notebooks of lyrics and chords for hundreds of songs: the blue one contained Ukrainian songs, the yellow one songs from the former Yugoslavia.

Uncle Teodor's family had lived in Banja Luka, some thirty miles down the road from Prnjavor. As the biggest city in the region with the greatest number of Bosnian Ukrainians, it was home to the Culture and Arts Association Taras Shevchenko (*Kulturno-umjet-ničko društvo Taras Ševčenko*), whose mission was to preserve and cherish Ukrainian culture, which mainly meant song and dance. For decades, Uncle Teodor and his wife, Štefica (who died as I was writing this), sang in the association's choir, their daughter, Ana, danced in their dance troupe, while Ivan played the accordion in the orchestra, which allowed him to learn, memorize and write down an enormous number of Ukrainian songs. He was also part of a band that played at parties and weddings, not just for Ukrainians but for others too; he learned, memorized and wrote down songs well-known in Bosnia and the soon-to-be-former Yugoslavia. The two notebooks he brought to Canada were compendia of not only the songs my family had always sung, but of many they hadn't—and now they could, and would, God knows, until their last fucking note, and then beyond.

The migration to Canada thus marked the beginning of the Hemons' musical renaissance. The trauma of war and displacement was fresh and overwhelming at first, and I don't remember them singing much then, certainly not with their customary intensity and abandon. By 1994, however, there was a critical mass of family, their nostalgia and hurt pressed for expression, while the need for some shared joy became acute, and they were back into it. A system was spontaneously established where regular get-togethers became an essential part of everyone's life itinerary. Thus the Christmas season involved a busy schedule: on Christmas Eve everyone went to my cousin Ivan's, on Christmas Day to my parents', then for New Year's they'd rent a hall with other former-Yugoslavia Ukrainians, on January 6 they'd go to my cousin Pedja's for Orthodox Christmas Eve, and then the next day to my uncle Bogdan's for Orthodox Christmas, and then a couple of days later to my uncle Štefan's for his name day; then on January 13 they would celebrate the arrival of the Orthodox New Year, thus singing their way through seven parties in three weeks. Whenever I called my parents to wish them a happy New Year, my father would thank me in a hoarse voice, while my mother complained that she was exhausted and they were only halfway through the season. The rest of the year was perhaps less hectic, but there would still be plenty of weddings, christening parties, picnics or nonrequired get-togethers, where they could sing for hours on end.

At the party my parents threw in their backyard for my firstborn daughter, attended by much of my Ontario-based family, the singing went on all day long. The variable line-up, which included my father, Ivan, Bogdan, Štefan and some cousins, never stopped singing for a moment, even if individual singers would take a break to eat, drink or relieve themselves. As vast as their repertoire was, they covered it at least a couple of times, and eventually had to go for the lesser-sung items in the notebooks—the rarities and B-sides, so to speak. They'd huddle over the blue or the yellow notebook, their heads touching; without glasses, they'd miss certain lines and would hum and howl to cover it up, figuring out the song they claimed they knew well as they went along. And they kept at it. Children played soccer in the backyard, got tired, ate, cried, fell asleep in their parents' arms, woke up to play soccer again, all to the soundtrack of the expanded Hemon repertoire. At some point all conversation ceased, for it was too difficult to speak over the belting voices, which was why I got miffed and insisted they end it. I'd forgotten that silence or conversation are far less commonly practiced at our gatherings, since the music is the main means of being together. I understand now that the ceaseless song was but an expression of joy, if expanded over a very, very long time. To be fair, they did try to wind it down after six hours or so, but then Stan, the neighbor, stopped by. Stan, the neighbor, was actually Stanislaw, a Pole, which is to say that his Slavic nostalgia had fully kicked in as he listened to the Hemons' backyard oratorio, so he'd had a shot of vodka, and then another one, and soon he wandered over all teary-eyed to gaze at them longingly across the fence. They sat him down, naturally, offered him another drink and then indulged him with the highlights of their repertoire, which took another two hours.

Over time, the Hemons' singing acquired a bit of fame among the Ontario Ukrainians. For one thing, the Hemons have never been shy about singing at other people's parties. Someone must have heard them and passed on the word, for Father, Štefan and Bogdan were recruited to sing for the Orion Men's Choir. This was a different game: they sang with thirty other men; they were required to attend rehearsals regularly; to submit to the conductor's authority and learn to read music; the choristers are divided into four voices; they're often accompanied by an orchestra, while Ukrainian and civilian songs are ambitiously arranged; performances ("showcasing liturgical, contemporary, traditional folk, and patriotic music," according to the website) take place in large venues; they're sometimes accompanied by a women's choir. Proper choral singing does not quite accommodate the Hemons' proclivity to belt it out from the top of their lungs as if the nearest audience were a couple of hills over, a style developed in their native Vučijak, but they've managed to adjust. They've toured with the choir, traveling as far as New Jersey and New York (which my father didn't like because it was "too crowded"), and they've recorded in a professional studio, where the sound engineer edited their singing, creating a kind of technological magic that appealed to my engineer father. When he heard the recording for the first time, he got goose bumps.

It must've been the choral experience of singing outside the context of backyards and weddings that encouraged the Hemons to undertake an endeavor that would've been inconcievable to my ancestors, who had happily sung to one another in a kitchen lit only by the stove fire. In the summer of 2015, the Hemons self-released a CD entitled *Hemons: Traditional Ukrainian Folk Songs*, their first (and possibly last) recording. The liner notes do not explain the absence of the definite article in the ensemble's name, but the artists are proudly listed:

Štefan: Tenor I
Petar: Tenor II
Bogdan: Baritone
Ivan: Accordion & Tenor I

Gregor: Guitar

Taras: Sound Engineer

For this project, a third generation of Hemons was added: Ivan's young sons, Taras and Gregor (Canadian-born). The CD was sold for twenty Canadian dollars, with all of the proceeds going to a "poor student's [sic] fund," that is, to college-age family members in need of financial help. My mother was put in charge of collecting the funds. As of the last audit, there was about $1,350 Canadian in the account, which has been disbursed to the young students in the tribe.

On the CD, the Hemons deliver what they've sung at every family gathering since I can remember hearing sounds. There is the perennial "Rospriahaite Hloptsy Konyi," in which the Cossack boys (*hloptsy*) unbridle their horses, and then one of them digs a well (what else?) and flirts with a maiden named Marusya, who is in turn jealous because the well-digger has chatted up another girl. And then there is "Tam Pid Lvivskim Zamkom," addressing the fact that Ukrainians have never won a war by way of depositing a dead young partisan, blond curls and all, under an oak tree just beneath the Lviv castle; there he lies dead as his mother informs the heartbroken audience that he was the youngest of her five sons, and that his father also died in a war; she wishes that the war hadn't been fought, as a mother would, but then there's that pricey thing called freedom. Another young soldier is dead in "Povijav Viter Stepovij," and another mother cries for him, this time aided by a maiden. There are a few more songs where the stories of tragic heroism might conceal plain sadness, and then there are inklings of joy, or at least some non-funereal flowers, as in "Nese Halya Vodu," in which the indomitable Halya fetches water, while one Ivanko trails her like a periwinkle (*barvinok*).

The song list is so familiar to me that some of the numbers I often hear in my dreams. It's the soundtrack for the part of the Hemon subconscious that houses our history, as the liner notes suggest:

The Hemon family left Ukraine in the early twentieth century, bringing with them the rich language, the delicious cuisine and the discipline of beekeeping to their new homeland. However, it is their love and memory of the beautiful songs of Ukraine that holds [sic] the strongest connection to their past, a love that has grown with them and has come to form a vital part of what it means to be Hemon. Through song the Hemons honor their past, enjoy the present, look to the future, but most importantly celebrate their strength, unity and love as a family.

"The discipline of beekeeping" slays me, while "a love that . . . has come to form a vital part of what it means to be Hemon" buries me. Much of my life, I've been trying to figure out what it means to be Hemon—or, as English grammar would have it, *a* Hemon. It's perhaps significant that the liner notes mention only the initial departure, while there is not a word about not one, but two arrivals in "their new homeland." The primary, unacknowledged source of inspiration for the music must be related to the fact that no one in my family dies in the country where he or she was born. Like the mythological Cossacks on their horses, we sing while passing from one place to another.

The *Hemons* CD notes also offer "special thanks to our wives for their love and support." One of those wives would obviously be my mother, who provided support by preparing the food the Hemons munched at the studio.

The gratitude notwithstanding, my mother has a complicated relationship with the Hemon singing. She enjoys music, likes to sing herself, but she does not speak Ukrainian and sometimes feels neglected due to my father's vocal obsession. It was her idea, in fact, to sell the CDs for the poor students' fund, so that there would be some actual purpose to all that singing.

There was a time when my parents sang a lot together. As students in Belgrade, where they met in the late fifties, they spent much of their non-studying time singing and dancing. There are a few pictures from those days taken at a party or picnic, where their joyful abandon, complete with ecstatic faces centered around a guitar, is conspicuous. Their music from their student days was rock, not only because it was conquering the world, but also because they were leaving behind their country roots to become educated urban dwellers. That might also be why they're fond of the particular genre of former Yugoslav songs known as *starogradske*—which could be translated as "old urban." These songs and their descendants tap into the late nineteenth-century bohemian, bourgeois nostalgia, where love is always unrequited, men drink to forget the woman, or their wasted youth, or both. Similar to the *sevdalinka*, which is infused with *sevdah*—a pleasant feeling of losing oneself to the hopelessness of love, to time passing, to life and the defeats it inflicts—the *starogradska* song generates *dert*, a kind of ecstasy where nothing but this moment—loaded with tears, wine, song, love—matters. My parents thus sang *starogradske* whenever temporary abandonment was available and permitted, which means on occasions like New Year's Eve or an evening with select friends. The abandon was never defeatist, the intended feeling always the joy of being with the people dear to their heart. If I want to recollect in my mind's eye Mother being happy, I imagine her singing—and there she is with her high-pitched voice, squinting as if to see better into her own soul, throwing up her arms as if discarding all her worries (and there have always been many), sometimes embracing a person next to her to make them turn it up. Nowadays, when the Hemons sing *starogradske* she might join in, but she usually sings under her voice, as if doing it only because she cannot refrain. The song list for my parents' relationship is thus different from the Hemon one. It was from this song list that my father drew for his performance marking my parents' fiftieth wedding anniversary.

The anniversary party took place in a Hamilton church-base-ment hall, which necessitated, to the consternation of my atheist mother, that a priest sprinkle holy water around and lead the guests in prayer; he also made her kiss the cross, which she did and which, we would be told later, left a foul taste in her mouth. Following the consecration, my daughter and nieces, accompanied by Felix, my brother-in-law, sang "Que Sera, Sera," and some congratulatory speeches were delivered. And then Father stepped in front of the microphone and announced that he would now tell the story of their first meeting, marriage and their fifty years of shared life, and he would do all that by way of song. The motto of his presentation: "The song sustained us, to her we're grateful." (*Pjesma nas je održala, njojzi hvala.*) There was no musical accompaniment; he was alone, armed with a one-page script in his hand. First came the story of how his roommate, Nidžo, introduced him to Mother, who shared lodgings with Nidžo's sister. When he saw her, Father said, she looked like an angel—whereupon he broke into a song about an angel-like woman. He addressed the fact that, in the course of their marriage, he'd traveled for work too much, leaving Mother alone to wrangle the life and kids, with a song entitled "Forgive Me That I Stole Your Love" ("Oprosti što sam tvoju ljubab krao"). The song includes the lines: "And I drank the red wine somewhere/ And I was happy with another woman somewhere/ And you waited for me"—but no one present would've considered the possibility that he'd actually done any of that. Still, at some point he posed a rhetorical question: "What is the secret of a successful marriage?" He responded in the same breath: "Constancy. I was bad at the beginning, I was bad for fifty years, and I am bad now." His being "bad," I knew, meant not being supportive, not being present when Mother needed him, not understanding what fueled her resentments, not being able to be rid of the burden of guilt. Toward the end of the performance, he related how, on the eve of the war, in April 1992, someone called to tell them that our cabin in the mountains above Sarajevo had been broken into, and he went up there to check and fix the damage. But then he had a hard time getting back home, because the Serb ring around the city was already in place and they would not let him get through. So he went off the road and followed a path through the woods, and the woods were still full of snow—as in the song, he said, "The Snow Fell on Trees in Bloom" ("Snijeg pade na behar, na voće"), which he then promptly belted out for the appreciative audience.

And thus he sang and talked solo for nearly an hour. It was an unforgettable performance of what can be accurately christened a "monomusical. " Throughout it I was alternately suppressing diluvial tears and chuckling on the verge of uproarious laughter. After the show was over, I asked for his script, as I knew immediately I would write about what happened. I put the script away for future use and now, of course, can't find it—it is in some file somewhere with all the other things I must never forget. My mother enjoyed his performance too, but with some ambivalence—on top of the annoying priest and cross-kissing, she must've felt that the musical rendition of their marital history was somewhat one-sided. Her songs would've been different, but she didn't get to sing them.

Not so long ago, my parents were visiting me in Chicago. On their way back, they listened to a CD of songs from the former Yugoslavia. When the classic Macedonian song, "Biljana platno belaše" ("Biljana Whitened the Cotton"), came on they spontaneously started singing, as they both loved it. They sang the next song on the CD as well, and then they turned off the stereo and sang together for hours, until they made it home.

ROSS RAISIN was born in 1979 in West Yorkshire. His first novel, *God's Own Country*, was published in 2008 and was shortlisted for nine literary awards, including the *Guardian* First Book Award and the John Llewellyn Rhys Prize. In 2009 Ross Raisin was named the *Sunday Times* Young Writer of the Year. In 2013 he was selected as one of *Granta*'s Best of Young British Novelists. He lives in London.

A Natural

ROSS RAISIN

As the season entered October the bright, immaculate pitches of summer were already beginning to thicken and spoil. Goalmouths knotted with mud, and the lower-lying areas of many of the division's slanted, undulating grounds were turning yellow with drowned grass. The non-league pitch on which Town played their reserve fixtures was even worse. During these matches Tom found it impossible to develop a settled rhythm. He would try to deceive himself into the actions that he had once done by instinct, conjuring the vision of belting down the smooth swathe of his academy-pitch wing, but whenever he tried to run with the ball now it would be up against his shins and knees bobbling out of control.

The reserve starting eleven was as unpredictable as the pitch: a mixture of eager scholars like Steven and Bobby—who sometimes, to the annoyance of the older pros, captained the side—trialists and fringe players desperate to impress but at the same time reluctant to commit themselves for fear of getting injured. Tom, who was playing in most reserve games and also as a substitute for the first team, was sometimes involved in two encounters a week now, yet did not feel like he belonged to either side. He was determined not to be associated with the seconds but performed erratically. In four reserve matches he had drifted in and out, but had still contributed the assists for two goals and scored once, a strike that he celebrated with the same muted animation as did the few dozen obsessives, scouts and parents in the crowd, who greeted each goal with cheerful seated applause, as if at a sports day.

Apart from the scholars, with whom he tried to appear confident and senior, Tom seldom mixed with the other reserves. Instead he increased his efforts to be around the first team. Ever since that fuzzily remembered night at the club, he found that he could hold the attention of most for brief conversations while stretching or taking fluids or changing. He joined the back of huddles to look at images on phones, laughed, hand-clasped, always feeling like a fool and a fraud but reasonably certain that nobody noticed.

He ensured that he was one of the last to board the first-team coach to Southend and sat himself with a rehearsed nod next to Richards, who nodded back but did not take his headphones off. When, nearly an hour into the journey, he did finally lift them from his ears, Tom was careful not to speak to him immediately, instead continuing to look at his laptop for a short time before turning towards his neighbour. 'You seen this? It's fucking class.'

Richards leaned in to look at the YouTube video that Tom had picked out the previous evening: a rival squad cheering and dancing in their training-ground lounge after hearing their manager had been sacked.

Richards laughed. 'Yeah, I can guess how that feels.'

They watched a couple more videos together, then Richards got up to join the group of players standing about the back stairwell, idly watching the Sky match on the monitor while they queued for the microwave to heat their Tupperwares of Mrs Davey's chicken pasta.

They lost. Afterwards Clarke refused to speak to them—in the tunnel, the dressing room or on the coach, where Tom, like many of the others, sat alone, staring out of the window at the burnished golden estuary mudflats.

Because of the length of the next away journey, to Morecambe, Tom did not intrude on Richards this time. He sat instead across the aisle from the table of card players, occasionally joining in a game of brag and, in the quiet spells between their playing and betting, offering them funny videos that he had spent several evenings finding on the Internet.

'What's that faggot's problem?' Easter pointed at Lewis, a few rows down by himself. 'You and him have a tiff or something, Yatesy?'

'Maybe his shrink's told him to steer clear of us.'

A few days earlier Lewis had let slip that he had started visiting a sports psychologist. To help him prepare mentally for games, he had explained while they fell about laughing.

'Hey, CL,' Price shouted. 'Your shrink told you yet why you never score any goals? It because your daddy never loved you?'

Lewis's head appeared above a headrest. 'He does have a theory about it, as it happens.'

'Go on. Enlighten us.'

'He says it's because our midfield is shit.'

Lewis, to a hail of peanuts and an energy bar, ducked out of sight. The goalkeeping coach had arranged, by calling in a favour, for them to use Blackpool's academy base that afternoon, then there was an hour for a nap at the hotel, followed by dinner. On these Fridays they were the perfect guests: quiet, preoccupied, sober. They ate all together around three large tables in the restaurant before going up to their rooms just after nine o'clock, leaving the travelling directors to eat and drink themselves into a state of pink untucked recline in the hotel lounge.

Tom still roomed with Easter. He knew that this continued arrangement was to do with the manager, and he wondered sometimes if it was the main purpose of his place in the travelling party.

They had established a routine: On going up to the room after dinner, Easter would immediately leave again, sometimes for a short while, sometimes for longer. Tom would switch Easter's bedside light on for when he came in—quietly, if Tom was asleep—to undress in the bathroom. In the morning they used Easter's phone to wake them, then Tom went first for a shower while Easter sat on his bed and drank coffee, watching the television. They did not speak much, but Easter did not seem to resent Tom's presence. He was quiet, considerate even. Tom suspected the reason he had grown not to mind the arrangement was because Tom left him alone. He had come to understand, with a certain amount of hidden pride, that there was a side to Easter, reclusive, reflective, that only he among the squad knew about.

So it came as a bit of a surprise that night when Easter got into bed and leaned over to hold out his phone.

'That's my son.'

Tom looked at the bug-eyed thing on the screen. He did not know what to say.

'He's big.'

Easter appeared not displeased with this response. He looked at the phone himself, smiling. 'Fat little bastard, isn't he?'

Tom was in two minds about whether or not to laugh at this so he took the opportunity to go and get them each a glass of water, staying in the bathroom until he was sure that the colour on his cheeks had died down.

They were both on the substitutes' bench. Tom was not used, but Easter came on to score the equaliser, a frantic, scrambled effort inside the six-yard box, in reaction to which he sprinted the full length of the pitch towards the eighty away supporters and, in the fervour of the moment, turned round once he was before them to stretch down his shirt and thumb blindly at what he intended to

be his number, but was in fact the lettering above it: YDV FINANCIAL
SERVICES.

With no league wins, five draws and seven defeats, firmly planted
at the bottom of the table, out of the League Cup, attendances
dwindling and the board increasingly agitated, Clarke pulled off, as he
himself described it to Peter Pascoe in the local paper, something of
a coup. He signed a very reputable higher-division midfielder, Andy
Jones, on a three-month loan. He did not state openly that he was
signing the player to replace Easter, but the interview with Pascoe left
nobody in any real doubt: 'Andy is somebody who will run through
walls for you. I've had him at previous clubs and I've always made
him run through walls. That's exactly what we're needing now. I'd
love to sign him permanent come January but the budget's not there
for it yet. If we can clear some of the wage bill by then, hopefully
we'll see what we can do with Andy.'

These words caused apprehension to ripple through the squad.
Even the established first-teamers who played in different positions
to Jones became unsure of their places. The January transfer window, still over two months away, loomed ahead of them, and they
viewed Jones with caginess because, in their eyes, he had arrived
as the embodiment of it.

Jones needed no time to settle in. He took charge straight away,
demanding the ball constantly during practice matches. He let them
know if they were not working hard enough. He injured a scholar.
He stayed behind after the rest of the squad had left the field to talk
privately with the manager, and returned to the dressing room to
plunge into the vacated ice bath, wincing and groaning in there for
longer than anybody else ever did before rising enormous, glistening,
his skin blue and purple with bruises that gave him the appearance,
under the stark dressing-room lighting, of butchered meat.

He marked his debut by galvanising the team to its first victory of the season. Tom, next to Easter in the away dugout, applauded Jones's first goal but did not stand as the others did, punching the air, slapping the roof. When they settled back down Tom looked round at Easter. His elbows were raised, head clamped between his fists, obscuring his face. For a second Tom thought about catching his eye, but the idea immediately dissipated and whatever sympathy he might have tried to communicate remained unexpressed save for the hot squash of their thighs, minutely increasing.

Upon Jones's second, decisive goal the tight pocket of Town fans came alight—dancing, jumping on seats, rushing down the aisles towards the pitch, and a steward sprinted all the way from his position by the dugout to accost a young boy standing on the grass in front of the advertising hoardings. He caught the boy unawares, lifted him in a bear hug and began dragging him across the side of the pitch towards a solitary policeman, all the while pursued by a group of fellow stewards who had realised, along with most of the crowd and the overjoyed away dugout, that the detained youngster flailing in the big man's arms was not in actuality an away fan, but a ball boy.

Hope grew that the team's fortunes might be on the turn. Training sessions took on a new competitive edge. Every player apart from Jones lived under the permanent threat of being bombed out if Clarke thought they were not keeping up to the new standard. Even Boyn was punished, judged not to be running fast enough between cones during a doggies drill. The squad all stood and watched him walk over to the scholars, who paused their session under the huge, balding sycamore tree to let him join their number. When the squad turned back to resume the drill, Clarke glared, with a slight smile, at Easter. Easter did not meet the challenge but continued to stretch, waiting for his turn to sprint. The others had begun keeping their distance from Easter in the dressing room and around the ground. If Clarke was present they avoided speaking to him, or even, except in the moments that he and Jones fought for the same ball, looking at him at all.

The improvement in the team did not bode well for Tom's standing either. Finch-Evans had played well in the win, replaced by Tom for only the last three minutes. Not enough for Tom to get into the game, barely enough to touch the ball. He had come in at the final whistle with his kit unmarked, ashamed to shower. A few days later, he was not even picked to start in the next round of the Johnstone's Paint despite his convincing performance in the first, which seemed to him now like a dream, and he walked off the pitch at the end without joining the celebrations of the others following another victory. In the showers afterwards, rinsing off a cursory lathering of soap, he realised that Easter, under the neighbouring showerhead, was laughing quietly.

'What's the fucking point?' He did not move his gaze from the wall. There was nobody else left near them, and Tom could not tell whether Easter was speaking to him. 'Seriously, what's the fucking point?'

'Showering?' Tom said. Easter turned to look at him. 'Yeah, if you like, showering.' 'Don't know.' 'No, me neither.' He moved away and reached for a towel to wrap about his waist. Tom did the same.

'Seriously. Tell me. What kind of operation is it he thinks he's running here?'

'Van hire?' Tom said on a whim, a remark that Easter found improbably hilarious, stepping forward to give him a short, aggressive hug.

'You're all right, you are, mate.' He laughed again. 'Van hire.'

Tom paused for Easter to go ahead of him into the dressing room, grateful that they had been alone in the shower room, that they had been wearing towels.

To Clarke's fury, the team's momentum was curtailed by a period of heavy, near-continuous rain. Within three days the lower half of the stadium pitch was submerged. A home fixture had to be called off. A section of the car park wall collapsed. Brown puddles formed on top of the Portakabin club shop, leaking into the stock room; water ran down the steps of the two uncovered terraces to collect in secret pools in the foundations; cascades from the corrugated roofs of the Kop and the main stand poured down in windblown torrents that left a flotsam of litter and bird shit floating over the pitch.

The training ground, however, held out for longer. The squad continued to slog and slide, Clarke refusing to give in to the rain. He walked the touchline in his wellies under a giant golfing umbrella, bawling commands into the drenched air. Daring them to complain. One morning the players stood by the side of a pitch, water up to their bootlaces, waiting for Liam to finish clearing the area near a corner flag with a brush mounted on the front of the compact tractor. He drove off around the edge of the pitch when it was done, but instead of continuing on across the floodplain towards the ground-staff shed, he turned the tractor again, and came straight at them, speeding up. The others scattered, but Tom could only stand exactly where he was, anchored, Liam coming directly for him, his eyes fastened on Tom, until at the last moment he swerved away, creating an arc of spray that showered several of the players and caused the flock of seagulls around the goalposts to launch themselves into the air.

Some of the squad chased halfheartedly after the tractor as it roared away, Liam standing like a jockey, one arm raised in the air. The players soon gave up and trudged back. Liam slowed the tractor down and, on reaching the ground-staff shed, cut the engine, turning round as he did so to look back briefly to where Tom stood now in the midst of the group.

For the final two mornings of the week training moved to a local secondary school. In public view the sessions were less intense, less combative, than usual. The size of the sports-hall pitch allowed only for small-sided games, and each time there was a break in lessons an ebullient pack of children crowded onto the two balconies, where, to the disbelief of the squad as the hall echoed with shrill cries, Clarke let them remain and sometimes even looked up to joke with them or offer a criticism of a player. Two Year Seven boys, arriving early for lunchtime basketball practice, ran into the changing rooms while the players were still there. For a few seconds they stood dripping in their coats by the door, completely stationary. Men walked about the room in complete nakedness. One was sitting on a toilet, the cubicle door open. The smaller of the boys nudged his mate to leave, but the other stood hypnotised.

'Hey Yatesy, I think he's got a thing for you.'

Yates, drying himself, stepped towards the boys. He moved his towel aside. 'What, you never seen one this big before?'

There was some giggling.

'I thought Asian lads were supposed to be huge. Bet your daddy's got one like a baby's arm.'

The two boys turned and fled. There was an explosion of laughter, which Tom joined in with as he stared through the doorway after the boys, away from Yates.

After a series of sucking footsteps and easily inserted fingers, Saturday's referee declared the Swindon pitch unplayable. Tom, the whole weekend free in front of him, rang his dad and within minutes of the call ending was in his car on the way home.

On the motorway his mind turned to the past couple of days at the school. Being in that hall had felt achingly familiar. The squeak and scuff of the AstroTurf. The rubbery smell of the storage rooms. The constellation of shuttlecocks and soft tennis balls caught in the ceiling nets. He slowed to watch a column of Aston Villa coaches come past in the other direction and wondered how so much could have changed. It was not so long ago—school. Everything had been so clear to him then. All he had wanted—to play football—and never a doubt in his mind that he would make it. Another sound he remembered from those days, so well that he could hear it now: *Give it, Tom*. Every lunchtime, every PE game, bouncing off the walls for years. *Give it, Tom. Give it, Tom.*

He arrived home to the sight through the kitchen window of his mum chopping vegetables. She waved when she saw him getting out of the car and moved to the sink to wash her hands as he came through the gate. The small lawn was waterlogged. Damp little flowers stood in solemn lines along both sides, like Town supporters. The image of his dad hunched with his trowel came to Tom, the door opening now, his mum waiting there, and it was an effort to hold himself together as he stepped into the house, her arms closing around him.

They pulled apart and she looked at him. 'Are you allowed a beer?'

'There's no match, Mum. And it's not like I'd be playing anyway.'

She smiled, shaking her head. 'No point feeling sorry for yourself. Go say hello to your dad. He's in there, wrecking his head at the football. Rachel's upstairs.' She turned round. 'Rach! Tom's here.' But his sister was already coming down the staircase, bounding towards him, hugging him. For an instant, her skin against his face, he remembered the girl in the nightclub.

'So, the Fourth Division footballer returns.'

'League Two.'

'Fourth Division. Dad's been explaining it to me.'

Their father was coming out of the living room. He shook Tom's hand at the same time as pulling him in close. Squeezing knuckles pressed against Tom's stomach.

'Heard the Chelsea score?'

'I was listening in the car,' Tom said. 'Crazy game.'

His dad was studying him. 'Very crazy game. Beer?'

They ate a late lunch, sitting on the two sofas in the living room, talking, the television on in the background. It made a nice change, he told them, not having to eat around a table. When nobody responded he feared he might have offended them, so he went on to say how good the shepherd's pie was, how much he'd missed his mum's cooking. He told them about life at the Daveys', concentrating on the lack of privacy, the Scottish pair playing Xbox into the night, the waiting for the bathroom. He felt somewhat sheepish pointing out these things, especially as it quickly had the effect of worrying his parents that he might not be happy in this place they had sent him to. They wanted to know if he was getting on with the other lodgers, if he was sleeping enough. He looked tired to them.

'He's fine, Dad,' his sister stepped in. 'He's only tired because he's out on the pull every night.'

Tom was at once hot with embarrassment. He was aware of his dad watching him, waiting for what he would say.

'I'm fine. Seriously. I'm not tired. It's a good place to stay. It's the club. The manager. That's the problem.'

His dad seized on the change in direction: 'Clarke's teams have always played the same way. Fine if you're winning, but if the results aren't coming he's got no plan B.'

'He's brought in Andy Jones, to be fair,' Tom said.

'Yes. I remember Jones when he was at Blackburn. Dirty player. Just the type Clarke likes.'

His mother and sister, with nothing to add to this conversation, began talking about the upcoming wedding of one of his mum's colleagues, another health visitor alongside whom she had run a baby drop-in clinic for years. When there was a lull and he was sure his dad had finished his point, Tom turned towards them on the other sofa.

'How's A-levels, Rach?'

'Hard. Coursework never stops. I shouldn't even be down here now. You should feel honoured.'

'You still planning on John Moores?'

There was a moment of silence.

'I'm not sure yet.'

'Thought you were dead set?'

'Well, I was. Bloody Tories, though.'

They all looked at the television. Tom did not understand, but he said nothing more. He had always been proud of his sister's cleverness, never threatened by it, because he had football. For as long as he could remember there had been an unspoken assumption in the house that they would both be successful. She wanted to do an events management degree, as far as he could recall, and he wondered now if he had got that wrong. But as he observed the look that passed between his parents, he thought that maybe he did understand; that it was about money.

He perused the small, immaculate room while they listened to the half-time reports coming in. It was a world away from the busy clutter of the Daveys. The pert, vacuumed sofas. The remote controls lined up on the television stand. His dad's neatly organised plastic desk tucked into one corner of the room; wage-slip, bank and utilities files boxed underneath it next to a pile that Tom had noticed the second he came in of printed-out Town match reports, which he knew his mum or sister must have shown him how to do. His dad was listening to the Bolton–Everton report. His plate and tray were on the floor by his feet. It struck Tom for the first time that he probably earned more than his dad. Barely playing, in League Two. He thought about the box upstairs, with all of his photographs and press cuttings and England age-group caps. For years his dad had driven him to school matches, county matches, Centre of Excellence and academy matches, England matches, reserve matches. Taking time off work. Paying for kit. Overnight stops. Relocating the whole family. All while Rachel had never asked for anything, never been given anything.

His mum collected the trays from the floor. 'You got plans for later, love?'

'Here, I'll do that, Mum. No, I've not told anyone I'm up. Thought I'd stop in, watch *Match of the Day*. I'll stick around tomorrow too, if that's all right.'

He followed her into the kitchen to help her with the dishes. He had thought about texting some of his old friends but decided against it. The last time he came up he had gone out and it had been awkward. Not at first, when they came to the door to say hello to his parents, lingering for an appearance from his sister, and his dad had made them stop for a beer, but later, when they had exhausted all talk about football and what the other former scholars were up to. The conversation of the other three then was about the gym that they worked out in—they had all put on muscle—and girls. Tom wanted to entertain them by taking the piss out of Town, but they didn't ask about his life playing football, and Tom did not feel that it was his place to bring the subject up.

He dried up the plates that his mum washed. He heard his sister going upstairs. In the other room his dad was on the phone.

'You can go out, you know, if you want,' his mum said.

'No, it's fine. Don't worry.'

'OK. But we won't be put out if you change your mind.'

His dad came into the kitchen. 'Just been speaking to John. There's a guy off sick at the sorting office and he's picking up the shift tomorrow. Says you're welcome to his ticket if you want it.'

After *Football Focus* his dad drove them over to Uncle Kenny's. Jeanette made coffee and they stood around in the kitchen, Jeanette and Kenny wanting to know all about his life down south, how he was getting on at his digs, what it was like playing senior football. Jeanette gave him a third cuddle as they were about to leave. 'Oh, Tommy. My Tommy. You're a man, look at you,' she said, and Tom looked down at the polished floor, feeling every inch a child.

Most of the familiar old faces were in the pub, his dad and Kenny's crowd, though Tom was glad that none of their sons was there.

'You drinking, son?' Kenny asked him, turning from the bar. Tom looked instinctively at his dad.

'Yes, he's drinking. Not playing this weekend, is he?'

Kenny waited to be served and Tom stood back from the group at the bar alongside his dad, hoping that they would move over to a quieter area of the pub where he would not have to speak to his dad's friends and hear, in their questions and their joking, the unspoken pity behind their words at his failure to gain a contract.

'First match in a while, isn't it?' his dad said.

'Since last season.'

His dad nodded. 'Must feel a bit strange for you.' He nodded again. Tom did not say anything and they both turned to look at the television above the pool table. Outside, a small group of Arsenal fans was coming towards the pub, the bouncer smiling, shaking his head at them. Kenny was approaching from the bar. He had three pints of lager in a careful stranglehold.

'It's all right, lads, don't give me a hand or anything.' He smiled, offering Tom the first pint, and they moved away from the bar.

As soon as they left the pub, Tom felt the old excitement start to build. The routine of the walk to the ground automatically made his senses tingle with anticipation, heightening at each of the normally empty pubs now overflowing onto the pavements, the stalls crammed together on derelict scraps of land selling programmes and badges and sweets, the tide of people thickening down the road, horse shit, police wagons, car horns, the tops of the floodlights appearing and the noise of the growing crowd riding on the air, soaring over the city. Throughout all the years no aspect of it had ever changed. The prematch sausage roll from the tea bar. The queue to buy a programme, which he would take home afterwards to pore over in his room. He followed Kenny and his dad into the toilets for the customary piss at the packed urinal, before hurrying out, up the steps and through the gangway for the sublime moment of seeing the pitch, the crowd.

They made their way to their row. The team was being announced on the tannoy. There was the smell of pie fillings, Bovril, farts. Old men and women, families, were in the same positions they had sat in since Tom was little. All of this was deep inside him, ingrained yet altered now by the knowledge—shared by his dad, Kenny, all of the season-ticket holders they nodded past on the way to their seats—that Tom was not part of the club any more. He was not going to play for it. He sat down in John's seat. Kenny, beside him, held out a Yorkie bar for Tom to break off a block.

'We're very proud of you, Tom, you know, me and Jeanette,' he said. 'Very proud.' And he turned to the pitch, where the players were coming out of the tunnel to an escalation of noise. The Town players did not know what this was like. None of them would be able to handle it, Tom thought as he gave himself up to the mass of the crowd, becoming a part of it, the collective voice entering him, joining with the increased pumping of his heart and his lungs.

One of the scholars that Tom had played with was on the bench. Jamar Daley. At each break in play Tom glanced over at him among the substitutes. He had been given a one-year deal. Inevitably, he would play only a handful of games, mainly in the cups, probably go out on loan and be released at the end of his year, but still the unfairness of it kept pulling Tom's attention away from the game. Jamar had been good, a tidy midfielder, strong, competitive, but through all their academy years together he had never been as good as Tom. He was on five thousand a week now, according to one of the old scholars Tom had seen the last time he came up. If not for the couple of goals Jamar had scored in the FA Youth Cup semi-final he would probably not have got the attention, or the agent, that had followed, although it was Tom who had been given the man-of-the-match award for that game. Everything he had done that afternoon had come off. Every dribble, every through ball, every decision the right one because he had not hesitated or overthought any action, he had played purely on instinct—and it had been obvious, to the large crowd, to the agents waiting in the car park, his family, his teammates bouncing and shrieking in the dressing room, that he was the one, out of all of them, who was going to make it.

A quick throw-in caught the Arsenal left-back by surprise, and Kenny, Tom's dad, everyone around them, were all onto their feet as he slipped and handled the ball just inside the edge of the area. The referee straight away indicated a penalty and a contained bellow went around the stadium. Tom remained standing, his stomach knotting. Kenny was making a low guttural sound as the crowd became quiet, waiting.

The ball went underneath the goalkeeper's dive. All around Tom people were jumping about, doolally, released from themselves. Kenny was shaking his fist in the air. He turned to Tom and they put their arms around each other, bobbing up and down, fastened together, Kenny's nose pressing into his cheek—'Yes, Tommy! Yes! Yes! Yes!'

The rain eventually gave way to a cold, dry spell. Tom stood by his bedroom window and viewed through the night sky the glowing cigarette tips of the weekend's rearranged bonfires on the hills. He drove Bobby and Steven to the stadium the following afternoon to look with the other players over the wasteland of the pitch. They walked up and down, shaking their heads, imagining injury. There was an atmosphere of abandonment everywhere. Small heaps of rubbish had accumulated on the grass and the terracing. Mildew flowered across the plastic roof of the dugout. Inside the bowels of the main stand the air in the dressing rooms and tunnels hung with damp. When they came past the referee's room, a rat skittered across the floor just in front of Steven, who yelped and jumped back.

'You little fairy,' Boyn, following behind, shouted. 'Look at the little bloody fairy, pissing herself.' And he got down on his hands and knees to give chase to Steven, pretending, it only dawned on Tom when Boyn was some way down the tunnel and started sniffing at the concrete, to be a rat.

Tom sat in thermals then played for the last ten minutes of a heavy Tuesday-night defeat in Dagenham. The small flame of hope, ignited before the rain came, was put out by this loss to another relegation-threatened side—extinguished, if not by the first four goals, then by the fifth and the ensuing squabble between Daish and Gale as the teams left the pitch to the backdrop of 'Girl fight, girl fight, girl fight' from the rapturous home support.

They stopped for takeaways on the way back, and the air of the coach became thick with the rich cheesy stink of two-for-one pizzas. Tom ate his slices slowly, looking out of the window at the hurtling dark while Clarke proceeded up the aisle, stopping at each seat to say, softly, 'Cunt' to every player along the way.

The squad was ordered in on its day off. They gathered together outside the clubhouse and one or two players took shots at the crowd of seagulls that still loitered after the flood while they waited for Clarke to arrive. As soon as he appeared, grey and faintly unsteady, he made them start running.

The ground broke up like cake under their feet and a track began to blacken around the perimeter of the pitches. Two players collapsed and were removed to the clubhouse. Tom, however, had no difficulty coping and found himself wanting more, and for it to be harder. He stayed at the front of the group, forcing the pace—past the clubhouse, the fencing, the hulking sycamore, the grass-wet mower outside the open doorway of the ground-staff shed—as if by running hard he might distance himself from the anxious mood that had settled on him since the visit home. He shut it out, focusing solely on the satisfying action of his heart, his blood, his limbs.

When the squad limped in to shower and change, Tom jogged over to the reserve goalkeeper, Hoyle, and asked if he would be up for staying behind to practise a few crosses and catches. Hoyle wavered a moment but agreed. A few of the others, near the back of the group, turned to look and exchanged words. They probably thought he was trying to impress the manager, Tom realised, regardless of the fact that Clarke had already left to drive to his company premises.

They practised together for about twenty minutes, at which point Hoyle said that he was done.

'OK,' Tom said. 'I might stay out a bit longer, though. Do a few drills.'

Hoyle laughed. 'You're not in the Premier League now, mate.'

When Hoyle had left, Tom spaced out half a dozen cones along the right-hand side of a pitch where the grass was still fairly smooth and emptied a bag of balls by the cone farthest from the goal. He repeated a shuttle: dribbling around each cone until he reached the dead-ball line, looked up and swung a cross in, aiming every time for the same spot at the near post. He did this until all of the balls were gone, scattered over the neighbouring pitch, which he now saw that Liam was approaching. Liam stepped towards one of the balls and, when he reached it, booted it. Tom ran to apologise and collect them all up, but Liam jogged to kick another ball, then another, and as Tom got closer he could see that he was enjoying himself, firing each ball with deliberate aim towards the goal.

When all of the balls were returned, many of them into the net, Liam came over to where Tom stood watching at the side of the pitch. 'Don't want to try a few penalties against me, do you?' He was striding towards the goal before Tom even replied.

Tom struck his first attempt low towards one corner, but Liam was quickly down to stop it. The second he aimed for the same corner and this one went in, just, despite Liam sprawling to get a touch on it. Tom smiled to himself as he turned to get another ball. Liam was surprisingly agile, even in his heavy boots and canvas trousers. For five penalties Liam threw himself about, attempting to get one of the leathery palms of his groundskeeping gloves to the ball. He stopped three.

'You're good, you know,' Tom said when they had finished.

Liam was sweating. He wiped a long muddy smear over his forehead with the back of a glove. 'Too good for you lot.' He grinned and walked away. Tom watched him go, then collected the balls and the cones and returned to the clubhouse.

The other players, including Hoyle, had all left, so he took his time getting changed, enjoying the quiet echo of his studs on the floor and the still-steamy warmth of the shower room.

Afterwards, collecting his things, he began to feel a sluggishness descend through him, as if the strength was being sapped from his arms and legs. He sat down, staring ahead at the pool of shower water struggling around the drain. When he tried to get up, his kitbag was a lead weight. For some time he stayed there, watching the last of the water eddy and choke down the hole, before he forced himself to stand.

He went out onto the field. All he could hear was the noise of cars in the distance beyond the fencing and undergrowth. He started towards the breeze-block outbuilding at the far side of the pitches, trying to ignore the exposed, self-conscious sensation of walking across the expanse of reeking cut grass.

As he got closer he could see Liam through the doorway. He was pouring the last of one pot of white paint into another on top of a trestle table. He looked up in puzzlement and, Tom thought, amusement.

'What, more penalties?'

He looked down again to shake the last of the paint into the pot. Tom stood in the doorway. The roller shutters of the tractor entrance rattled momentarily beside him. He knew he should say something but he did not know what. Liam, however, did not seem perturbed by the interruption and carried on with his work. On the walls, among hanging rakes and shelves of canisters, paint, pallets, balls of string, there were old team posters and a dirty red-and-green scarf nailed to a ceiling joist. Somehow the sight of these things filled Tom with a distinct but unplaceable sadness. He watched as Liam pressed the lids onto the paint pots then took the empty one towards a dustbin by the door.

Liam was about to open the dustbin when Tom reached forward to clasp his arm. Liam shifted his eyes to him. Tom let his hand fall to his side and gazed down at the paint pot still in Liam's hand, his boots, at his own trainers, stained green. He was conscious of how fresh and clean he was, this close to Liam's work clothes. A dim thrum came from the road. He could not bring himself to look up. Liam moved away and Tom watched him step back to the table, hearing then the unbearable clunk of the paint pot being put down.

Tom turned to stare, for a long time, out of the doorway at the wide abandoned field. He heard Liam's boots on the concrete floor. Then he felt the warmth of his body behind him. A hand touched Tom's side, pressing, gradually, against it. Tom pulled himself away. He twisted to look directly at the large face and he was charged with a sudden glorious sense of risk as the man stood there, inspecting him.

'I have to go,' Tom said.

He made for the clubhouse, not deviating to avoid the patches of mud. Above the road noise, the baying of seagulls, was the sound of blood in his ears. His vision was constricting, the sky, the world around him, closing in until all he could see was the door of the clubhouse ahead.

GREGORY PARDLO's collection *Digest* (Four Way Books) won the 2015 Pulitzer Prize for Poetry. *Digest* was also shortlisted for the 2015 NAACP Image Award and was a finalist for the Hurston/Wright Legacy Award. His other honors include fellowships from the National Endowment for the Arts and the New York Foundation for the Arts; his first collection *Totem* was selected by Brenda Hillman for the APR/Honickman Prize in 2007. He is also the author of *Air Traffic*, a memoir in essays forthcoming from Knopf. Pardlo is a faculty member of the MFA program in creative writing at Rutgers University-Camden. He lives with his family in Brooklyn.

Marine Boy

GREGORY PARDLO

After signing the papers in the storefront recruiting office, to psyche myself up for Marine Corps boot camp, I drove half a mile north to the video store in a competing strip mall and rented *Apocalypse Now*. This was how I planned to overcome my fear of death, wading unflinchingly into the tropics on that screen in our den, big as a car windshield where the red, green, and blue lenses combined, like clown searchlights, from their reflection in the cabinet's mirrored lid.

Ahead of me were three months of basic training. It wasn't the exercise I was scared of; having been captain of my high school tennis team for two years, I was prepared, at least in body. No, boot camp was scary because until now I'd only ever pretended at self-destruction, experimenting with gothic and moody phases, but never actually placing my life at risk. The Cold War had ended and Desert Storm was two years off yet. *Full Metal Jacket* and *Hamburger Hill* would come out later that summer, recalling national sentiments that predated my birth. War was purely conceptual for me, the fact of my enlistment the only real cause I'd had for contemplating my mortality. In this, it seemed, the best approach would be through deliberate and careful screening and analysis.

Within two weeks of my arrival on Parris Island, Ollie, my father's mother, died. There was insurance money involved. But instead of investing it in something or someone, my father, recipient of that money, bought a boat. Now, the reason I joined the Marine Corps was to get money for college. So let's just say I was confused and dismayed to find there was a financial need my father felt was more pressing, and that this need amounted to nothing more than vanity or recreation. If only to guard against the hives with which I typically responded to emotional stress, I had to make up a story that I could believe in, one that could make sense of my father's actions. "He came into some family money," I began explaining to people. It was part of the legend I tailored for exhibition, regalia for the humblebrag I'd begin by describing my father's new cabin boat, which I'd only ever seen in a photograph from below, dry-docked on a lift. After long suppression, I could no longer guess the truth from the shape it made beneath the legend, although it occasionally breached my unconscious like a nosey dolphin, forcing me to admit, to my immediate embarrassment, that my father had been so undisciplined as to blow fifty grand on a dumbass boat. The deeper, more essential truth, which I avoided altogether, concealed unmapped regions of dread that the father I had so long idolized and I were becoming two very different people.

For what it's worth, these were generally unstable times, the tail end of "white flight" all across America, but especially pronounced in my town. An unfortunate shorthand, I know, "white flight," jumbling class and race by assuming all members of the escaping class were white, and that their egress was uniformly motivated by racial fears, but, give or take a few statistical outliers, largely appropriate. What remained of the pioneer homeowners in my town of Willingboro, New Jersey, was a smidgen of retirees with little or no stakes in the school system, and a good number of households either blinded to race by their own enlightenment or comfortably disinterested in the declining value of their property. Or both. In any event, the community fabric, its tribal memory dimming, was as rent as the knees of our acid-wash jeans.

It had morphed in subtle and disorienting ways, my Levitt-built hometown, classmates who once measured themselves by their parents' hourly *rates* having been body-snatched and replaced by others who took pride in their parents' hourly *wages,* while rumored bonuses yielded to "windfall overtime" and "holiday pay." The average skin tone deepened by several shades, though we still wore neon-colored Izod shirts with our collars turned up, our sockless feet chafing inside cheap, leather boat shoes. Many families just learning to put on airs were guilty of conspicuous errors, the driveways of their "Gramercy" or "Ardsley" model houses now sentineled by concrete lions or plastic flamingoes.

Some of us, more chameleonic than others, had refined our sense of striving, even if we had no real concept of precisely what it was we were striving *for*. I, for one, distressed by my folks' flatlining financial narrative, devised ingenious yarns like the boat legend to revise that narrative, the way natives seek to explain a volcano's silence or pagans read motive into the motions of stars. To mask our stagnation, I became a mythmaker, and told stories that might foreshadow brighter futures than our demographics suggested. Only this town that had served as a stepping-stone for so many families en route to tonier districts displacing the orchards and cornfields of South Jersey, this town was beginning to harden around me like a final destination. I wanted out. I also wanted to take the entire apparatus of my emotional environment along with me.

And so I created a legend to obscure how it was that my father, despite his stumbling, lurching efforts to recover after losing his job in the 1981 air traffic controllers' strike, came to afford the 24-foot Bayliner just out of its shrink-wrap. For the truth of his swift depletion of my grandmother's life insurance, unembellished, surely would have placed my father on a par with some lucky drunk at the racetrack. Describing him as having fully anticipated this inheritance, receiving it nonchalantly, suggested . . . something else, unseen abundance, the notion that there might be more where this came from. So, yes, then: inheritance. It was the most appealing gambit I could fashion.

Of course, with my father himself, I refused to acknowledge the boat, as if it were some floozy stepmom. His invitations to come aboard I read as backhanded, a welcome that would serve only to lend him my witness so that he could better enjoy the fun-house spectacle of his own consumption, rattling off maritime trivia he'd learned from the bullshit course he'd taken at the marina.

How he got the boat was to his mind none of my business. I only got the news anecdotally, long after the money had been committed, when I returned home in October 1987, after my three summer months of boot camp in South Carolina and another six weeks of field communications training at Camp Pendleton, California. It wouldn't have been enough money to get me through college anyway. If it *had* been, and if, by some freak celestial alignment, 1) I had not gone off to boot camp that June after dropping out of college in a self-destructive funk; and 2) my father had not thought of using the money to repair his ego, still smarting from the strike's failure, and reward himself for having weathered, family and home intact, the intervening years of material deprivation—then I would have blown that shit anyway. Especially before boot camp. Because the kid I was before boot camp? I wouldn't throw peanuts at that kid.

As he frequently announced, my dad had long since fulfilled his obligation to the universe when one evening the previous June, under the lights in Carl Lewis Stadium, I moved the tassel on my mortarboard from one side to the other. Not so long after that, with the forbearance of one retiring from a job he'd always felt beneath him, he set me, my duffel bag, my guitar, and a secondhand cube fridge on the curb outside Quad 4 on the Rutgers-Livingston campus, and promptly drove away. At that point, as far as my father was concerned, he'd crossed the finish line. Imagine his surprise, then, when just a few short months later, he discovered me back home, as if waiting for him to dream up our next adventure: I had bailed on my second semester at Rutgers to save everyone the embarrassment of trying to pull it out of the fire.

It must have been late May because, even though I was not officially living at home, my dad and I had just opened the pool. Sean, a friend who'd graduated from Willingboro High with me in 1986, was back home, I remember. Seemingly minutes after commencement ended, Sean had left for Parris Island just as he had always planned to. Now, a year later, he was home from Twentynine Palms to serve on recruiting duty. For this he needed bodies to fill the seats at the Marine Corps recruiting office in the strip mall at the intersection of Route 130 and Beverly Rancocas Road. So Sean gathered up the chronically unemployed and a number of us who'd lasted little more than a semester in college, gathered us the way a preacher gathers winos and homeless people, with the promise of coffee and shelter in exchange for their mere presence in the pews.

In high school I'd cultivated a pampered bad-boy persona—or tried to anyway; scared of fashionable pharmaceuticals, I was but a stoner wannabe. I ran for class president and lost, courting a constituency that I discovered, for all their huzzahs and high fives, wouldn't actually vote. I'd joined half a dozen clubs just to be around the girls they attracted and was cool with a variety of crowds without being particularly popular in any of them. I played guitar. I played tennis. I sang in the choir. I ran track. I drank with those who drank in the woods behind the school during free period, but then I parked alongside the AP kids, and stood on the hood of my car proclaiming, "To thine own self be true!" without any idea whom or what I was quoting. Go ahead, cringe. Exceptional, I said. A piece of work, said others. I was a floater on the surface of life, hesitant even to place an oar in the water. And so, with mock courage, I cast my tube in wherever the current was swift enough to catch my eye.

Now Sean reappeared in my life as something more than another category or clique—something glinting and unique. He'd always wanted to be a drill instructor, Sean. While I didn't exactly admire this ambition, I was attracted to its intensity (that attraction, yet another symptom of the manic depression I thought was merely a byproduct of my devotion to Jimi Hendrix, but which I would many years later begin to puzzle out by connecting the genetic dots—great-grandfather, grandfather, mother, aunt, brother—of family members similarly afflicted). Sean's closest friend, Nate, had a hard-on for the Air Force, so I had always lumped the two boys together as sharing more or less the same ambitions. They strode the halls of 'Boro High, Sean and Nate, wearing their "Aim High" or "Swift, Silent, Deadly" T-shirts with equal pride. To some, they might have made an incongruous pair, considering the vast differ-ence in mission and ethos between these two branches of the armed services, but at least back then, they gave me the impression of differing chiefly in their choice of fashion. Military was military, if you asked me. But then, I couldn't have told you the Marine Corps from the Drum and Bugle Corps.

When I asked who it was calling downstairs on the phone, Bob, my mother's father, said he didn't know; he hadn't asked. My mother must have given out the number. "'Sup, Sean," I said a moment later, smiling into the receiver, and then cupping the mouthpiece while waiting for Bob to leave the room.

The tale of woe I'd begun telling myself was that my father had kicked me out of the house when I dropped out of college, and this was why I was practically homeless. Broke and staying in one of the upstairs rooms, a dusty, unused part of my grandfather's house across town from my parents', I looked forward to even the smallest plot developments in life that might break the monotony of my days. I imagined Sean must be home for some kind of military spring break, and hoped there was an invitation to hang forthcoming.

Sean said he'd heard I left school, and was hoping to catch up with me. Also he needed a few bodies to fill some seats. He said he had promised his "boss"—as if he worked at a car dealership—he could produce just that: a few bodies a week in exchange for this recruiting assignment allowing him to come home for a month. Otherwise they would ship him right back to the Mojave Desert.

"For real, dude?" I said. "Damn, but . . . Fuck *that* shit."

"Twenty minutes, OK? That's all I ask. I can come over and pick you up, huh?"

Couldn't leave my boy hanging.

The Marine Corps recruiter Sean was assigned to, a squat master sergeant, seemed laughable in his little blue uniform, walking around the office all tight and jerky like he was constipated or something.

"Sean tells me you're only home for a few weeks to regroup," he said, punctuating each phrase with a jut of his chin or an inverted nod. "I can sympathize, you know. It's tough. You're probably the first in your family to go to college, am I right? We usually don't have people at home to help us figure everything out—am I right?"

Every question was rhetorical, broadcasting its intended response, even when that response was in fact far from self-evident to me. "Last *I* checked college wasn't free," he continued. "*Somebody's* gonna have to pay for it. Might as well be the government, ooh-rah."

I winced at the hayseed contraction: *gub'ment.* The "ooh-rah," too, was odd. He dropped it into his speech like "Amen" or "praise God." He wasn't from the Northeast, I could tell, but he didn't seem to be from the Motherland either, that abstract and boundless place below the Mason-Dixon Line where, I believed, ancient peoples still walked the red earth barefoot. If not the South, then somewhere in the Midwest maybe? Which was about as mysterious to me as Canadian football.

The presentation was canned, I knew, but I nodded along anyway, feeling compelled to play my part, letting my mind wander as I was used to doing in school. There was a barnyard in my head, and I would unhook the rickety gate, let it swing open, and watch the animals waddle and trot out onto the open prairie. What must this man be like at home, I wondered, without the uniform and persona? Did he have children? And, if so, was he impatient and unforgiving with them while at work he pretended to be supportive and empathetic, offering absolution to any eighteen-year-old college dropout who walked through the door?

I was there to fill the seat, of course—just a body making itself useful by staring vacantly at a man in a uniform. I didn't have to agree or disagree or get caught up in any of the images he was busily conjuring. What I was or wanted didn't matter, I just had to keep blank until he let me go, even as strands of "Ride of the Valkyries" had begun to whisper through my head. By the end of his spiel— which turned out to be somewhat longer than twenty minutes—I had a handful of flyers and pamphlets and what I fully expected to be Sean's eternal gratitude.

Despite having been mercilessly turned out of my childhood home—"victim," in my own self-conception, fast replacing "rebel"—I still had keys to the front door, and felt like swimming. So Sean drove me, in that Ford Taurus with its government plates, to my parents' house on Tinker Place, where I tossed all the pamphlets on the glass-topped dining room table, forgetting about them even as they left my hand, and then shimmied through the sliding door, making sure not to let the dog out. I snaked out of my T-shirt and kicked off my sneakers before seal-diving into the pool in my khaki shorts.

All the stuff of my life—my practice amp, my tapes, my notebooks—all of that was now at Bob's. Everything but the cube fridge. Bob, my mother's bachelor father, had given me a folding cot (he wasn't prepared for boarders) in the room overlooking the garage, which I set up by the window so I could indulge in the cigarette habit I'd cultivated at Rutgers. This was on Bolton Lane, one of two streets cut off from the rest of Buckingham Park by the four lanes and tree-lined median of Van Sciver Parkway, wedged in behind the Rancocas Hospital—the hospital where my brother, Robbie, had been born and where I had been laid up for two weeks with tubes up my nose after an asthma attack in fourth grade, the one time in childhood I could remember my father saying he loved me. Bob's house, a Cape Cod he'd taken over from my Aunt Donna after her divorce, had been in the family almost as long as Tinker Place. Either address might appear under my name on a job application or an emergency contact form, and I had keys to both, a fact that did not prevent me from believing myself homeless.

Another friend had connected me with a temp agency, but whether out of boredom or depression I had a habit of just . . . walking off of jobs. More than once, I'd stood in line in the parking lot of some warehouse or tool-and-die shop to get a Saran-Wrapped tuna fish sandwich, only to find myself overcome by a mild terror when I saw the workaday world rippling in the diamond-patterned, stainless steel siding of the truck. Even today, the sight of a lunch truck kicks my pulse up a notch. Without connecting my sudden depression to the pixelated reflection of my face, I'd find myself taking refuge in the bucket seat of the rusty Chevette Bob had loaned me, jabbing pre-sets on the dash radio before reaching to light the roach that was either in the ashtray or beneath the foil lining of my cigarette pack, and erase the thought of work altogether before driving back to Bob's, one more awful job successfully ditched.

In the wake of the air traffic controllers' strike, I had convinced myself of the nobility of the labor class. I still believe in that nobility— far more romantically, in fact, than I might had I ever actually aspired to it. Maybe my father's experience in the strike broke my faith in the power of solidarity, broke my faith in the ability of unions to secure a stable domestic life, ruining me for that which I had so ennobled. Or maybe the snobbery I inherited from my mother had simply hardened into a shell of denial, shielding me from my own grim reality.

After my meeting with the Marine Corps recruiter, I hadn't much felt like going back to Bob's, back to my cot and the vale of cigarette ashes I was accumulating on the windowsill beside it. My parents' house was, at least, clean; and the refrigerator, reliably full. These small comforts were worth the risk of a run-in with my father.

See, whenever my father found me in his house, the look on his face, some combination of smug and regretfully judgmental, said *Lay down your king. Game over.* Being caught there with my head in the fridge only gave him additional grounds for the sort of chest-thumping displays he seemed to find so grimly satisfying. Thankfully, not having seen my dad's car in the driveway when Sean wheeled the Taurus onto Tinker Place, I was free to make myself at home. So to speak.

Despite my asthma and a developing taste for Marlboro Lights, my lungs were strong. I could drag myself through nearly three laps underwater before my chest felt like bursting. (Granted, the pool was only, like, twenty yards long; still.) My lung strength had perhaps been enhanced by a game I always played as a kid where I wadded sticks of Juicy Fruit in my mouth and sat at the bottom of the deep end, imagining I was no longer oxygen-dependent. *Marine Boy,* the anime cartoon, held me in such thrall as a kid that

I was willing to risk committing my terrestrial form to the deep in order to glimpse the amphibian divinity nestled in my brain stem. The "oxy-gum" invented by Professor Fumble allowed Marine Boy to patrol the depths, keeping the ocean safe, alongside his friend Splasher, the dolphin. Me, I just wanted to hide. In a minor escape, I liked to sit underwater with my back against the side of the pool closest to the patio door, so that anyone happening to look out from the kitchen just then might expand that eyeblink in their mind to fit a presumption that no one was in the yard *or* in the pool. Thus camouflaged, I was but a feature of the water, a trick of shadow and refraction if anyone registered a presence at all. A ghost. It was from these frontiers of Atlantis in an oxygen-deprived illusion that I veered off the gentle cobbles of my make-believe Bimini Road to reconvene with the air and my surface-mates, the water strider and the thirsty dragonfly.

He must have been standing over my subsurface perch boring a hole into the top of my head with his laser vision, and coming up, I inadvertently placed my hand on my father's foot as he waited, impatient for me to join him at the shores of his world.

Crouched on the balls of his feet, he was clutching the Marine Corps pamphlets. "This supposed to be some kind of joke," he grunted as he shook the fist of literature in my face like a rolled-up newspaper. Squatting only made his bulk that much more formidable, his broad shape blocking the sun.

"What?" I said, in a lame bid for time, for of course I knew just what he was talking about.

His strategy with me of late was to insist that I find regular, "gainful" employment. Just a few weeks ago it had become an outright ultimatum: If I didn't find a full-time job, he wouldn't allow me in his house at all. He'd given me some unrealistic deadline at the time—a week, perhaps—which I made a point of ignoring. Still, it took up a great deal of my energy not thinking about the ultimatum. Had I left the pamphlets on the table to provoke him? Given the balance of passivity and aggression in evidence, I can't rule out the possibility.

He didn't have to know I had so far only agreed to *consider* the Marine *Reserves,* and not a *full-time* enlistment anyway. Sgt. Ooh-Rah had repeated "one weekend a month" so many times it had taken residence in my mind with all the logic of a public television pledge drive, fitting right into the rhetorical space of "just ten cents a day." *That's nothing,* I heard a distant voice in my head exclaim. Surely I could spare a few cents a day for my country. The pamphlets agreed: One weekend a month was nothing. A reservist would have to serve two weeks each summer, too, of course, but that was mentioned so seldom it hardly even factored.

My father was afraid for me, I knew; just as he knew that if he expressed any form of disapproval, I might exploit his concern as a weakness. I had left him with but one move to play: the put-down.

"You wouldn't last two weeks in the Marine Corps."

It was *absolutely imperative* that I leave for boot camp in June, the Marine Corps recruiter told me. Otherwise, I would not be able to join the field communications training program, starting in September, which he said was the best job my middling ASVAB scores qualified me for. It didn't occur to me to ask to see my scores on this military placement test, and the fact I took it on his word alone that I was a dumbass, more than my allegedly poor scores, is what surely confirmed that I *was* one. Still, I was reluctant; starting in June would mean being in South Carolina through the three hottest months of the year—though it was the sand fleas, he said, not the heat, that would be the toughest part of boot camp. Perhaps because of this deft distraction from the physical and emotional hardships of training, which he accomplished with chitchat about bugs and weather, I soon enough found myself stepping in the yellow footprints painted on the roadside, outside the main doors of the Marine Corps Recruit Depot on Parris Island, South Carolina.

I lasted exactly two weeks before declaring I'd had enough. We were waiting to be issued rifles in the great hall of the armory that day, my platoon, 2069, along with five others. Roughly 480 of us stood rank and file, still redolent of the civilian malaise we were in the process of shedding. Someone's better-informed sibling or cousin could have sent word of the impending tonal shift, for Christ's sake. That information should have been filtering through our ranks like so much truth-telling samizdat. Yet, somehow not *one* of us seemed to have had any warning that on this day, the two-week mark . . . shit was *about. to get. real.* How could we have been so blindsided?

The first two weeks, it seemed, were just the adjustment period. How many studies or focus groups had the Marine Corps psychologists conducted to determine that this was the minimum time necessary for recruits to be acclimated just so? Far enough removed from home that we could be trusted not to revolt at the dawning awareness that our innocence had been swept away, unceremoniously, like the piles of hair shorn from our now gleaming skulls; trusted not to revolt at the certainty that we might never again place ourselves fully in our parents' emotional care. How, for that matter, had those Marine Corps shrinks decided that, two weeks in, we could be entrusted with firearms? How many gruesome tragedies must have occurred before that maturation period had been established? By now we were expected to have memorized the Lord's Prayer, which would come in awfully handy as we began receiving a kind of activity-based time-out, whereby, instead of being sent to sit at the bottom of the stairs or on a stool in the kitchen, we would be sent "digging," which included an especially punishing exercise routine.

Wherever we were on the island, I noticed, there was a sandbox or patch of dirt bared in the grass nearby, which dirt patches were innocently paired with a pull-up bar. You rarely saw one without the other. During that original two-week honeymoon phase, the domination we suffered had been mostly mental; I did not yet understand that these pseudo-playgrounds would frame the most lively and relentless disciplinary actions. Who knew, maybe they were historical fixtures predating modern gym equipment, evidence of some preservationist vogue? How quaintly antique, this old military installation, I thought, with its wood-frame barracks and coercive Christianity!

Digging consisted of a series of exercises performed in rapid succession to the barking rhythm of the drill instructors' whim. "Sit-ups now!" Shouting instructions as if from the deck of a storm-twisted ship, they'd direct this tormented pantomime with a crazed sort of urgency. "Push-ups now!" Whereupon the private would immediately exchange positions so as to execute this pressing new command. "Leg lifts now!" Another flip. "Toe touches now!" All of it delivered with increasing speed—a sadistic sort of "Simon Says." Only after a sufficient amount of dirt had caked his sweat-soaked face and cammies would the offending private be released.

As I say, no one in our platoon had yet experienced this form of punishment, though we'd been doing the exercises together, as a group, and at a pace mild enough to be sufferable even by someone as circumspect as myself. And so, given that all six platoons of men who arrived on the island at the same time were present in the armory that day, I believe I must have been the very first member of that entire company to be called out for demonstration.

We had just been issued our rifles, were still clutching the paperwork registering each serial number, as one of the island's innumerable flies bedeviling the space above our collective harassed my ears like a little air raid siren. The way we were instructed to stand, with our M16-A2 rifles held diagonally across our chests, my rifle's sight post near the end of the barrel was conveniently close to my face. Conveniently close to my left eye, where the dizzy insect seemed determined to lounge in the musk of my brow. Surreptitiously—not a popular word in the Marine Corps—I dipped the sight post toward the spot on my face just then bristling with the phantom itch of fly wings.

A word of advice: When Marine Corps drill instructors tell you to stand in formation, they don't mean stand there and chill for a bit; they expect you to stand *stock* still, like the Marines outside the White House or Air Force One—hell, like that guy covered in silver paint in Times Square who pretends to be made of aluminum.

Just then I heard my name as if it were a cheer—as if someone on the sidelines were cheering me on to a goal, like, "Go, Pardlo!" Or, "Yay, Pardlo!"

Suddenly, drill instructors were ringing me like white blood cells rushing a foreign body, commandeering my total attention as, mysteriously, the armory roof, without my ever noticing, was replaced by a pastel sky, the human-filled armory standing behind me now fully a hundred feet away; there might as well have been stagehands scurrying around us to effect this shift of scenery; it seemed we hadn't even moved. Now, though, the drill instructors overturned that calm, shiftless Southern heat like a crate of oranges, their words drumming all over my skull, their thundering, elaborate ad hominem assessments of my masculinity, my parentage. Inches from my face. At the back of my head. Chests bumped my shoulders. Seen at a distance, if you turned the sound off, I could have been a prince being fussed over by a retinue of tailors, one of whom had just relieved me of my weapon. But this was a very different sort of attention indeed.

Please, I thought, as they ordered me into the dirt, and my mind ratcheted like an old train station schedule board. I was afraid of the dirt. And it was—did I mention?—insanely fucking *hot* out.

At this point I undertook a very quick blame assessment. It was my father's fault, all of this. Right? Done. That was easy. What a huge, unnecessary production this had all become. What a misunderstanding. We could still fix this, couldn't we? They wanted me to say uncle? All right, then, fuck it: *Uncle*. I crumpled up the weapons requisition form, like I was drying my hands with it, and dropped it right on the ground, the kind of littering I would not ordinarily do. "Listen," I said as I put my hands up, "this is all a big misunderstanding, you know? I should be home smoking a joint, sitting on my diving board. I mean, you guys, you all take this very, very seriously. And I respect that, right? Just . . . It's not for me."

Respect was a word I'd learned listening to reggae and ska. Pronounced properly [REE-spect], it could have salvific effects. Naturally, I thought, as a final word of parting, it would clear things up. That we would all just shake hands and, like, "Peace Out."

Only now, my tormentors' barking took on a stereophonic depth, as if they were multiplying. When I realized they had no concern for decorum or appearances—OK, now I was getting embarrassed for *them*—I realized as well that they wouldn't tire easily. Nor could I out-pout them. Panicking, I wept. And continued weeping until my weeping was . . . existential. Now *I* didn't give a shit what anybody thought. No pretense, no masks left to shed. No gambits or distractions.

At some point, I relented, seeing as they were going to do no such thing. We were now standing on the edge of the pit. Dutifully, I climbed down into that dirt with all the showy indignation of a church matron, a vain attempt at dignity in the face of its opposite. Now I did *push-ups now* in front of the entire company. I did *sit-ups now* and knew: They were making an example of me. That's what they were doing—*Leg lifts now!*—trained to handle the likes of me. *Squat thrusts now!* They did not take me to be unique, exceptional. *Jumping jacks now!* They'd seen me coming a mile away, clearly—*Sit-ups now!*—and were not impressed. Damn, I thought. *Mountain climbers now!* My uniform is dirty as *fuck*.

There was talk of incarceration. Court-martial even. In hindsight, I see all of that must have been part of the drill, too, the staging of terror and discipline. Nor was this an empty threat. They could have been preparing to set me up with a blindfold and cigarette against a pocked cement wall just around the corner, for all I knew. I was toast, had committed suicide by military-industrial complex. And so, surrendering all sense of reasoning, all sense of subjectivity, I made myself a thing. It was almost a relief, except for the fact that they wouldn't allow me to sit. For what seemed like hours, I stood beside a picnic table outside the armory, looking like I had been run over by a truck, as I watched the others file past, freshly shorn and pressed, each with a greased black M16-A2, haughty as Egyptian gods marching in some perfectly stylized frieze.

For the next two days, while, I could only presume, the brass decided what to do with me, I was made to tag along with my platoon in a sort of limbo, following behind the formation like a POW. For hours I was made to stand off to the side while my former platoon-mates engaged in grueling training exercises on the parade deck, drilling, learning to march in formation (*Eyes right!*), which is just what we (they) were doing the day someone shouted for me from across the blacktop. I was told to follow this marine and report to my senior drill instructor's office. By this point, any resolution would be blessed relief, anything that would provide some category with which to identify. "Deceased" would have worked.

For twenty minutes, I had been standing there, alone, at attention, when he arrived. He seemed almost apologetic, the senior drill instructor, when he entered the room and installed himself behind his desk, a civility of which I was immediately suspicious. That he was African American made no impression on me; I had so little understanding of U.S. military history. Between him and the recruiting officer, I had begun to suspect the Marine Corps, the "first to fight" in a field of battle, and thus most disposable, had been especially established for black soldiers.

My grandmother had passed away, he told me. It took me a beat before I could translate his accent. Tinny with a bit of banjo. "Technically," he said, "because she's not an immediate family member, you won't be given leave to attend the funeral."

Given leave? That would suggest I had some official status to be given leave *from*.

"But you do have permission to call home," he sighed as he pushed a few coins across his desk and pointed me toward a pay phone at the bottom of the stairs.

"Thank you," I managed through my unsteady face, unsure what to feel; it was the first death in the family I'd been old enough to grieve.

"Don't thank me," Sgt. Brown said. "Never thank me."

Growing out of eighteenth-century maritime culture, with an honor code and caste system so austere as to account for horrors like human trafficking, summary capital punishment, and cannibalism, the Marine Corps can't afford to let interpersonal debts of gratitude impede the brute imperatives of rank. To thank Sgt. Brown, even *I* quickly saw, was to substitute the authority given to him by the chain of command with the unreliably coercive force of kindness, exchanging my obedience for common courtesy. No. Marines don't do favors. Still, no system is impartial, and I believe the man felt sorry for me. Maybe it wasn't personal. But I like to think he was expressing some more-than-bureaucratic concern. Whatever the case, I later chose to reimagine this gesture as kindness, and this kindness as paternal.

We have few rituals of passage in American culture. No secular age of accountability that hasn't been arbitrarily decided by our judicial system. No vision quests. But those first two weeks were enough to shift something fundamental in me. I'd like to avoid any metaphor that might suggest some sort of cleansing occurred; no, my soul was not cleansed. But after the full three months of Marine Corps boot camp, I was able to recognize the difference between me and whatever besmirched thing it was that I'd made of the quilted face on the lunch truck.

In the days that followed my grandmother's passing, I was sent back to the armory without discussion to re-requisition my weapon. For the remainder of boot camp, I would be given no assignments that showed me to be in the drill instructors' esteem or confidence. I was placed in no leadership roles. But I enjoyed, at least, the head-shaking deference of my peers, everyone having witnessed that rash leap into the abyss, and then my emergence therefrom, goopy and disoriented, like a newborn calf. Thus I had become my own spirit animal. And now I threw myself at all sorts of challenges, to test my strength and ring the carnival bell of redemption. No longer did I consider digging a punishment, but rather, like some arms demonstration in the middle of the Arizona desert, an exercise in controlled fear.

Once, Sgt. Brown called me out for something incidental I no longer even remember, something small enough it gave me the sense he might have been waiting for this opportunity. Our platoon just then was camped in a forested area alongside a decommissioned airstrip. Rather than send me to the dirt, Brown ordered me into the brambles. And like Br'er Rabbit, I dove right in, shouting my assent as welts rose up on my bare forearms, histamine flooding the thorns' countless abrasions. Many years later, reading Frederick Douglass's account of his fight with Covey, the slave-breaker, I recalled my contest with Brown. The earlier incident at the armory, but a prelude to this, to my mind was not nearly so pivotal. For here I stood, in the face of resistance, and my fear of it, and managed to see my way through. The difference between my experience and Douglass's, discounting the obvious, is that I was grateful to my master for staging this ritual do-over in which I might properly mourn my carefree-if-not-overprotected childhood, setting it adrift on a swift current of nostalgia.

I was only dug once or twice more after that. But, then, there was no need for it. I knew by now what was expected of me, and my bearing made it clear I considered the bargain perfectly reasonable. I was like the Ship of Theseus, replaced entirely with new parts, one random piece at a time.

Just six months had passed, when I graduated boot camp, since leaving Rutgers. Two more years would pass before I'd return to college, and ten years total, full of however many false starts and second thoughts, before I finally completed my undergraduate degree. The little bit of Nietzsche I'd read, in addition to the VHS rentals before boot camp, made me just ignorant enough to briefly think I might not need college after all. I could move through the world freely enough, I decided. Not with privilege, mind you . . . and not with any particular power to *remove* obstructions. But I could imagine what lay beyond them, and that long sight diminished my fear of the everyday ripples that might once have grown into levee-breaching swells. I imagined myself a phantom that has no need to decimate brick walls, for he can teleport right through them. I had become untouchable, you see, without seeing any downside—the emotional distance, the distaste for intimacy—of considering myself immaterial, a different kind of thing.

Need I point out that I didn't really believe I had super powers? Or perhaps I *did,* in a way. But I also believed that with every super power must come a fatal flaw. I knew what happens to Greek heroes who start thinking they've got it made. So I was reluctant to use whatever powers I had, unsure of how they even worked, and afraid of unforeseen consequences. What I didn't count on was that I could, even now, continue to be my own greatest foe.

I want to go back, like some time-travelling dolphin, and warn that young man—my eighteen-year-old self, the new Marine whose father had rented a Winnebago and driven the family from New Jersey to South Carolina to bear the prodigal home—of just how much he'll *need* his powers, and not for the open sea ahead, either, so much as for all the demons lurking in the unconscious fathoms below.

EMILY RABOTEAU is the author of a novel, *The Professor's Daughter*, and *Searching for Zion: The Quest for Home in the African Diaspora*, finalist for the Hurston/Wright Award in nonfiction and winner of a 2014 American Book Award. She teaches creative writing at the City College of New York in Harlem. Her next book, *Endurance*, is about the intersecting lives and problems of the residents in a gentrifying upper Manhattan apartment building as told through the eyes of the building's live-in superintendent.

The Curse

EMILY RABOTEAU

1

Is there anyone more maligned in popular culture than the mother-in-law? When I married, I became daughter-in-law to a woman from Uganda named D LaValle, whom I had previously called Auntie by her request, and was now supposed to call Mom. I wasn't sure how I felt about this, not only because I referred to my own mother that way, but also because now that we were family, we'd bypassed the familiarity of D's first name, which I found beautiful but had never been invited to say. Her first name nearly rhymes with mine. Three syllables, accent on the first. Neither did our names' similarity nor dissimilarity escape me. When she was a domestic she asked the white people whose homes she cleaned to call her Dilly. She felt it would be simpler for them to pronounce. Her maiden name was Kanyike. From my point of view, D's name was exotic while mine was commonplace. I wanted devotedly to know her, not merely as my husband's mother, but as a person.

I studied her. Like all children of all mothers, my husband was too biased to see her objectively. I had more distance and so, I believed, less prejudice. He'd told me plenty of stories about the woman but I mistrusted them all. They tended to make him look heroic for having survived his childhood and her look pathological for dragging him through it. The grisliest of these tales has my husband, at age three, seated in his mother's lap on the ledge of a window in one of the Midtown high-rise buildings whose offices she cleaned through an agency at night.

D has threatened to jump with my husband in her arms. Concerned onlookers yell at her not to do it from the sidewalk below. She hesitates long enough for the police to arrive, force their way into the office, and coax her down from the ledge. My husband, whose childish view of his mother cannot yet process her as menacing, tries to defend her against harm by rushing toward the cops and biting one of them on the leg. He's barely taller than the man's knee. D winds up at Creedmoor Psychiatric Center in Queens for a couple of years. During that interim my husband lands in the care of a grandaunt in Trinidad because his estranged white father has refused to raise him—a half-black child.

Heartbreaking material, but none of it considers what might have prompted D to the edge. The fatigue of motherhood has made me rethink that entire story from Mom's point of view. The crushing responsibility, the frustrated potential, the wasted intelligence, the frayed nerves, the unsexed body, and worst of all, the invisibility. When did she realize she now ranked as a nonperson? How many hours was Mom working for how little pay? How narrow were her opportunities as an immigrant from East Africa? How much childcare could she afford as a single mother? What kind of help did she have? How much sleep was she getting? How far was this reality from the life she'd dreamed for herself?

My husband wasn't wrong to describe her as paranoid, reclusive, fretful, self-loathing, and touchy, but there were all these other admirable qualities he couldn't see. For example:

- She cared deeply about the poor. In election year 2008 she stumped door to door for Dennis Kucinich out of ardent enthusiasm for his progressive politics. Until it was taken off the air in 2013, she listened religiously to the left-leaning talk radio station WWRL whose host, Ed Schultz, perfectly articulated her liberal views.
- Sidney Poitier and Harry Belafonte were her role models when she was young because they were activists as well as black superstars.
- She was no pushover. She had a habit of suing unlicensed contractors in small claims court for trying to screw her over with shoddy home repairs, such as uneven aluminum siding. She won these cases without fail.
- She was proud. She once painted the hands and face of a Christmas tree ornament brown to convey that angels shouldn't by default be rendered white.
- Most delightful of all, she could perform Johann Strauss's "Blue Danube" from memory on piano, and when she played, her face lit up from within from the flame of the waltz.

I collected these merits as evidence in her defense. "And just look at *you,*" I often told my husband, appealing to his ego as Exhibit A. "Your mother must have done something right." It would be fair to say that I loved her, and not only because I loved him.

2

After I bore her first grandchild Mom expressed relief that he was healthy, satisfaction that he was a boy, and displeasure with what we had named him. The first evening we spent alone together outside my husband's company, the baby (Geronimo) was ten days old, I was almost thirty-four, and my mother-in-law was thirty-four years older than I. Thunderstruck by exhaustion, I felt as vulnerable as a shelled egg. Nobody had warned me that every two hours the baby would need to eat, or if they had, I hadn't understood the toll it would take. My body was a wreck. My mind was bankrupt. My husband was as helpful as he could be without a pair of lactating breasts but now he had to abandon me to honor a prior commitment he couldn't refuse. He expressed reluctance about leaving me alone with the baby and questioned my choice of his mother as alternative company. Nonetheless, I persuaded him to invite her. Mom arrived at our apartment in Upper Manhattan with one of her African movies in her hands.

"Put the movie on and go," I encouraged my husband. "We'll be fine." I hoped this might be our moment, hers and mine. With my husband out of the picture, I would come to some crucial understanding about my mother-in-law that would finally allow me to call her Mom with ease.

Now, Mom's library of bootleg Nollywood films was prodigious. They had titles like *Man of Sin, Moment of Betrayal,* and *Possessed Lover 2.* She'd been entreating us to watch one of these with her for the four years my husband and I were together, as evidence that Africans were civilized as much as for our entertainment. I was game. Her son was not. Among other things, he resented her for suggesting that the titles of these films were cleverer than those of the novels he'd published. She'd read none of his books though they were proudly displayed on a shelf to the left of the TV. It embarrassed him that these were the only books in the house. When we visited her home in Rosedale, Queens, a stone's throw from JFK Airport, we usually agreed to watch true crime or home improvement shows instead of D's Nigerian movies, even as we disagreed about the volume at which to set the TV. She preferred it outstandingly high, as she did the heat in winter and the air conditioning in summer.

The 48-inch flat screen was the centerpiece of her living room and a point of pride. It stood in a wall unit surrounded by family photos and bibelots, such as an ostrich egg from Cape Town and a plaque engraved with the Serenity Prayer. The TV was on constantly. Dinner (Shake 'n Bake chicken or oxtail stew) was eaten before it on TV trays that might have been folded up and put away, but were used instead as furniture. On Mom's living room tray sat the remote controls, a shaker of salt substitute, a little jar of toothpicks, scratch-off lotto tickets, and a timer set to remind her when to take her blood pressure meds. Her drink was Diet Pepsi mixed with sherry over heaps of ice. My husband worried about her liver. At Christmastime there were Indian sweets from Jackson Heights that reminded her of her girlhood in Uganda before the expulsion of the South Asian merchant class by dictator Idi Amin. Plastic sheeting protected the wall-to-wall carpet from spills. Conversation was difficult.

The African touches in Mom's house interested me as prisms into her past. Over the light switch near her front door, which was bolted by seven or eight locks, hung a picture of the latest *kabaka,* king of the Buganda Kingdom. The kitchen clock was in the jigsaw-puzzle shape of Uganda itself, as established by the British Empire that ruled the nation as a protectorate from 1894 until its independence in 1962, when Mom would have been fifteen years old. A brightly patterned, woven-grass floor mat was rolled up and stashed behind the upright piano, growing mold. Exhibited atop the wall unit stood an eighteen-inch black collectible doll dressed in a marvelous red *busuuti* with a square neckline, puffed sleeves, and an orange sash, much like the dress Mom wore to our wedding. In its display box, this doll reminded me of Snow White in her glass coffin, waiting to be reanimated by some fated form of affection.

The reason Mom wanted us to watch one of her movies so badly was that she assumed her son and I held some backwards Tarzan image of Africa. She was given to saying accusatory, if legitimate, things like, "Most Americans believe we go around with bones in our noses." She only meant to make us see her more clearly, but recriminations like these pointed to the distance between us. Though she was a longtime citizen, we were the Americans in this equation. She was not. Who was she, then, our Mom?

3

My husband set up the DVD in the player for us, kissed me apologetically, and was gone. For now, the baby napped facedown on a sheepskin rug on the floor. The lights were dim. Mom and I sat next to each other somewhat bashfully on the love seat—her in her very best 1960s flip-hairstyle wig to cover the thin, gray cornrows beneath; me with cabbage leaves on my breasts to relieve nipples cracked from the violence of nursing. It hurt to sit. I wore a diaper to catch the uterine elements still sliding out of me. Encircling my slack waistline was a donut-shaped pillow to support the baby while he fed. In my hand was a tube of lanolin that I applied to my scabrous nipples after he finished. I was too drained to be respectable. She was too formal to be overtly critical or particularly helpful.

"Why don't you use formula? It's much easier," she said over the movie's title sequence. It was hard not to think of her as the archetypal mother-in-law at that moment: meddlesome, overbearing, and sour.

I snapped back viscerally, "Because I want to breastfeed," though this wasn't exactly true.

Her face slammed shut like a drawer and I immediately regretted my tone. I tried reassuring myself that it was okay to bare myself to her this way. To be raw. It was only natural for us to bicker. We were family. Her son had come out of her in more or less the same way that her grandson had recently come out of me. More to the point, the baby was here because her son had been inside both of us. Our genes were comingled. Our bodies were linked. I'd never seen it but I knew from my husband about the vertical cesarean scar beneath her sweater. I hoped that her showing me this film would be a proxy for lifting the sweater to reveal the scar.

Almost immediately something went awry, threatening to derail the evening's plan. Mom pushed the wrong button on the remote control and turned off the player. She'd only meant to adjust the volume, which due to shoddy sound production, vacillated wildly between blaring and inaudible. Neither one of us knew how to reset the system. In the uneven division of our household labor, the media hookup fell to my husband, who was fond of video games. Now the night stretched before us like a mysterious tunnel. It would be hours before my husband returned. I felt anxious in both senses of that word—eager and uneasy. Without the movie to occupy us we'd have to talk. I had a dozen burning personal questions for my mother-in-law, this woman who was my family, but still so much a stranger. The most impertinent and interesting question being: *What stopped you from jumping?* The most honest and intimate disclosure being: *I too have imagined jumping with the baby in my arms.*

Before I could open my mouth Mom happened upon the correct combination of buttons to get the Nigerian movie started again, the room was suffused with blue light, the operatic plot unfolded, and we settled into the usual silence. I've forgotten the name of the movie but I still remember the costumes, the theatricality of the acting, and the overall narrative because I paid it such close attention. It centered on a man who unintentionally impregnates his college sweetheart. Instead of proposing marriage, he pushes her against her wishes to abort the pregnancy for the sake of both their futures. The girlfriend leaves the scene in tears after rending her garments, pulling her hair, beating her chest, prostrating herself, and cursing the young man for refusing to legitimize his seed.

Let me pause here to interject that the thing I admired most about my mother-in-law was that she was a successful mother. I say "successful" because there is no such thing as a "good" mother.

Not only did she manage to buy her own house, and bring her own mother and brother over from Uganda, she also raised my husband with next to no support from his father (a corrections officer she divorced when my husband was still a baby), to earn two Ivy League degrees, publish four books, teach at Columbia University, and make the bed every morning. Before that, she procured my husband a scholarship to attend a private high school on Long Island while working as a legal secretary. Before that, she cleaned affluent homes and office buildings in Manhattan. Before that, she attended college in Canada. Before that, she dreamed of one day escaping to New York City to become an actress. Before that was the coup d'état of General Idi Amin, under whose brutal, eight-year military regime somewhere between one and five hundred thousand Ugandans were killed. My point is that she didn't jump. She climbed.

Back to the movie. Cut to several years later. The ex-girlfriend has not had the abortion after all. The child, a boy, is now seven. His mother has done well for herself by marrying a diplomat who is raising the son as his own. Meanwhile, the son's biological father has become rich. He now possesses a thriving business, a beautiful and doting wife, a sweet daughter, a fancy house, a cadre of servants, and a BMW. He is pleased with these acquisitions, full of preening self-regard. But then, conventionally enough, things start to fall apart. First, the servants begin stealing from him. Next, his business falters. The car is repossessed. His wife turns into a nag. His daughter grows dramatically ill and dies. The house burns down. Yet none of these is the worst tragedy in the undoing of the man's empire. He hits bottom when his penis retires like a snail and no amount of prodding will stiffen it. Impotence is the final straw. Absolutely degraded, he seeks the aid of a witch doctor. The wise man intuits that his patient is accursed. Is there someone the man has wronged in his past, the witch doctor enquires, some error he needs to correct to set his manhood back on course? The man's face lights up with recognition.

Mom and I were by this point over three hours into the movie. The baby had woken and fussed and fed and fallen back to sleep more than once. We'd eaten our take-out Chinese food and read our fortune cookies. (*Even the person who appears most wrong is quite often right.*) Against the odds, I'd managed to stay awake. I believed I knew exactly where the plot was heading and how it would resolve. I'd seen this formula played out in the third act of countless Hollywood films, even if a witch doctor wasn't part of the cast. The antihero would have to find the woman he'd wronged in his youth and apologize for his arrogant cruelty. He would effectively end his curse having made humble amends, the music would swell, his erection would return, and the movie would end, but not before the drama pivoted to validate, however briefly, the woman's point of view. The *mother's.* Good, I thought, leaning in. There's something satisfying in formulas. I was so sure I knew this story.

Permit me another digression to share some of the other unsavory things my husband has told me about D. I have resisted them for fear of making her appear one-dimensional:

- Out of the conviction that her nose was too broad, she had it "fixed" in the late sixties when she was still hoping to become an actress in New York.
- She married my husband's father not because she loved him, but because she wanted to raise a light-skinned baby. She believed her child's life would be filled with misfortune if he were dark, like her. Before he introduced us, my husband showed his mother a photo of me. "Thank God she's not any darker than you," he says she said.
- When my husband was a child, she forced him to listen to elocution cassette tapes so that he'd learn to speak proper English, meaning with a British tinge instead of a Queens accent—ah-loo-MIN-ee-um for aluminum, WAH-ta for wodder.

- My husband returned from elementary school one afternoon to find his mother chasing his pet budgie around the room with a garbage bag like a woman possessed. She caught the parakeet and swiftly killed it by thwacking it against the wall. At the time she was dating another white man who'd made a comment to the effect that caged birds were filthy creatures. Evidently, she'd believed him.

- When he went through his black power phase in college, my husband says he asked Mom to place his jawbone on the wall unit in the tragic event that he should die before her. He'd read somewhere that it was a Bugandan custom to showcase the jawbones of deceased loved ones in the family compound. In his macabre way, he meant to lay claim to her culture. Probably he also desired demonstrative proof of her love. "*Muzungu*, why would I ever do that?" he says she laughed in his face. *Muzungu* means foreigner or white person.

Let us return to the loveseat where Mom and I watch the African movie, our thighs nearly touching. To my surprise, it goes on for yet another hour. It consists of five acts, not three. The crazed man attempts to kidnap his son. From my point of view, he now seems entirely like the antagonist. Instead of apologizing for not taking the woman's perspective into account, he bullies her, claiming that because the boy is his seed, his stepfather has no right to raise him. The poor woman is terrified. The man harasses her and her husband, angling to get to the kid, who is equally terrified. Eventually, he succeeds in absconding with the frightened child. He explains his actions to the boy thusly: "A child belongs with his father." FIN. The credits begin to roll. Stunned, I looked to my mother-in-law.

"Did you enjoy the movie?" she asked, sweetly.

"I don't get it," I admitted. "Was that the end? The son belongs with the father?"

"Yes, that's right," she answered.

"That's the message?"

"That is the moral of the story, yes," she said.

"And you agree with it?"

"Of course."

I felt as if I'd been slapped. I'd wanted her to be better than this. How could my mother-in-law, who had, in spite of her son's stories to the contrary, become my picture of feminist independence, immigrant grit, quiet heroism, progressive politics, black power, and resilient grace, subscribe to that patriarchal baloney? Here I sat, in my raw body, and this was what she had to offer—received wisdom that risked her nothing to impart.

Later that night, after my husband, the gentleman, had walked his mother to the subway train back to Queens, he asked me how it went. We lay in bed while the baby stirred nearby in his bassinet. At any moment our son, the tyrant, could detonate, disrupting the promise of sleep. I didn't have words yet for the terror of being in the baby's thrall, of having lost my interior life, of no longer recognizing myself, of being somebody's Mom. But I did know this. I had made a mistake in thinking I could get to the heart of D's character in one night. It would take a lifetime to know her.

Because it would have corroborated my husband's view of his mother as uncaring to summarize the movie she'd screened, I evaded him with a cheap joke. A husband pours his wife a glass of wine, describing it as full-bodied and imposing, with a nutty base, a sharp bite, and a bitter aftertaste. The wife asks, are you describing the wine, or your mother?

4

There is something else I haven't mentioned. The main reason I was reluctant to call my mother-in-law "Mom" was that she already had a daughter. My husband's half sister, S, is ten years younger than he, and still lives at home. She looms large in his family lore, so large in fact that her character threatens to overshadow their mother's entirely, as Godzilla would a Komodo dragon. S's mental illness first reared its head when she hit puberty and she's been in and out of mental hospitals ever since, including Creedmoor, where D spent the mid 1970s. I mistrusted my husband's stories about S too, such as the one where she'd temporarily blinded their mother by throwing nail polish remover in her eyes; or the one about the cop who was so tired of domestic violence calls coming from their house that he threatened to throw one or the other woman in jail; or the one about how their mother cautioned my husband against having children because—she implied—to be childless would be easier than living with a child like S.

The first few times I met S she was actually very sweet. If anything, she seemed suspended at age thirteen, poring over celebrity gossip and black hair care magazines, or cooing over her pet turtle. Then, after my first international trip with my husband, I realized he hadn't been exaggerating. *Even the person who appears most wrong is quite often right.* Mom (still Auntie to me then) and S picked us up from JFK sometime before midnight. The plan was to stay the night in Queens, but our flight from Entebbe had been delayed several hours, and when it finally landed they'd already gone to bed. He called to tell them not to bother collecting us, but Auntie insisted. When the Kia Sephia with its decal of my husband's alma mater on its rear window pulled up to arrivals, S sat behind the wheel in her nightgown. Auntie sat in the passenger seat without her wig. She told us as we climbed into the backseat that she'd bought my husband's favorite soda for us and we'd find it in the fridge. I don't know why she added that it was not for S to drink, but that is what set off my husband's little sister.

"Why the fuck would you think I'd want to drink that shit anyway, you old black bitch?" began S as her foot pressed down on the gas pedal. "You shouldn't even have sugar in the house. You know my meds make me eat too much. You're trying to make me fat like you, you smelly alcoholic whore." The worsening tirade continued for two exits. "The only reason I'm even in this car is you're too drunk to drive," she spat. S's vitriol astonished me. I feared she would drive us off the road. I looked to my husband for some kind of reassurance, but he had slumped down spinelessly in the seat like a crash test dummy and his eyes had gone dead. Later on he told me this stance was a kind of passive resistance. To engage with S when she grew confrontational would be a tactical error. She shouted at the three of us, "You better sleep with one eye open or I might just bash in your heads with a lead pipe." With a sharp turn of the wheel, she took the next exit, parked haphazardly outside a 7-Eleven, dashed out of the car, returned with a packaged honey bun she hadn't paid for and, I was glad, ordered my husband to drive the rest of the way home. Next to me in the backseat, she scarfed down the snack in two bites, breathing heavily through her nostrils. She glared at me mutinously, as if daring me to speak. I said nothing. Was it any wonder, I thought, that Auntie drank?

Back at the house, S slammed shut her bedroom door. Auntie made up the pull-out couch for us, apologizing profusely for S's behavior. "I believe it's that she's jealous of you," she explained in low tones. "Tomorrow you'll tell me all about your trip, but first, there's something I want you to see." She pulled out an accordion folder from a cabinet in the wall unit. Other folders contained elaborate records of S's medical history that Auntie kept on file to aid in her tireless advocacy for S's health care under Medicaid. But this folder was different. It held glossy head shots and commercial photography of S when she was a child. S in a red cowgirl dance costume with white fringe, spinning a baton. S in pigtails, holding a beauty pageant trophy, second runner-up. My husband bit his tongue. The pictures infuriated him because they reminded him that the lion's share of his mother's attention had gone to S, who once again sucked up all the air in the room without even being inside it.

"I want you to see that my daughter had a career in the performing arts," Auntie implored. "She's more than just a mentally ill person."

I understood that Auntie was speaking about herself as much as she was about S. She wanted me to have a fuller picture of who she was. I could see it then, how Auntie had projected her aborted dream of stardom onto her light-skinned daughter, meaning to shape her like Pygmalion, but how, in a cruel twist of fate, S had instead inherited the inner darkness she'd struggled to overcome, like Pandora, spewing out Auntie's worst fears about herself from the contemptuous box of her mouth. And I could hear it, not just Auntie's desperate need for my approval but the unasked question hovering in the air—will you help to care for her when I am gone? Caretaking was women's work. She didn't trust her son to do it. I studied the contact sheet of determined little S in a black leotard and lurid makeup, suggestively posed like a harem dancer with a diaphanous hot pink scarf. *Love me,* the pictures screamed. Could I love her? I nodded my head.

That night it was hard to sleep, in part because I didn't know if S really did own a lead pipe, and in part because the springs of the pull-out couch pressed into our backs. "Are you sure you want to be part of this crazy family?" my husband asked, sheepishly. I'd already decided the answer on the trip we'd just taken to his mother's homeland, where, somewhere on the road between Entebbe and Kampala, we'd stopped at a tomb to visit the wife of the ghost of a former king—for it is thought in the Bugandan Kingdom that a *kabaka* cannot die but is lost in the forest forever, and may still be consulted (if I have this right) through his spouse, who continues to dream his dreams. The queen lay on a mat in the palace of wattle and daub and received the goat meat we had brought in obeisance, which would be cooked without seasoning on an iron hook over a fire to feed the entire village, and explained through a translator in a story that lasted hours, interspersed with drumming by a bored little boy with flies on his skull, the lineage of the *kabaka* back to Kintu, earth's first man, tracing my husband's specious attachment to the kingdom through his mother's last name, Kanyike, which indicated that D belonged to a royal clan, meaning that if she had not made the mistake of diluting her bloodline by leaving the country and marrying his American father, my husband would be an African prince. I watched my husband's jawline tremble with defiance as he made his comeback, which the translator refused to repeat. I knew then that I would marry him, among many other reasons, because he could not countenance anyone speaking ill of his mother. In spite of it all, she'd raised him right. He looked so much like D in that moment. Prideful, defensive, and slightly unhinged. *You tell 'her highness' I'm glad my mother made me exactly what I am.*

5

We scorn the mother-in-law because we can't tolerate her own dismay at having been replaced. She is mother no longer now that her child belongs to another. Now that this child has children of his own, her utility fades. She is passed over, used up, no longer young, and yet she clings to the sailing ship of her family like a barnacle—an irritant with crusty advice. That, anyway, is the stereotype. It does not fit D, whose most defining trait is her indefatigable nurture of S, the daughter who will never grow up. What does it mean to be D's other daughter? I have said yes to her son, and to her, and to S, and to calling her Mom. I have chosen to be part of the crazy puzzle of this family.

Mom had been free to visit with me on the night of the disappointing African movie because S was interred again at Creedmoor. The next day she would visit S at the mental hospital, as she did every day S was hospitalized, bringing her a deck of cards, a stack of entertainment magazines, and a packaged honey bun so that she would feel loved, and seen. I wondered about the movie she had brought me that night, long after my husband and son had drifted into sleep, and I marveled at her level of maternal sacrifice. I doubted my own such abilities. I had thought, erroneously, the movie might show me who Mom was, whereas she had billed it all along as proof of civilization. Perhaps she was right in this regard. The making of a new family, like the making of a new nation, involves a terrible, bloody unmaking.

In those early days as a new mother I anguished over the loss of my independence, as I had known it. My boundaries had been redrawn and I no longer knew where I ended or began, just as I could hardly distinguish night from day. Taking my resources into account, I estimate my anguish then to be a tenth of what D felt when she sat on the ledge, maybe less, I can't really say, except that the dread of having to submit to a force that would suck me dry was real. Perhaps the truest reason it was hard for me to call D Mom was that I feared being called Mom myself. I was bereft of my own proper name.

Presently, the baby began to cry. His hunger was also real. My husband slept through this alarm. I envied and pitied him his deafness. My breasts were engorged. I'd never felt weaker, or more powerful. I picked up the baby and brought him into the raft of our bed. I had said yes, and now, like the man in the Nigerian movie, I had to say yes to my child.

I cradled him without knowing if I was doing it right. He fumbled for my breast, and finding it, grew calm. We settled against the pillows into a dim accord. This, then, was civilization—forgiving the woman her madness, allowing the man his misapprehension, placing the nipple in the baby's mouth, feeling the latch and the mingling of bloodlines as the milk let down.

MARIE DARRIEUSSECQ was born in 1969 in Bayonne, France. Her debut novel, *Pig Tales*, was published in thirty-four countries. Her most recent novels translated into English include *All the Way* (*Clèves*) and *Men* (*Il faut beaucoup aimer les hommes*), for which she was awarded the Prix Médicis and the Prix des Prix. She lives in Paris.

PENNY HUESTON is an editor and translator. Most recently, she has translated novels by Marie Darrieussecq and Patrick Modiano.

Being Here
The Life of Paula M. Becker

MARIE DARRIEUSSECQ
TRANSLATED FROM THE FRENCH BY PENNY HUESTON

Translator's Note: In Being Here, *her biography of the German Expressionist painter Paula Modersohn-Becker, Marie Darrieussecq ignores the commonplace details of Paula's life, focusing instead on the pressures she faced as a female painter at the turn of the twentieth century; on Paula's style and choice of subjects—"real women", "real babies" (Paula was the first to paint herself not only naked, but pregnant); her fraught marriage; her ambivalence about combining her career as an artist with motherhood; and her tragic death at thirty-one, days after giving birth. In this extract, Paula is torn between Paris and her home in the artistic community of Worpswede, in northern Germany. Paris is where she can focus on her work, her art. Paula's close friend Rainer Maria Rilke (who is married to Clara Westhoff, Paula's childhood friend) is in Paris too. Germany is home, where her husband, Otto, is, as well as her mother.*

Thirty. Like Nora in *A Doll's House*, Paula leaves everything, house and husband, for something else, for the unknown.

273

Her diary, 24 February 1906: 'I left Otto Modersohn and I'm poised between my old life and my new life. I wonder what the new life will be like. […] Whatever must be, will be.'

For a few days now, she has been carrying the things she will need to the Brünjes' studio. She confides in Rilke. Could he lay his hands on a bed base, an easel, and a table and a chair that are not too ugly? She will go back to Rue Cassette. She doesn't know how to sign off:

'I'm not Modersohn and I'm not Paula Becker anymore either.

I am

Me,

And I hope to become Me more and more.'

At the same time, Herma [Paula's sister] writes to their mother, saying how pleased she is that Paula, for once, is by "dear Otto's" side for his birthday, and has stopped gallivanting round Paris for good.

Urbane as ever, generous as he often is, Rilke puts himself at Paula's service. 'I am grateful that you have allowed me into your new life. […] Know that I am happy for you and share in your happiness. Your servant, Rainer Maria Rilke.' He tries to source money to help her. He lends her a hundred francs, and speaks to the banker and patron Karl von der Heydt: 'I was profoundly surprised to find Modersohn's wife in the throes of a deeply personal transformation: She paints—in a very spontaneous and direct way—subjects that, while still in the "Worpswede" style, could not be perceived or interpreted by anyone other than her.' And he buys a painting from her, the little child with the fat cheeks like large drops. It is the first painting she has sold in her life.

Paula moves out from the room in Rue Cassette, which proves too expensive, and finds a studio at 15, Avenue du Maine. The studio is still there today, even though the district of Montparnasse has been comprehensively rebuilt. Rilke did not end up dealing with Paula's furniture needs; indeed, he had already left Paris, in one of his customary quick moves. Fortunately one of the Bulgarians [fellow art students] is around: He knocks together a table and some shelves that she covers with colourful material. Herma describes it all to their mother in a tone of forced cheeriness. Paula, on the other hand, thinks Herma is depressed.

At first, Paula's letters to Otto are distant and sad; she speaks about other things. And a bit about the Bulgarians, making it clear that they are not around. Then, after the avalanche of his tearful and insistent letters, she tries to convince him that their separation is inevitable.

And could he go to her studio and send her six of her better nudes, so that she can enroll at the Beaux-Arts. He'll find the drawings in the large red portfolio hanging on the door. Could he roll them up in a cylinder and post them to her new address, with a label marked 'No Commercial Value', in order to avoid customs charges. And she must have left her passport papers at the studio as well; she needs them to enroll. Failing that, a marriage certificate will do. Oh yes, and the anatomy book she left on the bookshelf. And also, she has no more money. Is it still all right if he sends her some? Thank you very much. All the buds are ready to blossom in Paris. Thank you to Elsbeth [Otto's daughter from his first marriage] for her pretty embroidery. Fond wishes.

In a desperate effort, Otto quotes from his old letters, his love letters to her. And tells her about their garden, where the yellow flowers are blooming. Spring is on its way.

'Dear Otto, How I loved you. [...] I *cannot* come to you *now*. I *cannot* do it. And I do not want to meet you in any other place. And I do not want any child from you at all; not *now*.'

She has made up her mind. She had to. He is suffering, she is suffering, but she has to live and work. And once more she tells him all about Paris. And Brittany: the huge expanse of sea only a ten-hour train trip away, the apple trees, the sunshine, the warmth and the roses, Mont-Saint-Michel and the omelettes at La Mère Poulard restaurant. She sends him a postcard of the rock sculptures at Rothéneuf, which these days would qualify as Art Brut. She thanks him for financing her trip, as well as for last month's two hundred marks, which allowed her to pay her rent and her settling-in expenses. But if he feels obliged to help her, why doesn't he just send her two hundred and twenty marks on the fifteenth of every month without her always having to ask him.

Otto drags all the still lifes out of Paula's studio. He places them around the house and tries to draw inspiration from them, to discover the life force, the spark, the spirit. But according to Paula's mother, who keeps the poor man company, all he produces are 'mathematical proofs'.

And when [their friends] the Vogelers want to buy one of Paula's paintings, they have to insist that Otto part with it. Frau Brockhaus, a friend who visits the Brünjes' studio, also buys a still life. The money allows Paula to reimburse Rilke, via Otto, whom she entrusts with the transfer. Along with the little painting bought by Rilke, they are the only three paintings she sells in her lifetime.

As for Otto, he has sold five paintings so far this year. Paula asks her sister Herma to write to him and ask him for money . . . And asks her other sister, Milly, for sixty francs for models' fees.

Money pressures: the mainspring of her solitude, the dilemma of her independence.

'I am becoming someone.' This is the mantra echoing through Paula's letters. Neither Modersohn nor Becker: someone.

Bernhard Hoetger encourages her. Hoetger is a German sculptor she meets in Paris. He admires her talent, is astonished by it. Paula also meets his wife. It is looking to be a repetition of the early days with Modersohn: admiration, the need for approval, the only opinion that matters, I was feeling so alone, you believe in me, I'm weeping with joy, you open doors that kept me locked out . . . But Hoetger loves his wife. Paula does several portraits of her: a beautiful rectangular head, a square neck, a braid above her forehead, great strength in her upright bearing. 'There is something very grand about her, and she is quite magnificent to paint'. Her hand in the shape of a tulip.

Hoetger himself is working on a 'wonderful reclining nude, simply monumental'. Paula is gazing at a version of her future funerary monument. She has one spring and two summers left to live.

She works. Still lifes, self-portraits, lots of large nudes. More than eighty pictures just during 1906. A painting every four or five days. Feverish. She lives with her canvases, wakes in the night to look at them in the moonlight, starts work on them again at first light. She tries to slow down, to spend more time on each one. But to linger on a canvas is to 'risk ruining everything'.

Rilke is still Rodin's secretary and returns at the end of March after a trip with him. Along with a crowd of admirers, Paula and Rilke attend the unveiling of *The Thinker* in front of the Pantheon. But on May 10, after a misunderstanding, Rodin dismisses Rilke as if he were a 'thieving servant'. Driven away from Meudon, destitute and hurt, the poet takes refuge at the old address of 29, Rue Cassette.

Then he poses for Paula, in this time regained. They stand opposite each other, looking at each other, speaking or silent, in the mutual generosity of a shared gift; they forge this painting the way you forge friendship. A portrait that is the vestige of long hours together. Rilke is orange, white, black, and green. He looks young. A pharaoh's beard, a Hun's moustache, a high, stiff collar, a broad forehead, dark-ringed, watery, bulging eyes, the whites of which are violet, raised eyebrows, his mouth open, thick-lipped. His nose is big, his beard rectangular. It is as if his face is skewed towards the right. Rilke looks into the distance, somewhere else, within; he seems struck by what it is that, for the rest of his life, will make him write without really knowing how to live.

Paula sees what others do not see. Twenty years later exactly, on 30 April 1926, the painter Leonid Pasternak writes to Rilke: 'I saw two portraits of you in a journal, *Querschnitte*. I forget the name of the artist of one of them, which does bear some resemblance to you; by contrast, in the other one—by Paula Modersohn, a quite well-known woman painter, not without talent, in my opinion—I found no resemblance whatsoever. Is such an alteration possible? I assume it's a misunderstanding or a mistaken attribution, perhaps . . . Anyway, enough of that . . .'

During this spring of 1906, Paula and Rilke spend every Sunday together, in Fontainebleau or Chantilly, sometimes in the company of Ellen Key, a Swedish feminist friend of Rilke's, much older than them. The two of them dine together on Saturday nights chez Jouven, on the corner of Boulevard du Montparnasse and Rue Léopold-Robert, a bistro described thus by Ramuz, a contemporary: 'The tables were so close together, there could be no secret conversations [...]. We heard so many different languages spoken [...] And there were so many women painters! What sort of painting were they doing? They wore long skirts, it was the era of the *jupe entravée,* the narrow 'hobble skirt', and enormous hats laden with flowers and fruit.' Paula loved ordering the asparagus and Rilke the melon.

On May 13, returning from a walk to Saint-Cloud, Paula notices that she no longer has her bag. Rilke tries everything, weaving back and forth the way they had come: 'I went back to our bench in Saint-Cloud, to the Blue Pavilion restaurant, to the spot where we had tea, to the park police station and to the Bateaux-Mouches office. At the last two places, I described your bag and the contents and I left your address. They will contact you if they find it, but I wouldn't count on it. I was told that it would already have been handed in, if the person was planning on handing it in. But most thieves do not intend to return things. I am sad that the memory of our afternoon is now imbued with such loss. I am especially sad that irreplaceable things were in that little bag, but there is nothing more we can do about it.'

There will be more loss. The world is heading rapidly along the road to ruin, to unfathomable loss in the trenches at Verdun. And Paula has five hundred days left of her life.

In the beginning of June, Otto turns up in Paris without warning, to convince Paula to come home. Herma witnesses a difficult week. Perhaps because of it, the portrait of Rilke was never finished: The poet seems to have fled in the face of the husband's arrival. The eyes, so preternaturally black, might not have been finished. But I like to see this as a deliberate breakthrough: Rilke's vibrant gaze, and the opening for his ghost.

Paula does not go home. The summer of 1906 is scorching. Her studio is infested with fleas, and she can't see the sky because the glass roof is made of thick yellow glass. She wonders where to spend this summer. How to get through it. How to contend with the waste-land of heat, how to live the next minute. She does not know that life will be short, but right now it is unliveable. She yearns for fresh air and the countryside. 'I hope to have many more summers, when I will be able to paint outside.'

August 3: She has never been so hot in her life. Her head spinning, she writes to Rilke, asking him to let her know if he has found a nice place for the summer holidays. If so, she'll come. She signs the letter with a question: 'Your Paula—?'

Rilke replies that he is with Clara and Ruth [their daughter] near Furnes, on the Belgian coast. He doesn't mention the name of the village. 'This is not the sea you are looking for.' And it's expensive, almost as much as Ostende. Places like Morlaix and Saint-Pol-de-Léon would be much better. He writes out a list of train stations and advises her to buy the 1906 official guide of *Swimming and Outings in Normandy* at the Gare Montparnasse for fifty centimes. She should stay at the hotel Saint-Jean et des Bains. And not miss the Pointe de Primel cliffs. At Saint-Jean-du-Doigt, she should see the fifteenth-century Renaissance fountain and church, and walk along the treelined path to the beach.

A strange, incongruous letter, written from Belgium and extolling the virtues of Brittany. 'We all send you our best and wish you happy travel plans. The best train for Roscoff: 8.24 in the evening.'

So Paula gives up. A coolness in the heat. Silence.

A year later, Rilke writes her a letter full of regrets. 'Now I can tell you that during all this time I have felt I made a mistake not writing to invite you to stay with us when your short letter was forwarded to me in Belgium. At the time, I was preoccupied by my reunion with Clara and Ruth, and I did not have a very favourable impression of East Dunkirk. It wasn't until later that I had the feeling I had been grossly unfair in my reply, as well as inattentive to you at a time in our friendship when I should not have been. [...] What makes me especially sad is that I am not going to see you now.'

They see each other for the last time on 27 July 1906, for dinner chez Jouven. They don't know it—at that age, you don't know it's the last time, and when the person who is still alive thinks back over what was said, the meaning of the words is reduced to nothing. They will never again share their summers, they will never again go for walks together, there will be no more Sundays with Paula.

On August 12, the heat wave has passed. Paula is coping better with being cooped up in Paris, and with being alone. There is a small pencil drawing of her studio. On the wall is a portrait of Frau Hoetger, and a large reclining nude with a child.

It is through this nude that I first met Paula. I think it was in 2010 that I received an advertisement, in my junk mail, for a psychoanalysis symposium on motherhood. The image was a tiny illustration on the flyer, and at first it reminded me of a poster I had been fascinated by as a child. My parents had bought it, already framed, to hang in their bedroom. It was a reproduction of a picture of a mother and child, by Toffoli, that artist of the seventies or eighties who mass-produced semi-abstract paintings of roundish-shaped people in vibrant colours. But it wasn't by Toffoli.

And the child in the image was a very young infant. Who was this artist, and where did this knowledge about breastfeeding come from? It was the first time I had seen a portrayal of that extremely comfortable breastfeeding position, not then taught in maternity wards and never featured in paintings of the Madonna and Child: not seated, not encumbered with the child on your arm, but lying down on your side with the child against you. Milky drowsiness, zoned out with milk and the warmth of the two of you. In 2010, I was breastfeeding my third child, and I continued for two years, ignoring advice to the contrary, including the rules I had set for myself.

In 2001, I had written *The Baby,* an attempt to counteract clichés, and to counteract questions like, 'What does it mean to be a mother?' When the book was published, I learned that some men cannot take motherhood seriously. Mother and child—the truth about this ordinary and fundamental experience is that men cringe if the mother is not represented as a Madonna (Virgin and Child) or a whore (Venus and Cupid).

Paula is a painter, and she sees that the female model has fallen asleep with the baby lying opposite her. She does several pencil drawings and paints two canvases. The breasts have large areolas, the pubic area is black and luxuriant, the belly is round, the thighs and shoulders sturdy. In the drawings, the mother and child are cuddling, the ends of their noses touching; in the canvases, they are languorous and symmetrical, both in the foetal position, the large woman and the tiny child. Not sentimental, or pious, or erotic: another sort of sensuality. Vast. Another sort of power.

All I knew when I saw this painting was that I had never seen anything like it—a woman shown like that, in 1906. Who was Paula Modersohn-Becker? Why had I never heard anything about her? The more I read, and the more I saw (other powerful depictions of breastfeeding, the mother holding her breast as only a woman painter, perhaps, could allow us to see), the more I said to myself that I had to write the life of this artist and help to make her work known. [...]

At the Paula Modersohn-Becker Museum, her museum in Bremen, is her most famous self-portrait, the one people talk about when they talk about her. Naked to the waist, standing three-quarters on, a big amber necklace and small pointed breasts. Her belly is swollen. Four or five months pregnant. She has, unusually, written a sentence on the back of the canvas: 'I painted this at the age of thirty, on my sixth wedding anniversary, PB.'

But the dates are impossible to determine. On 25 May 1906, Paula is not pregnant. A month earlier, she was specifically explaining to Otto that a child was not on the cards now, and not with him. And yet here she is holding her belly in that proud and protective gesture that many pregnant women have.

The Modersohn-Beckers, all thirty of them on the planet, debate the issue. They bring up her diet. Too much cabbage and too many potatoes. The self-portrait of a bloated woman: Care for a bit more soup? But she could just as easily have been *imagining* herself pregnant. Making a game out of sticking out her belly, arching her back, her navel protruding. *Just to see.* The self-portrait as auto-fiction. She paints herself as she would like to be, and as she imagines herself: She paints an image of herself. Beautiful, happy, a little bit playful.

And, take note: it is the first time. The first time that a woman has painted herself naked.

The gesture of taking her clothes off and setting up in front of her canvas and going ahead and doing it: Here is my skin, I'm going to show my belly, and the shape of my breasts, and my navel . . . The nude self-portrait of a woman, one-on-one with herself and the history of art.

Is it because models are expensive? Is it deliberate? This healthy, sporty, pretty, well-rounded, nudist German woman loved her body. The act of painting herself naked had nothing to do with narcissism; it was work. It was all there for her to do. Using either a mirror or a photograph. It was all there for her to discover. I don't know if she is aware of it: of being the first one to do it. In any case, she always looks happy naked.

KATIE FORD is the author of *Deposition, Colosseum,* and *Blood Lyrics.* Her next book is forthcoming from Graywolf in 2018. She teaches at the University of California, Riverside.

#21

KATIE FORD

My room is small, but not too small—
my room is green, green, succulents and sea,
the green of a peony so red it pinkens
the comb-y string of lights I hang now in my room.

Not cavernous and no space to fear:
my room.
No dank closet where someone may have died
(or buckled carefully her shoes, then died).

I make my bed every morning.
I don't know where to start
so I start with the bed.
Then I fall to my knees against it.

Without knowing what I'm falling to,
no mind makes it do it, my body just falls.

KJELL ASKILDSEN was born in 1929 and made his debut with the short story collection *From Now on I'll Follow You All the Way Home* in 1953. The Critics' Prize winning book *Thomas F.'s Last Notes to the Public* (1983) established his status as the greatest living Norwegian short story writer, and his laconic, minimalist style has been a great influence on younger Scandinavian writers. In 2015 he published a new collection of stories, *The Cost of Friendship*, his first book in nineteen years.

BECKY L. CROOK is a translator of Norwegian and German literature and founded *SAND Journal* in Berlin in 2010. She lives with her husband and daughter on Bainbridge Island where she recently finished writing her own first novel.

The Red House

KJELL ASKILDSEN
TRANSLATED FROM THE NORWEGIAN BY BECKY L. CROOK

A red house, beyond it only heather and sky. Never a soul to be seen, yet it remains unknown whether or not it is inhabited, for you never venture over.

The red color shifts with the day's hour and the sky's moods. At times the house stands screaming: a raging fleck on a deserted clearing facing a billowing, close horizon. Other times, subdued as a faded flag.

No one lives there, you think, but still you do not venture over, you keep your distance of a few hundred feet without really wanting to know why.

Beyond it is the sky—gray, blue, red, nearly white. And the heather. You do not know quite what color that is, you are not a painter. At times it seems the house has taken a stiff step forward or back, and it happens that you simply turn away so as not to see it.

Days pass in this way—a week. Then one night, just before the sun rises, you glimpse a person silhouetted against the sky to the right of the house. You stare to assure yourself that you haven't erred. The figure walks over to one of the walls, sort of leans against it—and is suddenly gone. You wonder. It is difficult to sleep. The next day the house appears as empty and uninhabited as before.

New days pass. You should be able to go over and investigate, take a closer look at the subdued flag/red scream, but you do not go.

A new night, toward dawn, the figure is standing there again, almost but not quite in the same place, there is no chance that it is an optical illusion: one simply cannot say whether it is a woman or a man. She/he takes some steps to the right, then back again—and thereafter she/he vanishes behind the house.

Does someone live there after all? Possible, but not likely, because if you look at the house from a certain perspective you can see straight through it, that is through two windows, and you have never seen someone crossing the field of light. Does the person in question have a reason to crawl back and forth on the floor? Not likely, but possible.

You tarry the night, draw it out one extra hour to see whether there's anything to see, go to bed at three o'clock instead of two, waiting in vain, until one evening following a rain-heavy day, the house is a subdued flag, wind gust from the west, there she is again, it is a woman, she stands perfectly still, the wind tears at her, her hair upright like a bundle of reeds.

You open the door and walk outside, to show that you have seen, to put a final end to her imagined invisibility. Then she walks, without having revealed whether or not she has seen you, over to the white door, it should have been a little less white, silhouettes herself almost black against it, her long hair settles to rest, the wind is nearly warm, it is July, she opens the door and walks inside.

You remain standing there, you do not conceal your staring at the empty windows, you believe perhaps she is standing and observing you behind one of the dark panes. Does she light a candle? No. It grows darker. She does not light a candle. The wind is nearly warm, but strong, and you walk inside, without doing what you had thought of doing, drawing a kitchen chair over to the window, staring in vain.

Tomorrow you will, you think, go over and knock, say that you've run out of sugar or flour, if she is even still there, but the next day you do not do it; darkness is for plans, light is for timidity.

The wind has quieted, the sun attempts to render the blue-gray rug of the sky. You've risen early, woken by a dream, but are at once aware that there is a red house standing nine hundred feet away; it is as though you have slept yourself into loving. But that cannot be possible. Can one fall in love with a person one has not seen?

Now, in any case, you behave differently, you consume your breakfast while pacing, walking between the kitchen counter and the window facing south, toward the white door, no longer so white at dawn; and when you then try to gather your thoughts on "faith and knowledge," the page remains unwritten, like a white door. Nothing gets done, and no woman reveals herself.

You turn more and more restless, gulp three quick drams and one somewhat slower dram of beer, your peace is gone, you gather courage, walk out into the gray day, pass the house with less than twenty steps' distance, observing no one, continue through the wet heather, five hundred feet, eight hundred feet, turn and walk back, on the other side of the house, see no one, pull the door shut behind you, leave your wet shoes and socks on, one must have reason to believe that in spite of everything one is in love, or if not in love, then . . . yes, then what? You have always changed your socks . . . wrong. You have never before gone out through the wet heather without putting on the appropriate footwear. It's ridiculous, after all she could be—it is even statistically likely that she is neither pretty nor . . . nor? Besides she is obviously absent again.

For two days you have no peace, do not get anything done, see no one. Then suddenly she is standing there, in the midpoint of the sun, a hot day with a breeze from the east, clad in red, as though to blend with the house, you should go into town to buy binoculars, you should at least hurry outside and show your existence, and you do so, you have every right to, although you have the feeling that opening your own door is about courage. You have thought so much about her that you almost can't believe she doesn't know—could so many thoughts have missed their mark? What does the mark say? The target has no reason to feel itself struck.

And so you go outside, and you believe she turns and sees that you are there, but you cannot be too certain, though yes, you are. She sees. You remain standing; you are in love with a not-yet-identified woman, but you do not conjure the potential, the probable disappointment, which she statistically is, and so on. You do not take a step forward, the sugar and flour don't even cross your mind, you carry your nature within you, it is like a clenched fist; if only you could open your hand and let arrows soar from each finger!

There she stands—she takes a step forward or back. You take a step forward, she may think it is back. She rotates her head from right to left, then from left to right, toward the sun. It is eleven o'clock, the house is screaming, the flour and the sugar do not exist, she exists, she and the distance—those three hundred feet, five hundred steps through the heather, insurmountable, irrepressible as one's nature. Then she walks, disappears behind the house, does not show herself further, but in the evening a lighted candle hangs to the left of the white door; peculiar—that must mean something.

You drink two drams, then two more; then you brush your teeth— you never know what might happen, a lighted candle makes the impossible possible. Couldn't you, yes, certainly: you light a paraffin candle and hang it beside the door, so that two lights are burning in the still evening, one for her and one for . . . no.

Do you celebrate your audacity with another drink? With two! One for each of the two candles—cheers! And then you position yourself behind the window, weighing, knowing deep inside that those four hundred steps are too many, you think, if only I had a carrier pigeon, if only I had a bow and was Robin Hood—nonsense, you are drunk. Yes, but not only from those six small glasses, six glasses have never before provoked such sudden madness, never!

You press your nose to the glass, and there! There she comes! You could not have expected that, you turn sober, sit down at the desk, prepare your feigned surprise, check whether your palms are sweating, a knock. Yes?

The door handle presses down, the door opens, slowly—as though to illustrate that time is a relation. You stand slowly, think better of it, return to sitting, she enters, she does not adhere to the statistical probability. She has bound a thin scarf around her light blond hair.

Good evening, and excuse my interruption, but I saw there was a light; would you mind lending me a bit of margarine?

Would you mind! Of course! Yes, so then, margarine—isn't it reasonable to ask her to sit down to wait? Please, oh, you do not wish to sit . . . Thank you, but I don't want to be a bother.

Why don't you say that she is not being a bother? Why do you go fetch the margarine directly, without taking time to consider? How oafish can you be?

She is supplied with the margarine, smiles, says thanks, it's no small wonder you were in love already days ahead of time, you are indescribably clumsy, she has smile-wrinkles at her eyes. Thank you so much. No problem. Good-bye.

She departs, the red fades, step by step, you leave the door ajar, it will not be shut tonight. But only turn, and observe you who are standing there!—and when she reaches her door she puts out her hand with the packet of margarine into the air, and then she is gone. But she has not taken the candle with her, she will have to return outside again, this gives you something to wait for, and as the summer flies and mosquitoes and moths swarm in through the open door, a buzzing diversity, right this way, free entry, here is your candle, you have one of your own.

Are you bitter over your own clumsiness? No. You have a happiness within you, a whole orchestra of trumpets and bassoons. Tomorrow you will borrow flour and sugar, you better believe it! Tomorrow you will say: You must excuse me that I allowed you to leave, I wanted nothing more than that you should stay. Tomorrow you will speak, you are, after all, a man of your word.

ADONIS, born in 1930 as Ali Ahmad Sa'id, is a Syrian poet who led the modernist movement in Arabic poetry in the second half of the twentieth century. He is responsible for founding the radical political journal *Positions*, in 1968 and for the seminal critical volume *An Introduction to Arab Poetics*. He has written more than 20 books in his native Arabic. In 1957 he helped found the avant-garde poetry review, *Poetry*. His volumes of poetry translated into English include *Adonis: Selected Poems* and the forthcoming *Concerto for Jerusalem*, both translated by Khaled Mattawa, published by Yale University Press in the Margellos World Republic of Letters series.

KHALED MATTAWA is Assistant Professor of Language and Literature at the University of Michigan. He is the author of two books of poetry, *Zodiac of Echoes* and *Ismailia Eclipse*, and has translated five books of Arab poetry (by Saadi Youssef, Fadhil Al-Azzawi, Hatif Janabi, and Maram Al-Massri). Mattawa is the recipient of a MacArthur grant, a PEN Award for Literary Translation, a Guggenheim Fellowship, the Alfred Hodder Fellowship from Princeton University, an NEA translation grant, and two Pushcart Prizes.

E. A hymn bracing for the end

ADONIS

TRANSLATED FROM THE ARABIC BY KHALED MATTAWA

Many gray hairs on my head,
but in my insides only the down of childhood.

Take away your alchemy, dear poetry, raise it, discipline it, and
        teach it to
mingle our bodies with our dreams,
how time can earn a place among our days and nights,
how minutes grunt in our veins like wild horses.

In your name, I flee myself to be myself,
and in your name I become joy and sadness in one inhale
and I clamp my lips on your secrets.

GERALD MURNANE was born
in Melbourne in 1939. He has
been a schoolteacher, an edi-
tor, and a university lecturer.
His debut novel, *Tamarisk Row*
(1974), was followed by nine
other works of fiction, including
The Plains and, most recently,
A Million Windows. In 1999,
Murnane won the Patrick White
Award, and in 2009, he won the
Melbourne Prize for Literature.
His memoir, *Something for the
Pain*, won the 2016 Victorian
Premier's Award for Non-fiction.
He lives in Victoria.

On Winning the Melbourne Prize, 11 November 2009

GERALD MURNANE

A few years ago, I felt somewhat less well disposed towards the Melbourne Prize Trust. The year was 2006, and I was filling out my entry form for the Melbourne Prize for Literature for that year. I happened to be reading some of the fine print when I learned something that dismayed me. The Melbourne Prize for Literature was then, as it is today, a sum of $60,000. However, in 2006, half of that sum had to be spent by the prize winner on international travel. This I could not understand. Here was a prize meant to celebrate the city of Melbourne as a centre of culture, and yet the winner of the prize was compelled to *leave* Melbourne. As of 2006, I had lived in Melbourne almost continuously for forty-six years and had never felt during those years the least urge to leave. Being compelled to leave Melbourne seemed to me not a prize but a punishment, and so I was not an applicant for the Melbourne Prize for Literature in 2006.

Earlier this year, my publisher, Ivor Indyk of the Giramondo Publishing Company, phoned to tell me that he was nominating me for the Melbourne Prize for Literature for 2009. I told him to stop at once. I told him that nobody was going to compel me to leave Melbourne for overseas, even if my travel expenses were fully paid for. Ivor then read to me from information supplied by the Melbourne Prize Trust: "With this prize, the Trust encourages *local* and overseas travel . . . " I was very relieved to hear this. If I happened to win the Prize, I could fulfil the wishes of the Trust by filling my car with petrol and driving around the back streets of Pascoe Vale, where I lived in 1950. I might even travel to Bendigo, where I lived from 1944 to 1948, or to Strzelecki, where I taught in a one-teacher school for three weeks in 1960. I told Ivor to go ahead and nominate me, and I thank him now for doing so.

I understand that this prize is meant in part as a celebration of Melbourne. I'm now going to celebrate Melbourne in my own way. It's true that I haven't always lived in Melbourne. I was born in Coburg, but my parents took me in my childhood as far away as Wangaratta, Bendigo, Timboon, Port Campbell, Naringal, Mepunga East, The Cove, and Monbulk. Even so, I can tell you that I've lived for sixty-four of my seventy-one years in the suburbs of Melbourne. And now I'm going to end this speech by reciting the names of the streets and suburbs that I've lived in. I hope my recitation sounds to you not like some sort of obsessional rant. I hope it sounds like a litany of praise to a city that was once called, and still deserves to be called, "Marvellous Melbourne."

The Avenue, Coburg . . . Breese Street, Brunswick . . . Plenty Road, Bundoora . . . Ray Street, Pascoe Vale . . . Bakers Road, North Coburg . . . Peter Street, Oakleigh South . . . Legon Road, Oakleigh South . . . Filbert Street, Caulfield South . . . Caroline Street, South Yarra . . . Powlett Street, East Melbourne . . . Argyle Street, Fitzroy . . . Rosedale Avenue, Glen Huntly . . . Wheatland Road, Malvern . . . Gweno Avenue, Frankston . . . Fitzroy Street, St Kilda . . . River Street, South Yarra . . . Lygon Street, Carlton . . . Barkly Street, East Brunswick. . . Park Street, Brunswick . . . Falcon Road, Macleod . . . .

Contributor Notes

Leila Aboulela was the first winner of the Caine Prize for African Writing. She is the author of four novels, *The Kindness of Enemies; The Translator*, a *New York Times* 100 Notable Books of the Year; *Minaret*; and *Lyrics Alley*, Fiction Winner of the Scottish Book Awards. Her collection of short stories, *Coloured Lights*, was shortlisted for the MacMillan Silver PEN Award. Leila grew up in Sudan and moved, in her mid-twenties, to Scotland.

Adonis, born in 1930 as Ali Ahmad Sa'id, is a Syrian poet who led the modernist movement in Arabic poetry in the second half of the twentieth century. He is responsible for founding the radical political journal *Positions*, in 1968 and for the seminal critical volume *An Introduction to Arab Poetics*. He has written more than twenty books in his native Arabic. In 1957 he helped found the avant-garde poetry review, *Poetry*. His volumes of poetry translated into English include *Adonis: Selected Poems* and the forthcoming *Concerto for Jerusalem*, both translated by Khaled Mattawa, published by Yale University Press in the Margellos World Republic of Letters series.

Rabih Alameddine is the author of the novels *The Angel of History*; *An Unnecessary Woman*; *I, the Divine; Koolaids*; *The Hakawati*; and the story collection, *The Perv*.

Kerri Arsenault is a writer, editor, and serves on the Board of the National Book Critics Circle and is a founder of the Western Maine Water Alliance. She writes a column for *Literary Hub*, and her work has appeared in the *San Francisco Chronicle*, *American Book Review*, NBCC's *Critical Mass*, *Kirkus Reviews*, and *Bookslut*. She is currently working on a book about Maine, from which this piece is excerpted.

Kjell Askildsen was born in 1929 and made his debut with the short story collection *From Now on I'll Follow You All the Way Home* in 1953. The Critics' Prize winning book *Thomas F.'s Last Notes to the Public* (1983) established his status as the greatest living Norwegian short story writer, and his laconic, minimalist style has been a great influence on younger Scandinavian writers. In 2015 he published a new collection of stories, *The Cost of Friendship*, his first book in nineteen years.

Nir Baram was born into a political family in Jerusalem in 1976. His grandfather and father were both ministers in Israeli Labor Party governments. He has worked as a journalist, an editor, and an advocate for equal rights for Palestinians. He is the author of five novels, including *Good People*, which was translated into English in 2016. His novels have been translated into more than ten languages and received critical acclaim around the world. He has been shortlisted several times for the Sapir Prize and in 2010 he received the Prime Minister's Award for Hebrew Literature. His book of reportage, *A Land Without Borders*, will be published in English by Text Publishing in 2017.

Poet and journalist **Adisa Bašić** was born in 1979 in Sarajevo. She has a degree in Comparative Literature and Librarianship and a master's degree in Human Rights and Democracy. She has published four poetry collections, *Eve's Sentences* (1999), *Trauma Market* (2004), *A Promo Clip for My Homeland* (2011), and *Motel of Unknown Heroes* (2014). Her poems have been included in all recent anthologies of Bosnian poetry.

Philip Boehm has translated over thirty books and plays by German and Polish writers such as Herta Müller, Franz Kafka, and Hanna Krall. For these translations he has received numerous awards including fellowships from the National Endowment for the Arts and the John Simon Guggenheim Memorial Foundation. He also works as a stage director and playwright and is the founding Artistic Director of Upstream Theater in St. Louis.

Velibor Božović grew up in Sarajevo, Bosnia-Herzegovina. When he was in his twenties the country of his youth became a war zone and he spent the duration of the siege of Sarajevo honing his survival skills. In 1998, Božović moved to Montreal where, for eight years, he worked as an engineer in aerospace industry until he gave up his engineering career to devote time fully to image creation. His work has been exhibited internationally. He collaborated with Aleksandar Hemon on his novel *The Lazarus Project*. Most recently he completed the projects *My Prisoner* and *Encore, Odyssey*. In 2015 he was awarded the Claudine and Stephen Bronfman Fellowship in Contemporary Art. He holds an MFA from Concordia University where he currently teaches.

Jessica Cohen is a freelance translator born in England, raised in Israel, and living in Denver. She translates contemporary Israeli prose, poetry, and other creative work. Her translations of critically acclaimed works by major Israeli writers include David Grossman, Etgar Keret, Rutu Modan, Dorit Rabinyan, Ronit Matalon, Amir Gutfreund, and Tom Segev.

Becky L. Crook is a translator of Norwegian and German literature and founded *SAND Journal* in Berlin in 2010. She lives with her husband and daughter on Bainbridge Island where she recently finished writing her own first novel.

Edwidge Danticat is the author of several books, including *Breath, Eyes, Memory*, an Oprah Book Club selection; *Krik? Krak!*, a National Book Award finalist; and *The Farming of Bones*, an American Book Award winner, and the novel-in-stories, *The Dew Breaker*. She is the editor of *The Butterfly's Way: Voices from the Haitian Diaspora in the United States, Haiti Noir* and *Haiti Noir 2*, and *Best American Essays 2011*. She has written six books for young adults and children, *Anacaona, Behind the Mountains, Eight Days, The Last Mapou, Mama's Nightingale*, and *Untwine*, as well as a travel narrative, *After the Dance: A Walk Through Carnival in Jacmel, Haiti*. Her memoir *Brother, I'm Dying*, was a 2007 finalist for the National Book Award and a 2008 winner of the National Book Critics Circle Award for autobiography. She is a 2009 MacArthur Fellow. Her next book, *The Art of Death: Writing the Final Story*, will be published in July 2017.

Marie Darrieussecq was born in 1969 in Bayonne, France. Her debut novel, *Pig Tales*, was published in thirty-four countries. Her most recent novels translated into English include *All the Way* (*Clèves*) and *Men* (*Il faut beaucoup aimer les hommes*), for which she was awarded the Prix Médicis and the Prix des Prix. She lives in Paris.

Stuart Dybek's most recent books are *Ecstatic Cahoots* and *Paper Lantern*, both released by FSG in 2014.

Katie Ford is the author of *Deposition, Colosseum*, and *Blood Lyrics*. Her next book is forthcoming from Graywolf in 2018. She teaches at the University of California, Riverside.

Xiaolu Guo is a novelist and filmmaker. She was born in China in 1973 and moved to the UK in 2002. She studied at the Beijing Film Academy and the UK's National Film and TV School. Her most notable novels are *A Concise Chinese-English Dictionary for Lovers* (nominated for the Orange Prize for Fiction), *20 Fragments of a Ravenous Youth*, and *I Am China* (longlisted for the Baileys Women's Prize for Fiction). She has also directed several feature films, including *How Is Your Fish Today?* and *Once Upon a Time Proletarian*. They were officially selected by the Venice Film Festival, Sundance, and MoMA in New York. Her fiction feature *She, a Chinese* received the Golden Leopard Award at the Locarno Film Festival in 2009. She divides her time between London, Beijing, and Berlin. Her memoir, *Nine Continents* (in the US) and *Once Upon a Time in the East* (in the UK) is due to be published in 2017.

Rawi Hage was born in Beirut, Lebanon, and lived through nine years of the Lebanese civil war. He is the author of *De Niro's Game*, which won the IMPAC Dublin Literary Award; *Cockroach*, which was shortlisted for the Giller Prize, the Governor's General Literary Award, and the Rogers Writers' Trust Fiction Prize; and, most recently, *Carnival*, which won the Paragraphe Hugh MacLennan Prize for Fiction. He lives in Montreal.

Tal Haran is a bilingual Israeli activist who translates occupation-related materials. Her translation work includes *The One-State Condition* by Ariella Azoulay and Adi Ophir, *The Girl Who Stole My Holocaust* by Noam Chayut, and numerous reports and testimonies for journalists and organizations such as Breaking the Silence, Zochrot, and Machsomwatch.

Amira Hass is a correspondent for *Haaretz*, an Israeli daily, in the Occupied Palestinian territory, and author of *Drinking the Sea at Gaza*.

Aleksandar Hemon is the author of *The Question of Bruno*, *Nowhere Man*, and *The Lazarus Project*. His latest short story collection, *Love and Obstacles*, was published in May 2009. His collection of autobiographical essays, *The Book of My Lives*, was published by Farrar, Straus and Giroux in March 2013. He was awarded a Guggenheim Fellowship in 2003 and a "genius" grant from the MacArthur Foundation in 2004. His latest novel, *The Making of Zombie Wars*, was published by FSG in 2015. His book on the United Nations, *Behind the Glass Wall*, is forthcoming from FSG Originals. From 2010 to 2013 he served as editor of the *Best European Fiction* anthologies, published by Dalkey Archive Press. He is currently the Distinguished

Writer-in-Residence at Columbia College Chicago. He lives in Chicago with his wife and daughters.

Penny Hueston is an editor and translator. Most recently, she has translated novels by Marie Darrieussecq and Patrick Modiano.

Thom Jones is an American writer, primarily of short stories. Jones was raised in Aurora, Illinois, and received an MFA from the Iowa Writers' Workshop at the University of Iowa. The *New Yorker* published a series of his stories in the early 1990s, leading to his first collection, *The Pugilist at Rest*, which was a National Book Award finalist. Jones's other collections include *Cold Snap* and *Sonny Liston Was a Friend of Mine*.

Lawrence Joseph's sixth book of poems, *So Where Are We?*, will be published by Farrar, Straus and Giroux in 2017. He is also the author of two books of prose, *Lawyerland* and *The Game Changed: Essays and Other Prose*. He is Tinnelly Professor of Law at St. Johns University School of Law and lives in New York City.

Barry Lopez, a winner of the National Book Award, is the author of *Arctic Dreams* as well as nine works of fiction and six other works of nonfiction. His stories and essays appear regularly in *Harper's*, the *Paris Review, Orion*, and the *Georgia Review*. He is the recipient of an Award in Literature from the American Academy of Arts and Letters, as well as fellowships from the Guggenheim, Lannan, and National Science Foundations. His new book, *Horizon*, will be published by Knopf. He lives in western Oregon.

Allison Malecha is an assistant editor at Grove Atlantic and the assistant editor on *Freeman's*. She lives in Brooklyn.

Benjamin Markovits grew up in London, Oxford, Texas, and Berlin. He left an unpromising career as a professional basketball player to study the Romantics. Since then he has taught high school English, worked at a left-wing cultural magazine and published six novels, including a trilogy on the life of Lord Byron (*Imposture, A Quiet Adjustment*, and *Childish Loves*). In 2013, Markovits was selected as one of *Granta*'s Best of Young British Novelists, and in 2015 he won the Eccles British Library Writer in Residence Award. *You Don't Have To Live Like This* won the James Tait Black Award in 2016. It was followed by *Playing Days*. Markovits has lived in London since 2000 and is married, with two children. He teaches creative writing at Royal Holloway, University of London.

Khaled Mattawa is Assistant Professor of Language and Literature at the University of Michigan. He is the author of two books of poetry, *Zodiac of Echoes and Ismailia Eclipse,* and has translated five books of Arab poetry (by Saadi Youssef, Fadhil Al-Azzawi, Hatif Janabi, and Maram Al-Massri). Mattawa is the recipient of a MacArthur grant, a PEN Award for Literary Translation, a Guggenheim Fellowship, the Alfred Hodder Fellowship from Princeton University, an NEA translation grant, and two Pushcart Prizes.

Herta Müller is the winner of the 2009 Nobel Prize in Literature, as well as the International IMPAC Dublin Literary Award and the European Literature Prize. She is the author of, among other books, *The Hunger Angel* and *The Fox Was Ever the Hunter*. Born in Romania in 1953, Müller lost her job as a translator in a machine factory and suffered repeated threats after refusing to cooperate with Ceaușescu's secret police. She succeeded in emigrating in 1987 and now lives in Berlin.

Gerald Murnane was born in Melbourne in 1939. He has been a schoolteacher, an editor, and a university lecturer. His debut novel, *Tamarisk Row* (1974), was followed by nine other works of fiction, including *The Plains* and, most recently, *A Million Windows*. In 1999, Murnane won the Patrick White Award, and in 2009, he won the Melbourne Prize for Literature. His memoir, *Something for the Pain*, won the 2016 Victorian Premier's Award for Non-fiction. He lives in Victoria.

Viet Thanh Nguyen was born in Vietnam and raised in America. He is the author of the short story collection *The Refugees*, and *The Sympathizer*, which was awarded the 2016 Pulitzer Prize for Fiction, the Andrew Carnegie Medal for Excellence in Fiction, the Center for Fiction First Novel Prize, the Edgar Award for First Novel, the Asian/Pacific American Award for Literature, and the California Book Award for First Fiction. He is also the author of the nonfiction books *Nothing Ever Dies*, which has been shortlisted for the National Book Award, and *Race and Resistance*. He teaches English and American Studies and Ethnicity at the University of Southern California and lives in Los Angeles.

Gregory Pardlo's collection *Digest* (Four Way Books) won the 2015 Pulitzer Prize for Poetry. *Digest* was also shortlisted for the 2015 NAACP Image Award and was a finalist for the Hurston/Wright Legacy Award. His other honors include fellowships from the National Endowment for the Arts and the New York Foundation for the Arts; his first collection *Totem* was selected by Brenda Hillman for the APR/Honickman Prize in 2007. He is also the author of *Air Traffic*, a memoir in essays forthcoming from Knopf. Pardlo is a faculty member of the MFA program in creative writing at Rutgers University-Camden. He lives with his family in Brooklyn.

Emily Raboteau is the author of a novel, *The Professor's Daughter*, and *Searching for Zion: The Quest for Home in the African Diaspora*, finalist for the Hurston/Wright Award in nonfiction and winner of a 2014 American Book Award. She teaches creative writing at the City College of New York in Harlem. Her next book, *Endurance*, is about the intersecting lives and problems of the residents in a gentrifying upper Manhattan apartment building as told through the eyes of the building's live-in superintendent.

Ross Raisin was born in 1979 in West Yorkshire. His first novel, *God's Own Country*, was published in 2008 and was shortlisted for nine literary awards, including the *Guardian* First Book Award and the John Llewellyn Rhys Prize. In 2009 Ross Raisin was named the *Sunday Times* Young Writer of the Year. In 2013 he was selected as one of *Granta's* Best of Young British Novelists. He lives in London.

Kay Ryan is a lifetime Californian whose honors include the Pulitzer Prize for Poetry and the National Humanities Medal. She served two terms as U.S. Poet Laureate and is currently a MacArthur Fellow.

Danez Smith is the author of *[insert] boy*, winner of the Kate Tufts Discovery Award and the Lambda Literary Award for Gay Poetry, and *Don't Call Us Dead*. They are a 2014 Ruth Lilly and Dorothy Sargent Rosenberg Fellow, a Cave Canem and VONA alum, and recipient of a McKnight Foundation Fellowship. They are from St. Paul, Minnesota, and are a MFA candidate at the University of Michigan.

Una Tanović is a doctoral candidate in the Comparative Literature program at the University of Massachusetts Amherst and has dual focus in comparative literature and translation studies. Her translations of Bosnian literature have been published in the *Massachusetts Review*.

Juan Gabriel Vásquez was born in Bogotá, Colombia, in 1973. He is the author of five novels and a book of short stories that have been translated into twenty-eight languages. His most recent book is *Reputations*, winner of the Premio Real Academia Española.

About the Editor

John Freeman was the editor of *Granta* until 2013. His books include *How to Read a Novelist* and *Tales of Two Cities: The Best and Worst of Times in Today's New York*. He is executive editor at the *Literary Hub* and teaches at the New School and New York University. His work has appeared in the *New Yorker*, the *New York Times*, and the *Paris Review*.